BUILDING BRIDGES, CARVING NICHES

AN ENDURING LEGACY

Grace Loh

Goh Chor Boon

Tan Teng Lang

OXFORD
UNIVERSITY PRESS

OXFORD
UNIVERSITY PRESS

Oxford University Press is a department of the University of Oxford.
It furthers the University's objective of excellence in research, scholarship,
and education by publishing worldwide in

Oxford New York

Athens Auckland Bangkok Bogotá Buenos Aires Calcutta
Cape Town Chennai Dar es Salaam Delhi Florence Hong Kong Istanbul
Karachi Kuala Lumpur Madrid Melbourne Mexico City Mumbai
Nairobi Paris São Paulo Shanghai Singapore Taipei Tokyo Toronto Warsaw

with associated companies in Berlin Ibadan

Oxford is a registered trade mark of Oxford University Press
in the UK and in certain other countries

Published in Singapore
by Oxford University Press Pte Ltd

© Oxford University Press Pte Ltd 2000

First published 2000

Printed in Singapore

ISBN 0 19 594005 9

CONTENTS

Acknowledgements   *iv*

Introduction   *v*

Chapter 1
Winds of Change   *1*

Chapter 2
The Establishment of the OCBC   *21*

Chapter 3
Widening the Horizon   *33*

Chapter 4
In the Face of Adversity   *45*

Chapter 5
Building Firm Foundations   *91*

Chapter 6
Extending the OCBC Family   *120*

Chapter 7
Expansion through Prudent Conservatism   *154*

Chapter 8
The Logic of OCBC's Family Network   *190*

Chapter 9
The Magnificent Obsession   *202*

Chaper 10
On Ethical Principles and Management Leadership   *224*

Bibliography   *263*

Index   *274*

ACKNOWLEDGEMENTS

A book of this magnitude is the progeny of many hands, and there are a great many people without whose help we could not have written it. We would like to thank:

- Tan Sri Tan Chin Tuan, for so generously giving us his time and energies, and for his unstinting support of this project. We also thank him for opening to us his private papers and materials, and allowing us to use many of the photographs in this volume.
- The staff at the Tan Foundation, Singapore, for facilitating our research and who left no stone unturned in providing us data and materials and in helping us verify our narrative.
- Professor Lim Chong Yah, Associate Professor Ernest Chew, Mr Teo Cheng Guan, Mr Allen J. Pathmarajah, Mrs C. C. Lee-Tan, Mr Lee Hah Ing, Mr Chin Nyuk Fui, Ms Tan Kheng Choo, Ms Yeo Kheng Sian and Mr David Goh, who read and kindly commented on earlier drafts of this book.
- Professor Cham Tao Soon, President of NTU, for suggesting we undertake this project, and for his confidence and trust in us.
- Professor Leo Tan, Director of NIE, for his support and encouragement throughout the writing of this book.
- Our research assistants, Ivy Maria Lim, Chew Ee and Soon-Lee Lay Hong for their diligent work and invaluable help in researching this book.
- The National Archives, Singapore, who has generously allowed us to use many of the photographs in this book. Special thanks to Messrs Lim Kheng Chye, Lim Chin Tee, and Paul Yap, who gave us permission to use photographs they have deposited at the National Archives.
- The Straits Trading Company Limited, United Engineers Limited, Wearne Brothers Limited, Dr Kwa Soon Bee, Mr Lee Seng Wee, Ms Lim Sing Yuen, Mr Allen J. Pathmarajah, Mr Tan Tock San, Dr Tony Tan, Mr Teo Cheng Guan, Ms Yeo Kheng Sian for kindly letting us use their photographs for this book.
- All others who have helped in some way to make this book possible.

Of course, all errors and opinions remain strictly those of the authors.

Introduction

Against the changing skyline on Boat Quay, the imposing OCBC Building stands as a concrete symbol of its celebrated reputation "Solid as a Rock". Few people, however, know the history behind OCBC's spectacular ascent in the local banking firmament. It is one that reads like a rags-to-riches epic, animated with literal and metaphorical battles.

This book chronicles the drama behind the rise of the OCBC, from its humble beginnings in the days of the Great Depression, through its triumph over major adversities and political changes to its current distinguished status as one of the top 500 banks in the world. Many players contributed in different ways to the unfolding of the OCBC story; this book spotlights the few main players who dedicated the better part of their lives to the Bank and saw it through thick and thin, and whose leadership made a difference to the fortunes of the OCBC. Using a business model that combined Chinese values with Western management, these decision-makers transformed the bank from a dialect-based family concern into a modern, innovative institution. Forefront in this illustrious group is Tan Chin Tuan, whose 51-year career with the bank — much of it as managing director and chairman — made his name synonymous with the OCBC. Much of the story of the OCBC is inextricably linked to Tan Chin Tuan, his philosophy, his management style and his leadership: areas which the writers discuss extensively.

The title of this book, *Building Bridges, Carving Niches: An Enduring Legacy,* evolved naturally after the completion of the manuscript. The title captures the essence of what the OCBC leadership and more specifically, what Tan Chin Tuan did to develop the bank into a leading player in the industry. Tan helped widen the OCBC's contacts by "building bridges" with both the Chinese community and the Western world through an extensive system of networking based upon personal cultivation of goodwill or *guanxi*. In the process, he catapulted the OCBC into a regional and, increasingly, an international player. Tan Chin Tuan was also chiefly responsible for broadening the business interests of the bank and led it in "carving niches" in industries which were unrelated to banking or finance. This he did by aggressively acquiring substantial stakes in selected sound European companies when opportunities presented themselves to OCBC. Consequently, he built a vast OCBC group comprising a stable of blue chip companies and strengthened the influence of the bank within the group through a strategic system of interlocking directorships. What Tan Chin Tuan bequeathed to the OCBC then was "an enduring legacy" which emphasized solid foundations, solid linkages, solid relationships and, above all, a solid sense of loyalty, integrity and responsibility.

We trace the beginnings of the OCBC story to the colonial era when three Chinese banks decided to amalgamate their resources to form the Oversea-Chinese Banking Corporation in 1932. The first part of the book examines the growth of the OCBC from its inception to the beginning of the Second World War. Emphasis has been placed on the contributions of people who were at the helm of the bank. In particular, the section examines how one such person, Tan Chin Tuan re-defined the role of the Chinese banker by reaching beyond the confines of the Chinese community by building bridges through public service. The second part of the book begins with the onset of the Second World War. Here, the OCBC's operations in Singapore and overseas are discussed. With the end of the war, the focus shifts to Singapore and describes how the bank contributed to the reconstruction and rehabilitation of the Singapore economy. The role played by Tan Chin Tuan during this crucial period is also discussed at some length. As Singapore moved into the turbulent 1950s — when political and economic changes came fast and thick — we show how Tan Chin Tuan tackled a complexity of labour problems and formulated a comprehensive staff welfare system for the OCBC and companies closely associated with the bank. We also see how Tan created opportunities for the OCBC by cultivating a network of excellent connections for the bank, thus laying strong foundations for the OCBC to further its business and influence. Like many great entrepreneurs, Tan Chin Tuan also embraced methods that enabled the OCBC to expand beyond its financial interests. The third part of the book traces how Tan acquired, through the bank, companies that were once the proud strongholds of the British and "localised" them subsequently. We also examine this acquisition strategy and the OCBC Group or Family it spawned in the 1950s and 1960s. As the city-state of Singapore enjoyed its economic "take-off" in the 1970s, OCBC grew in tandem. In that context, the OCBC group's prudent global and domestic expansionary strategies under Tan's meticulous guidance is examined in some detail. The final part of the book is devoted to a deeper understanding of the ethical principles and management leadership of Tan Chin Tuan.

Building Bridges, Carving Niches adds to the limited literature on the history of local banks in Singapore. More importantly, many of the documents and much of the material relied on for this volume have been made available for the first time through the kindness of Tan Chin Tuan himself. These personal papers, painstakingly archived by a long succession of secretaries and staff, have never previously been consulted or made public. We are also grateful to the many hours Tan spent in personal interviews which helped fill many gaps in OCBC's history. Nonetheless, this book offers but one view of the story as the story we tell derives mainly from Tan's archives. As such we were unable to offer more than cursory treatment of many of Tan's able lieutenants mentioned throughout the saga. Their roles should not, however, be underestimated, for in Tan's own words, "I could never have done it without them".

The story of OCBC provides an interesting case-study of Chinese firms, which still dominate the majority of business enterprises in Singapore and Southeast Asia. It has been shown that the key to the successful transformation of the traditional family firm into a modern economic institution is the paramount role of leadership. The ideals and thinking of Tan Chin Tuan were firmly grounded in the cultural traits of trust, honesty and righteousness, and these were instrumental in the evolution and institutionalisation of OCBC. These then, are lasting legacies bequeathed by the merchant banker, business leader, institutional builder and public figure.

Grace Loh
Goh Chor Boon
Tan Teng Lang

September 2000

CHAPTER 1

WINDS OF CHANGE

It is not true that history cannot satisfy our appetite when we are hungry, nor keep us warm when the cold wind blows. But it is true that if younger generations do not understand the hardships and triumphs of their elders, then we will be a people without a past. As such, we will be like water without a source, a tree without roots.[1]

This wall inscription in New York's Chinatown emphasises not only the importance of appreciating our heritage but also the necessity of having a historical perspective. By learning from the experiences of our counterparts in the past, we will be able to deal more effectively with the challenges ahead.

As Winston Churchill once said, 'The longer you look back, the farther you can look forward.'[2] His comments are certainly applicable to the banking industry in Singapore. In order to understand the changes that are occurring in the domestic banking sector, we need to step back, look beyond the obvious, pose historical questions and gain in-depth knowledge of how commercial banking developed.

European Banks in Colonial Singapore[3]

In colonial Singapore, trade and banking were intertwined. Trade was financed from Singapore, and advances to outpost middlemen secured for the Singapore dealers' a line on the produce collected from the actual growers' in the Malay Archipelago.[4] This gave Singapore a financial hold over sago factories in the Archipelago, and the Macassar rattan trade and timber *panglongs* in Sumatra.[5] The Chinese brought the collection of produce to staple ports like Singapore or Penang, to be sold to European merchants. After being sorted, graded and bulked, the produce was then exported. Later, when Singapore's trade was largely dependent on main exports like tin and rubber, the country again played a key role in financing the export of these staple products. Huff explains that this was because Singapore opened 'channels to the London money market for both short-term credit and long-term finance'.[6]

Short-term credit, which was essential for trade, came mainly through the branches of a few European banks, usually with London head offices.[7] The Union Bank of Calcutta, a British bank, was the first institution to open a branch in Singapore in 1840 but its existence was short-lived; it suspended its operations after a few years.[8] In the 1850s, other British banks, like the Commercial Bank of India, were established in Singapore. However, as a result of their speculative activities, limited capital and poor management, these banks soon also failed. Three other British banks were more successful. These were the Mercantile Bank (originally the Chartered Mercantile Bank of India, London and China), the Chartered Bank (originally the Chartered Bank of India, Australia and China) and the Hongkong and Shanghai Banking Corporation.[9] The Mercantile Bank commenced operations with the opening of a branch in 1856; the Chartered Bank had an agency in 1859; while the Hongkong and Shanghai Bank started a branch in 1877.[10] The banks operated in a rather unregulated banking environment, however, and this was largely due to the absence of government controls over the industry.

As the British government in Singapore was primarily concerned with the promotion of trade and commerce, it adopted a free-trade principle that applied not only to trade but also extended to other sectors of the economy. As a result of this laissez-faire economic policy, the government made no attempt to establish a central bank to supervise the activities of commercial banks. Thus, there were no government regulations on minimum reserves, liquidity ratios or credit policies; nor were there periodic examinations of accounts to prevent fraud.[11] Without such controls, many banks were plagued by bad debts and fraud. For example, in 1872, the Mercantile Bank was cheated of £90,000 by long-time customers, the Joshua Brothers.[12]

Despite these problems, the three British banks dominated the banking industry in Singapore. Davenport-Hines and Jones explain that the British banks were so influential that they 'also acted as government bankers to various authorities in Malaya'.[13] The Chartered Bank and the Hongkong and Shanghai Banking Corporation were bankers to the governments of the Federated Malay States and the State of Johore respectively while the Mercantile Bank was the government banker in the states of Kelantan, Trengganu and Pahang.[14]

The three banks were so important they even issued bank notes. The Chartered Bank, especially, played a key role in the banking industry because of its control over foreign exchange. In fact, other banks and businesses had to obtain their foreign exchange from the Chartered Bank. To enable the colony's currency to become freely convertible with sterling, the sterling exchange standard was adopted in 1906 and the exchange was fixed at 2s. 4d. and backed by 100 to 110 percent sterling reserves.[15] The adoption of the sterling exchange standard benefited the British banks as they could 'invest surplus funds in London without significant risk of exchange loss'.[16]

In Singapore, the foreign banks were mainly interested in financing the colony's exports of staple products like rubber and tin to the West. As a result of their orientation towards financing the export trade, the foreign banks adhered to 'a policy of short-term, strictly commercial lending'.[17] The banks provided short-term credit to agency houses and other European businesses as well as to the more prominent members of the Asian business community. Initially, very few Chinese used the European banks. This was primarily because the banks would not accept small accounts and they were also unfamiliar with the way the Chinese did business. According to Huff, 'in 1896 less than 50 Chinese traders had European bank accounts; although a decade later the number had risen.'[18] Brown also pointed out that 'the Hongkong Bank's clientele in Singapore was 40% Chinese in the 1920s and 60% in the 1930s'.[19] In the case of the other British Exchange Banks, she noted that 'smaller banks like the Mercantile and newcomers, like the Eastern, had few good European accounts [and] had to rely almost entirely on Asian business'.[20]

Role of Intermediaries

To secure business from the local community, the European banks relied heavily on intermediaries like the Chinese compradores.[21] This was because few of their staff could converse, read or write in Chinese. The banks also did not have any information on the Chinese business community or contacts to do business with members of that community.

The compradores provided the European banks with the means to lend to Chinese traders and entrepreneurs. This was because the compradores usually had a wide range of contacts in the Chinese community and were able to use these contacts to introduce customers to the banks. Based on the assumption that the compradores were well-versed with the credit-worthiness of their clients, the European banks accepted the latter as 'safe' customers. However, to safeguard the loans, the compradores were held responsible for their repayment. But, in view of the volume of loans guaranteed by the compradores, it was evident that such loans were not adequately secured. In fact, failures as a result of over-borrowing were not uncommon.

According to Jones, a further disadvantage of the compradore system was that the bank depended greatly on the reliability of the compradore. As the latter 'frequently engaged in business on his own account, there was always a risk that the bank's funds would be misused and when this happened a bank could suffer serious loss.'[22] Consequently, this system introduced an element of instability in the banking system. As Brown observed, the 'Western banks encouraged Asian borrowing to the point of recklessness'[23] and large transactions were made without due care as they were made on the basis of compradore guarantees. As a result, there were cases involving fraudulent practices. One such incident occurred in November 1930 when the Chee Seng Rubber Works in Singapore failed with debts of $1.75 million. This sum was owed to the Hongkong and Shanghai Banking Corporation and the total security was only $600,000.

The Emergence and Growth of Chinese Banks

Given the shortcomings of the compradore system, the European banks had to rely on the indigenous Chinese banks established by enterprising Chinese who learnt to operate the banking system from the European banks. According to Huff, the 'Singapore Chinese began deposit banks, and several, reversing the European pattern, set up international branches with the head office in the staple port.'[24]

These local Chinese banks played a crucial role in the economic development of Singapore as they helped mobilise Chinese savings for investment purposes. According to Lee Sheng Yi, the local Chinese banks were an 'outgrowth within the economy, as distinct from the overseas banks with head offices in London or other financial centres'.[25] He further explains that they were 'commercial banks in the modern sense and were different in organisation and policy from the Chinese old-type banking and remittance houses prevalent in China or Hong Kong.'[26] Indigenous Chinese banks in colonial Singapore accepted deposits, provided loans, popularised the use of the current account system among the Chinese merchants and shopkeepers and financed trade bills along the line of modern commercial banks. Huff noted that the success of the Chinese banks in the Straits Settlements was evident when their estimated liabilities (effectively deposit liabilities) rose from $3.3 million in 1914 to an annual average of $40.4 million in 1925/27 and $55.5 million by 1937/39.[27]

There was also a complementary relationship in Singapore between the European and local Chinese banks. The European banks were international financial organisations with large capital and a world-wide network. On the other hand, the local Chinese banks, which usually started from a family or communal basis and therefore had fewer overseas branches, were essentially domestic banks and had relatively smaller assets. In view of their familiarity with the local market, indigenous Chinese banks were used as intermediaries to provide European banks with indirect access to the Chinese community. They were also used to transact business on a personal basis and in dialect. Whilst the local Chinese banks helped the European banks extend credit to the Chinese community, the former in turn relied on the European banks for credit in the event of a liquidity crisis. This arrangement was essential as the Chinese banks were exposed to a high degree of risk whenever the prices of commodities, especially rubber, fell sharply. Since many of their customers were rubber planters, the banks' money supply would contract leaving them to face liquidity problems. Brown explained that the 'Chinese banks used the Hongkong Bank and Chartered Bank to secure a high proportion of their working capital, particularly during periods of trade crises when a squeeze on trade-profits created diffi- culties and only a loan from western banks could stabilise the position.'[28]

As local Chinese banks pursued a policy emphasising money-lending, it became imperative for them to safeguard their reserves and reduce their risk exposure. To do this, local Chinese banks followed a conservative reserve ratio policy by depositing a large proportion of their capital with the European banks. According to a former banker, Yap Pheng Geck, 'foreign banks were glad to have the support of the local Chinese banks, for ultimately all the spare cash of the local banks were deposited with the European banks.'[29] He further explained that 'Chinese banks' reserves were largely held by the European banks partly because they could earn interest from the European banks and partly because their own strong-room facilities were inadequate.'[30] Huff concurred and stated that 'as a rule, Chinese banks kept 50% of their current account money liquid, and maintained large reserves as currency and deposits with the British banks.'[31] In this way, the European banks helped to enhance the reputation of and public confidence in the Chinese banks.

By having reserves with the British banks, the local Chinese banks were able to meet the liquidity demands of their customers. This was essential because the 'Chinese banks appear frequently to have made unsecured loans, often in the form of overdrafts and without any very specific time limit.'[32] Whilst the emphasis was on short-term credit financing of trade and other commercial activities, the banks did extend credit to finance investment by Chinese entrepreneurs in estate development and manufacturing. This practice proved useful because it had been difficult in the past to secure long-term loans from the European banks. In fact, before the emergence of local banks, many Chinese traders had to obtain their business capital from pawnshops, chit funds and Chettiar moneylenders.[33] For example, the latter charged exorbitant interest rates of between 24% and 36%, which made it difficult for the Chinese to earn profits from their business ventures.

Not only were local deposit banks established, but banks by the different dialect groups within the Chinese community were also opened. According to Cheng, this was not surprising as 'in the nineteenth and early twentieth centuries, the Chinese community in Singapore and Malaya was so rigidly segregated by dialect differences, that the Chinese tended to socialise exclusively within the dialect groups to which they belonged'.[34] The Chinese were effectively isolated and socially locked into their respective dialect groups.

Various dialect groups set up associations to meet the needs of their respective members. Depending on available resources, the associations provided members with initial free accommodation, assistance in finding employment, medical services and even free burial! In a society where government welfare benefits were absent, Yen observed that the idea of mutual assistance was an attractive one. He pointed out that 'one striking fact about the early Chinese dialect organisations is the domination of the minority groups. Thirteen out of the fourteen dialect associations founded in Penang, Malacca and Singapore in the period between 1801 and 1839 belonged to the Hakkas and the Cantonese, who were minorities in the local Chinese community'.[35] This might be due to the fact that the Kapitan China system[36] that the British adopted to exert control over the Chinese community made the minority groups within that community insecure.[37] The colonial authorities tended to appoint the leader of the major dialect group as the Kapitan, who was in charge of the security and welfare of the Chinese community. As the Hokkien community was not only numerically the largest group but also in a strong economic position, its leaders tended to be appointed to the position of Kapitan by the British. For example, in Singapore, Tan Tock Seng was the de facto Kapitan of the Chinese community.[38] However, the minority groups felt that the Kapitan would only safeguard the interests of his own dialect group and as he was not conversant in the dialects of the other groups, they perceived him as not being able to understand their problems. Thus, to safeguard their interests, the minority groups also formed their own dialect associations.

Dialect-based Banks

It was not surprising then that it was the Cantonese who established the first local bank in Singapore in 1903. Wong Ah Fook[39], a Chinese gambier planter and building contractor, formed the Kwong Yik Bank. But, the latter was not success- ful. Lee Sheng Yi noted that 'because of the lack of banking principles and experience, the Kwong Yik Bank got into financial difficulties in 1913 as some of its directors had obtained big loans from the bank'.[40] In November of that year, the Supreme Court appointed liquidators to clear its debts and the government amended the Bank Ordinance to protect the interests of depositors by restricting the amount of loans which banks could advance to their directors and officials.[41] However, because the early banks depended on successful businessmen as founders and organisers and as these people were involved primarily in the declining industries, such banks never became important institutions.

This situation changed when entrepreneurs in the rubber-pineapple sector and the manufacturing industry started their own banks. As many of these entrepreneurs were Hokkien speaking, they established Hokkien banks: the Chinese Commercial Bank (1912), the Ho Hong Bank (1917) and the Oversea-Chinese Bank (1919). These banks were to play a significant role in the banking industry in colonial Singapore.

The Chinese Commercial Bank (CCB) for instance, helped to popularise the use of the current account system among the Chinese merchants and shopkeepers. According to Chee Swee Cheng, this facility was utilised mainly by insurance companies and rubber estate owners to earn interest of 1% per annum on their money that would otherwise have been left idle.[42]

The Ho Hong Bank (HHB) under its general manager, Seow Poh Leng, impressed upon Chinese businessmen the advantage of the limited liability company system.[43] It further had the distinction of being the first Chinese bank to be externally-oriented. The Ho Hong Bank opened branches in Malacca and Muar in Malaya simultaneously with the start of its head office in Singapore.[44] The bank rapidly expanded by setting up branches in other towns in Malaya like Penang, Ipoh and Kuala Lumpur. It also ventured overseas with the establishment of branches in Hong Kong, Shanghai and Batavia. The Ho Hong Bank was determined to break into the foreign exchange market that had been previously dominated by the European banks. It intended to carry out independent arbitrage operations in sterling or US dollars.

Accordingly, the bank started foreign exchange operations in Hong Kong in 1923 and in Shanghai in 1925.

The Oversea-Chinese Bank (OCB) emulated the policies adopted by the Ho Hong Bank. The OCB set up branches in Malaya as well as overseas in places like Rangoon (Burma), Jambi (Sumatra) and Amoy (China). The bank even entered the foreign exchange business. At home, the bank also worked closely with the Overseas Assurance Corporation, an insurance company that was founded in 1920. The Overseas Assurance and the Eastern United Assurance were Singapore's main Chinese insurance companies and they dealt in fire, marine, and motor insurance as well as workmen's compensation.[45] Thus, it was evident that the three Hokkien banks made significant contributions towards the banking industry.

These Hokkien banks were not only affected by fluctuations in rubber prices but their major shareholders were also influential rubber planters. In fact, rubber magnates like Lim Nee Soon served as Vice-Chairman of the Chinese Commercial Bank with Lee Kong Chian initially as a director and later as Vice-Chairman. Other rubber estate owners included Lee Choon Guan who was not only the founder of the Chinese Commercial Bank but also a supporter of the Ho Hong Bank. This tendency for prominent people with rubber interests to have a stake in several banks was further evident when Lim Nee Soon became the second Chairman of the Oversea-Chinese Bank and Lee Kong Chian was made a director of this bank. The development of this network of interlocking directorates characterised early Chinese banking.

The early banks therefore had a closely-knit elite at the helm. The directors were not only from the same dialect group but they knew each other well and were also related through marriage. Lim Mah Hui cited instances of such links when he pointed out that the families of Tan Cheng Lock and Lee Choon Guan were connected through marriage and that S. Q. Wong's daughter married Lee Kong Chian's nephew.[46] In view of the close ties that were established among members of the elite business community, it was not surprising that the early banks encountered difficulties as a result of kinship and friendship links.

Problems Faced By Chinese Banks

According to Yap Ee Chian the problems of serious over-lending arose because 'directors of the banks obliged their friends by lending money to them'.[47] Unfortunately, as Lee Sheng Yi noted, since the loans were 'based on good faith arising from personal and communal relationship rather than on property or security for the loans', such debts were difficult to recover.[48] The banks faced problems when these loans could not be repaid. For instance, the banks were in financial difficulties when major customers like Tan Kah Kee could not repay his loans. According to Brown, 'Tan Kah Kee's borrowings from the Chinese Commercial Bank were sufficient to lead to a run on the bank in 1931.'[49]

It was difficult for banks to establish any form of internal controls to prevent directors from extending credit to their friends and relatives. This was because of the power held by the directors in the banks. Brown commented that directors like 'Lim Peng Siang managed the Ho Hong Bank as a personal asset, Tan Ean Kiam exerted similar influence over the Oversea-Chinese Bank, while Lee Kong Chian and Tan Kah Kee dominated the Chinese Commercial Bank'.[50] Yap Pheng Geck, a former employee of the Chinese Commercial Bank, was of the same opinion when he stated that 'anybody holding a position of importance in a Chinese bank had to be rich in his own right or related to one of the directors or big shareholders.'[51] This was certainly the case with Lee Kong Chian. On 10 August 1923, Lee Kong Chian bought 100 shares of the Chinese Commercial Bank from Tan Kah Kee and on 17 December 1923, he was elected to the Board of Directors of that bank. Later when he bought 50 shares of the Oversea-Chinese Bank, he was again elected to be a director of the bank. Zheng held the view that Lee occupied these positions because he was an astute business-man and was also the son-in-law of Tan Kah Kee, a prominent member of the Hokkien community and an important customer of the two banks.[52]

As power and ownership were so closely linked in Chinese banks, the banks were in effect managed like typical Chinese family businesses. Redding noted that 'personalism' was prevalent in such businesses as 'personal relationships and feelings about other people are likely to come before more objectively defined concerns such as organisational effi-ciency.'[53] Thus, in a Chinese bank, whom you know is more important than, or at least as important as, what you know. Redding explained that this meant that nobody outside the owning group could generate for himself truly legitimate authority and this became a 'significant handicap to the grafting on of a middle and senior management group made up of competent professionals.'[54]

This undoubtedly was a problem for many of the early Chinese banks. They hired staff mainly on the basis of kinship and dialect affiliations and did not focus on employing well-educated staff who could speak and work in English. Yap Siong Eu stressed that his entry into the Singapore branch of the Ban Hin Lee Bank in 1936 was one based on village ties between his father and Yap Chor Ee, the founder of the bank. He added that he called Yap Chor Ee 'uncle' only be-cause Yap Chor Ee and his father came on the same boat and were from the same village. He noted that most of the employees of the bank were also of the same surname, Yap.[55] This suggested that there was a tendency to employ people who, in reality, were totally unrelated but regarded as trustworthy only because they had the same surname or they originated from the same village in China. Such employment practices naturally placed banks at a disadvantage because to survive, they needed people not only to contribute to the administrative and legal aspects of banking but also to establish close ties with the European banks and the colonial authorities.

To make the situation worse for the banks, it was not easy to hire such well-educated people. This was because the colonial government did not promote higher education in Singapore. For instance, whilst a medical college was started in 1905, there was no university. Raffles College, together with the King Edward VII Medical College of the University of Malaya, only opened in 1928.[56] In the case of the Chinese elite, they had to continue their studies in China because tertiary education in Chinese was not available in colonial Singapore. The Chinese-language Nanyang University in Singapore was established only in 1956. In view of this situation, very few employees of Chinese banks had higher education.

Another difficulty encountered by Chinese banks was the prevalence of some customers' fraudulent practices. As there was no requirement for partnerships to be registered, partners were not legally responsible for the loans taken up by their firms. There were therefore cases of partners absconding. The banks called for the registration of Chinese and European partnerships to tackle the problem of fraud.[57]

Apart from having to deal with such difficulties, the Chinese banks encountered other problems as a result of their lack of exposure to modern banking practices. The early Chinese banks were mainly involved in money lending activities though a few like the Ho Hong Bank and the Oversea-Chinese Bank had entered the field of foreign exchange through their overseas connections. However, as they were new to the business, Yap Pheng Geck noted that the banks did not have a proper understanding of the subject of cover against exchange risks.[58] Consequently, both banks were badly affected by the decision of the British government to abandon the gold standard. The British government supported its action by arguing that, due to the Japanese invasion of Manchuria on 18 September 1931, there had been an excessive amount of withdrawal of funds from London. As these funds were backed by gold, the government had no alternative but to abandon the gold standard on 21 September. This meant that the pound sterling was in effect devalued. This was disastrous for the banks that were involved in foreign exchange operations as they were caught in an overbought sterling position. The local Chinese banks in Singapore suffered even more as their exchange operations were based mainly in Hong Kong and Shanghai. Their problems arose because the Straits dollar was pegged to sterling and when sterling was devalued, the Straits dollar followed suit. As they had been most active in the foreign exchange business, the Ho Hong Bank was the hardest hit, followed by the Oversea-Chinese Bank.

Although the Chinese Commercial Bank (CCB) did not suffer as much as the other two Hokkien banks, it did not emerge unscathed. Many of its customers were rubber planters who were already feeling the effects of a fall in the price of rubber. When prices plummeted even further during the Great Depression that began with the Wall Street Crash on 24 October 1929, the overseas demand for commodities like tin and rubber was further reduced. When rubber prices fell drastically from $1.14 per pound in 1925 to 35 cents in 1929 and 7 cents in 1932, many rubber planters had to cease operations.[59] Naturally, this affected the bank because loans could not be repaid. One client who was unable to pay back his loan was Tan Kah Kee, one of the richest men in Singapore. He had invested heavily in the rubber industry. According to Yong, 'it was clear by 1928 and 1929 that Tan Kah Kee had invested 75 per cent of all his assets in rubber manufactory, estimated to be $9 million in 1928 and $10 million in 1929.'[60] With the fall in prices of rubber, he had liquidity problems. He could not repay the loan of $2.5 million that he had earlier taken from the CCB at the request of its managing director, See Boo Ih. This was an incredibly large sum of money to lend an individual, especially since the bank's capitalisation was, at that time, only $1 million and its reserve, $1 million.

In an attempt to deal with this financial problem, the CCB invited Yap Twee to be its new managing director. Yap Twee had no previous knowledge of banking when he was asked to succeed See Boo Ih. He was then a proprietor of a successful hardware business, Chin Ho and Co. Ltd. According to Yap Pheng Geck, despite this lack of banking experience, Yap Twee was able to revitalise the bank and put it on such a firm footing that the bank emerged from the economic crisis in a stronger position than the other two Hokkien banks.[61]

His success could also be attributed to capable staff like Chew Hock Leong[62] and Tan Chin Tuan.[63] Yap Pheng Geck, a former colleague of both men, observed that Chew was 'very practical in his approach to problems and was adept at financial management and control' whilst Tan was 'another outstanding character' who was 'very deliberate and thorough in everything he undertook. He would look at a problem from all angles and come to conclusions only after long and thorough deliberations.'[64] Apart from depending on efficient staff, Yap Twee himself was also a dynamic person. According to Yap Pheng Geck, 'he was a veritable human dynamo to whom work was a passionate obsession.... In the bank, he made it a point to know every customer, his business and how it was faring, his account and how it was operating.'[65] Yap Twee was also persuasive and convinced Chang Kia Ngau, the chairman of the Bank of China, to buy 30% of the CCB's shares. This transaction helped to introduce an element of stability into the bank as well as increase the public's confidence in the CCB. Chang also agreed to persuade his board of directors to contribute a further $1 million dollars on the understanding that the CCB would raise the equivalent amount. However, the CCB's merger with the other two Hokkien banks put an end to this plan. Later, the Bank of China was to relinquish its CCB shares to facilitate the formation of the amalgamated bank — the Oversea-Chinese Banking Corporation Limited.

NOTES

1 G. B. Nash, C. Crabtree and R. E. Dunn, *History on Trial* (New York: Alfred A. Knopf, 1997), p. 3.

2 Cited in S. F. Hayward, *Churchill on Leadership* (Rocklin: Forum, 1997), p. 8.

3 See generally, Lee Sheng Yi, 'The Development of Commercial Banking in Singapore and the States of Malaya', *The Malayan Economic Review*, vol. XI, no. 1 (April 1966): 84.

4 Straits Settlements, 'Report of the Commission appointed by His Excellency the Governor of Straits Settlements to enquire into and report on the trade of the Colony, 1933–34' (Singapore: Government Printing Office, 1934), p. 34.

5 Ibid.

6 W. G. Huff, *The Economic Growth of Singapore: Trade and Development in the Twentieth Century* (Cambridge: Cambridge University Press, 1994), p. 18.

7 Ibid.

8 Lee Sheng Yi, 'The Development of Commercial Banking in Singapore and States of Malaya', *The Malayan Economic Review*, vol. XI, no. 1 (April 1966): 84.

9 Ibid.

10 Ibid, pp. 84–85.

11 R. A. Brown, *Capital and Entrepreneurship in Southeast Asia* (London: St Martin's Press, 1994) pp. 164–165.

12 Stuart Muirhead, *Crisis Banking in the East: The History of the Chartered Mercantile Bank of India, London and China, 1853–93* (Aldershot, Hants, England: Scolar Press, 1996), pp. 106–107.

13 R. P. T. Davenport-Hines and Geoffrey Jones, *British Business in Asia since 1860* (Cambridge: Cambridge University Press, 1989), p. 176.

14 Ibid.

15 Huff, *The Economic Growth of Singapore*, p. 18.

16 Ibid., p. 19.

17 Ibid.

18 Ibid., p. 230.

19 Brown, *Capital*, p. 158.

20 Ibid., p. 159.

21 *Compradores* or *compradors* are native-born (usually Asian) go-betweens, agents or intermediaries in commercial transactions; from the Portugeuse word meaning 'buyer'.

22 Geoffrey Jones, *Banks as Multinationals* (London: Routledge, 1990), p. 90.

23 Brown, *Capital*, p. 158.

24 Huff, *The Economic Growth of Singapore*, p. 19.

25 Lee Sheng Yi, *The Monetary and Banking Development of Singapore and Malaya*, 3rd ed (Singapore: Singapore University Press, 1990), p. 46.

26 Ibid.

27 Huff, *The Economic Growth*, p. 231.

28 Brown, *Capital*, p.159.

29 Yap Pheng Geck, *Scholar, Banker, Gentleman Soldier — The Reminiscences of Dr Yap Pheng Geck* (Singapore: Times Books International, 1982), p. 36. [thereinafter Yap, *Scholar*]

30 Ibid.

31 Huff, *The Economic Growth*, p. 232.

32 Ibid., p. 231.

33 The *Chettiars* hailed from Chettinad in the south-eastern tip of the Indian Sub-continent close to Ceylon or Sri Lanka. The most well-known of them were the Nattukottai Chettiars who lived permanently in 75 places in the Ramnad & Pudukottai districts. The Chettiars came to Malaya primarily as moneylenders. See Khoo Kay Kim, 'Contributions of the Chettiars in Malaya', *The Sunday Star*, 26 Jan 1996.

34 Cheng Lim Keak, *Social Change and the Chinese in Singapore —
   A Socio-Economic Geography with Special Reference to Bäng Structure*
   (Singapore: Singapore University Press, 1985), p. 78.

35 Yen Ching Hwang, *A Social History of the Chinese in Singapore and
   Maluyu, 1800–1911* (Singapore: Oxford University Press, 1986),
   p. 42.

36 On the Kapitan China system generally, see Chan G. G., The
   Kapitan Cina System in the Straits Settlements (unpublished copy);
   and Mona Lohanda, *The Kapitan Cina of Batavia 1837–1942: A
   History of Chinese Establishment in Colonial Society* (Jakarta:
   Djambatan, 1996).

37 Ibid.

38 Ibid.

39 Wong Ah Fook (1837–1918) was not only involved in the construction business in Johore, but was also active in the gambling, opium
   and spirit revenue farms. He was decorated as the Tuan Besar of
   Sungei Mersing and owned many gambier, pepper and rubber
   plantations in Mersing and Segamat, Malaysia. He was the father
   of Dato S. Q. Wong. See page 19 and Chapter 4, Lee Kam Hing and
   Chow Mun Seong, *Biographical Dictionary of the Chinese in Malaysia*
   (Malaysia: Pelanduk Publications, 1997), pp. 176–177.

40 Lee, *The Monetary and Banking*, p. 43.

41 Ibid., p. 44.

42 Straits Settlement Report, 1934, p. 26417.

43 Dick Wilson, *Solid As A Rock* (Singapore: Overseas-Chinese Banking
   Corporation Limited, 1972), p. 17.

44 Ibid., pp. 17–18.

45 Huff, *The Economic Growth of Singapore*, p. 231.

46 Lim Mah Hui, 'The Ownership and Control of Large Corporations
   in Malaysia: The Role of Chinese Businessmen', in *The Chinese in
   Southeast Asia, vol I: Ethnicity and Economic Activity*, Linda Y. C.
   Lim and Peter L. A. Gosling, eds (Singapore: Maruzen Asia, 1983),
   p. 288.

47 Interview, Yap Ee Chian, 13 August 1980, p. 46.

48 Lee, *The Monetary and Banking Development*, p. 47.

49 Brown, *Capital*, p. 166.

50 Ibid.

51 Yap, *Scholar*, p. 27.

52 Zheng Bingshan, *Li Guanqian Zhuan* [A Biography of Lee Kong
   Chian] (China: Zhongguo Huaqiao Chubanshe, 1997), p. 55.

53 S. G. Redding, *The Spirit of Chinese Capitalism* (Berlin: Walter de
   Gruyter, 1990), p. 165.

54 Ibid., p. 163.

55 Interview, Yap Siong Eu, 23 July 1983.

56 See Edwin Lee and Tan Tai Yong, *Beyond Degrees: The Making of the National University of Singapore* (Singapore: Singapore University Press, 1996).

57 Straits Settlements Report, 1934, p. 523.

58 Yap, *Scholar*, p. 231.

59 Wilson, *Solid As A Rock*, p. 5.

60 Yong C. F., *Tan Kah Kee: The Making of an Overseas Legend* (Singapore Oxford University Press, 1989), p. 68.

61 Yap, *Scholar*, p. 28.

62 Chew Hock Leong started his banking career in the Chinese Commercial Bank. Upon the amalgamation of the three banks in 1932, Chew, who was then the general inspector of the Chinese Commercial Bank, became one of the managers of OCBC. Chew was responsible for making the arrangement (on behalf of OCBC) with the Directorate-General of Postal Remittances and Savings Bank of China to become the latter's sole agent for family remittances to China in 1938. During the War, Chew refused to leave his family behind in Singapore to secure OCBC's interests abroad. In 1946, just shortly after the war, he was appointed Joint General Manager with Kwa Siew Tee of OCBC, and he later succeeded Kwa Siew Tee as General Manager of the Bank in 1951. Chew retired from the Bank in 1955 and was succeeded by Yeo Tiam Siew as General Manager. After the war, Chew wrote a pamphlet entitled *When Singapore Was Syonan: Being a Brief Account of What Transpired During the Three and a Half Years Japanese Occupation of Singapore* (Singapore: OCBC, 1945) which was published by the OCBC, describing what transpired during the Japanese occupation.

63 The story of Tan Chin Tuan's involvement with the bank is covered extensively in the ensuing chapters.

64 Yap, *Scholar*, p. 29.

65 Ibid., p. 28.

CHAPTER 2

THE ESTABLISHMENT OF THE OCBC

The merger that resulted in the formation of Oversea-Chinese Banking Corporation (OCBC) occurred as a result of lengthy discussions between the directors of the three Hokkien banks. These men knew each other as members of the same clubs and associations. During one of their morning walks, Chee Swee Cheng, the chairman of the Ho Hong Bank, discussed his problems with Lee Kong Chian, the Vice Chairman of the Chinese Commercial Bank (CCB). Lee suggested a merger to solve Chee Swee Cheng's problem. As Tan Ean Kiam, the managing director of the Oversea-Chinese Bank, had earlier also shared his problems with Chee, it was agreed that the OCB should be included in the merger. However, the bankers had to settle the terms of amalgamation. Their primary concern was to evaluate the worth of the shares of each of the three participating banks. As the market price of the CCB's shares was $60 whilst those of the other two banks were $20 each, the three boards of directors decided that their banks would exchange their respective shares for the new bank's shares. It was agreed that one share in the Oversea-Chinese Bank or the Ho Hong Bank would be equal in value to one share in the amalgamated bank. In the case of the Chinese Commercial Bank, it was decided that one of its shares would be equal in value to three shares in the new bank.

Apart from agreeing to the terms of merger, the directors also reached a consensus regarding the name of the new bank. They kept the name 'Oversea-Chinese' because they felt that the name was appropriate, but to differentiate the new bank from the old, they added the words, 'Banking Corporation'.

As a result of these negotiations, the Oversea-Chinese Banking Corporation Limited (OCBC) came into being on 31 October 1932 with an authorised capital of $40 million and a paid-up capital of $10 million. The new bank was incorporated to take over the businesses of the Chinese Commercial Bank Limited, the Ho Hong Bank Limited and the Oversea-Chinese Bank Ltd. When the OCBC opened for business on 2 January 1933, it was the strongest and largest local bank in the Straits Settlements. In fact, it was the only Chinese bank with 17 branches in Malaya (including Singapore), the Dutch East Indies, Burma, China and Hong Kong.[1]

Continuity

At first glance, the newly-established OCBC was very similar to the early Chinese banks formed in colonial Singapore. This was not at all surprising as it was also a dialect-based bank and its top management was drawn from the three predecessor Hokkien banks. As was the case with the earlier banks, the men at the helm of the OCBC were closely associated with the rubber industry. For example, Chee Swee Cheng, the first chairman of the OCBC and the former chairman of the Ho Hong Bank, had extensive properties and rubber estates. He owned 5,000 acres of land in Borneo which were initially used for the cultivation of tapioca and later for rubber. Lee Choon Seng, the vice-chairman of the OCBC and Tan Ean Kiam, one of the first joint managing directors of the bank, also had extensive rubber interests. Tan had invested in rubber estates and owned the milling firm of Bing Sing & Co. In 1933, the latter operated two rubber mills with 57 of the 582 machines in Singapore.[2] Yap Twee, the other joint managing director, was a close friend of Tan Kah Kee. Lee Kong Chian, who became the OCBC's second chairman in 1938, also had connections with Tan Kah Kee and the rubber industry. Lee previously worked in Tan Kah Kee Rubber Company as head of its rubber department. He later married Tan Kah Kee's daughter and started his own company, Lee Rubber Company. Lee subsequently acquired thousands of acres of vacant land and turned them into rubber and pineapple plantations. Thus, it was evident that rubber entrepreneurs were once again in control of the newly formed OCBC.

Power and ownership of the early Chinese banks were very closely linked. A few Chinese families had minority but controlling interests in the OCBC. According to Lim Mah Hui, examples of these 'owner-directors' were the families of Lee Kong Chian and Lee Choon Seng who owned 20% and 5.3% of OCBC stock respectively.[3] In Lim's view, the 'OCBC is thus a Chinese family-dominated bank, with most of the families keeping a low profile, tending their own family businesses and allowing a few selected directors to play a public role representing their interests'.[4] In the case of OCBC, the ownership and controlling interests have been rather stable. As Lim Mah Hui pointed out, the 'OCBC, which was founded by some prominent Straits and Singapore Chinese businessmen continues to be under their control'.[5]

As the bank's top positions were filled with people who were not only from the rubber industry but had also previously been in control of other Chinese banks, it was not surprising that they would continue with some of their old practices in the OCBC. This was confirmed by Yap Ee Chian who recalled that the directors of the OCBC 'obliged their friends by lending money to them'.[6] As these loans were made on the basis of personal relationships, such debts were difficult to recover. Apart from the directors, the OCBC also retained many of the best staff from its predecessor banks. For example, managers like Kwa Siew Tee and Lim Bock Kee from the Ho Hong Bank, Chew Hock Leong from the Chinese Commercial Bank, Ong Piah Teng from the Oversea–Chinese Bank, continued to work in the OCBC. Assistant managers like Tan Chin Tuan, who had been from the Chinese Commercial Bank were also retained. These people assisted the fledging bank in beginning its operations. Tan Chin Tuan, for example, was to make significant contributions to the bank in the decades to come. One of his first efforts was to resolve a situation involving the great Tan Kah Kee. The bank had inherited a major problem from its predecessor banks that approved enormous loans to Tan Kah Kee & Co. which eventually failed. In order to recoup bad debts from Tan Kah Kee & Co., the local banks and the British banks like the Chartered Bank and the Hongkong and Shanghai Banking Corporation organised a consortium. The latter was necessary because the British banks had made massive short-term loans to Tan Kah Kee & Co. For example, Brown points out that in 1932, the Hongkong and Shanghai Banking Corporation faced losses of $3 million[7] through Tan Kah Kee & Co. alone. The primary objective of this consortium was to dictate the company's financial policy, restructure its board of directors, reassess its assets and transform Tan Kah Kee & Co. into a private liability company.[8]

The consortium appointed a young employee from the newly-formed OCBC to negotiate with Tan Kah Kee, and that young man was Tan Chin Tuan. Despite his youth, he was considered the most appropriate person to act as a mediator. This was because Tan Kah Kee had known him since he was a child. His father knew Tan Kah Kee and the young Tan Chin Tuan even played marbles with the latter's son! The consortium felt that it would be easier for Tan Chin Tuan to present the banks' plans to Tan Kah Kee. Above all, if the latter did not respond positively to the consortium's proposals, it was believed that the OCBC's young employee would be able to accept reprimand from the older man with better grace than the more senior staff. In any case, the more senior managers of OCBC found the task of negotiating with Tan Kah Kee rather daunting. It was therefore agreed that Tan Chin Tuan be made a director of Tan Kah Kee & Co. The banks wanted Tan Kah Kee's factory at Sumbawa to start working again, but Tan Kah Kee was not interested; he told them, 'I have given you everything. I have nothing more and I don't want to do anything more.'

In the face of Tan Kah Kee's adamant refusal to cooperate, the banks asked Tan Chin Tuan to mediate. The latter persuaded Tan Kah Kee to get the factory re-started. Tan Kah Kee wanted a fee of $4,000 a month, insisting that as the banks had taken away all his assets they should pay him this salary if they wanted him to work for them. The banks were furious but finally accepted his terms. Tan Kah Kee then asked his former employees to return to work at the factory in Sumbawa Road.

At the end of the month, Tan Kah Kee dealt another blow to the consortium when he informed the banks that he wanted the $4,000 to be sent to Amoy University in China. The banks found this demand unacceptable and asked Tan Chin Tuan to convey their disapproval to Tan Kah Kee.

The latter stressed that the banks had no cause to complain especially since the factory had recommenced operations. Furthermore, the $4,000 was his to do as he pleased. As he wanted the sum of money to be given to Amoy University, he maintained that the banks should not object. Tan Kah Kee further added that he needed only $200 a month for living expenses and was able to get this sum of money on his own. After due consideration, the banks agreed to remit the money to China.

Unfortunately, the banks decided to wind up the factory at Sumbawa Road together with the rest of Tan Kah Kee's business empire by April 1934. The collapse of his business enterprises did little damage to his standing as a public figure. He continued to be respected by the Chinese community.

Through his association with Tan Kah Kee, the young Tan Chin Tuan also gained in esteem and influence in the eyes of that community. This would later prove helpful when he himself entered politics. Furthermore, his fortitude and deft handling of the consortium's negotiations with the formidable Tan Kah Kee did not escape the attention of the top management of the OCBC.

Apart from having to deal with the problem of Tan Kah Kee & Co., the 'new' management needed to streamline the organisation to reduce overheads. Although the OCBC was the largest Chinese bank when it was established, its assets were small in comparison with the European banks. In addition, the scope of its business was rather limited, servicing mainly the needs of the Hokkien community. According to Yap, 'business [was] on a small scale, only local business, and Federation business, only Muar and Malacca.'[9] This was because the bank was primarily involved in money-lending activities and initially did not go beyond the 'traditional Chinese role of middleman between native producers and European exporters'.[10]

The task of cutting down expenses was given to Yap Twee. He toured all the branches of the OCBC before deciding to merge the two offices in Malacca as well as the two branches in Penang. Meanwhile, Kwa Siew Tee stabilised the bank's exchange operations, Chew Hock Leong inspected all the offices and revised the control systems of the branches whilst Yap Pheng Geck completed the task of issuing new share certificates to all the shareholders.[11] These men were selected for specific jobs primarily because of their expertise and experience in working for the OCBC's predecessor banks.

Like the earlier Chinese banks, the OCBC was also concerned about liquidity. In its first year of operations, the OCBC attempted to build up its reserves so as to preserve a strong liquid position. According to their Annual Report,[12] the bank's balance sheet at the end of 1933 showed that it had achieved its results when the bank had cash holdings of $17 million, representing a liquid position of 63.14%. As the OCBC's clients included insurance companies and rubber entrepreneurs who kept large sums of money in their current accounts, Chee Swee Cheng, the chairman of the OCBC, explained the bank had to keep at least 50% of its assets liquid. This was to ensure that in the event of these clients withdrawing a large proportion of their funds, the bank would have enough funds available.[13] The bank continued to follow a 'safety first' policy and its liquidity ratio in 1940 was 1.00 compared with 0.55 in 1933.

The bank was able to build up its reserves not only because it pursued a conservative policy but also because the economy was improving. Six months after the bank was formed, the economy started to recover from the effects of the Great Depression. The prices for commodities like tin and rubber increased. Rubber prices went up from six cents a pound to 20 cents at the end of 1933. As many of the bank's customers were associated with the rubber industry, this naturally led to a rise in the bank's deposits from $34 million at the end of 1934 to $59 million at the end of the decade.[14]

The bank also took advantage of the improved trade conditions to expand overseas. It followed a strategy that had been used by the other Chinese banks when it concentrated on opening branches abroad. The OCBC set up a branch in Bangkok in 1934; and in the Dutch East Indies, the bank reactivated a branch in Jambi and opened a new office in Surabaya. Another branch was established in Haiphong in Indo-China in 1938. More agents were appointed to serve the bank's interests in key foreign cities. It was not long before its foreign exchange business became extensive. All these measures signalled the beginning of further changes in the management and orientation of the OCBC.

Looking Ahead

Whilst the OCBC was in many ways a traditional Chinese bank, the bank differed from the other Chinese financial institutions like the Sze Hai Tong Bank in the way it was managed. Without a doubt, the OCBC was controlled and managed by experienced people from its predecessor banks, but it was significant that a few of them were not only responsible for introducing changes within the organisation but they also modernised its practices. In fact, it was due to the influence of experienced bankers and entrepreneurs like Lee Kong Chian and Yap Twee that the OCBC was gradually structured along modern lines. According to Brown, 'they abandoned nepotism to install a management with checks and balances.'[15]

This was especially the case when Lee Kong Chian became the chairman of the OCBC in 1938. As he was previously on the boards of directors of the early Chinese banks, he was aware of the influence directors exerted over these financial institutions. As owner-directors used to dominate the banks, Lee realised that there would be problems if the OCBC were managed in the traditional Chinese manner. In a letter to Tan Cheng Lock, he explained that he intended to be impartial and 'act as a sort of referee or umpire when clashing opinions prevail among the Directors'.[16] Lee went on to observe that he was aware that, unlike a European company, the Chinese firm had a tendency to 'reduce principles into personalities, so that the real issues are completely lost sight of and no effective action could be taken after that.'[17] Thus, to avoid 'this common pitfall', he stressed that he 'would not be taking sides, or supporting individual members against others, but will deal with all matters in as impartial a manner as possible in the best interests of the Bank.'[18] Lee was therefore against personal favours when he was conducting the bank's business. According to Harada, his preference was for the directors to 'make independent investigations and raise up the matter at Board meetings'.[19]

Lee Kong Chian also supported the modernisation of the entire operations of the bank, in line with the practices followed by the British banks. All records were kept in English and the only difference between the OCBC and the British banks was that the former honoured cheques made out and signed in Chinese. The OCBC now had more bilingual employees. In fact, to encourage the use of English, the bank even published a bilingual house journal called *The OCBC Echo* twice a year.

Unlike the earlier Chinese banks which focused on meeting the needs of merchants and entrepreneurs, the OCBC went a step further with the institutional mobilisation of Chinese savings when it set up a savings branch in South Bridge Road to cater to the working class. Apart from increasing its customer base, the bank also provided their clients with a wider range of facilities. To this end, it set up a safe deposit box department at the bank's headquarters, the China Building,[20] a warehouse department as well as a hire-purchase department.[21]

The OCBC also strengthened its property arm by appointing the capable Tan Chin Tuan as the manager of OCBC (Properties) and concurrently manager of the newly incorporated subsidiary, Eastern Realty Company Limited. The latter was formed in 1933 to deal in and manage real estate and landed properties. The Eastern Realty Company Limited would essentially take over properties that had been mortgaged to the bank when owners defaulted. By transferring the property to the Eastern Realty Company Limited, the bank would then wipe out the balance of debt. As these properties were usually neglected, Tan's task was to improve the property or maintain it and later sell the property on behalf of the bank. With his experience in managing his late father's Kambau rubber estate, he reclaimed the rubber estates at minimal cost and when the property market recovered, sold them at a profit. To prevent fraudulent practices, he insisted that if the bank did not want to purchase a certain property, the staff of Eastern Realty Company could not bid for that property at an auction. He also showed initiative when he set up the Chinese Bankers Trust as part of Eastern Realty. As his late father's rubber estate in Johore had not been managed properly, he realised that a trust company would help others in a similar predicament. Such an innovation met the needs of people who did not know how to manage a rubber estate.

Under Tan Chin Tuan's astute management, the bank became a property developer. For example, it built 52 houses along Kim Seng Road. It was not easy to build in that area because the land was swampy. However, as a result of his experience in property development, Tan was able to solve the problem by using paco piles for the foundation. Such piles were then driven deep into the ground. Therefore, by venturing into related areas, the bank was able to go beyond money-lending and diversify its activities.

The OCBC also brought a fresh perspective to the traditional way of sending money back to China. Previously, remittance houses were in charge of remittance flows. However, these remittance houses could only send money to certain places in China and they were not able to guarantee that the money would be safely delivered to the payees. In 1938, Chew Hock Leong completed arrangements with the Directorate-General of Postal Remittances and Savings Bank of China to make the OCBC its sole agent for family remittances to China. This arrangement gave the OCBC a monopoly in the remittance business. The new service was very well received by the remitters and was popular with the payees because it provided access to more areas in China. The OCBC also guaranteed the safety of the money sent. As a result of its involvement in this business, the OCBC received many invitations to open branches both within and without Malaya. Although the volume of this business was not very big, the bank was able to maintain a high profile in the Chinese community in Singapore and in other countries. Thus, the OCBC went beyond the traditional role for a Chinese bank as an intermediary between the Chinese community and the European banks by establishing international business networks that were not dependent on British finance and commerce.

NOTES

1 Dick Wilson, *Solid As A Rock* (Singapore: Overseas-Chinese Banking Corporation Limited, 1972), p. 47.
2 W. G. Huff, *The Economic Growth of Singapore: Trade and Development in the Twentieth Century* (Cambridge University Press, 1994), p. 220.
3 Lim Mah Hui, 'The Ownership and Control of Large Corporations in

Malaysia: The Role of Chinese Businessmen', in *The Chinese in Southeast Asia, Vol. I: Ethnicity and Economic Activity*, Linda Y. C. Lim and Peter L. A. Gosling, eds (Singapore: Maruzen Asia, 1983), p. 288.

4   Ibid.

5   Ibid., p. 289.

6   Interview, Yap Ee Chian, 13 August 1980, p. 46.

7   R. A. Brown, *Capital and Entrepreneurship in Southeast Asia* (London: St Martin's Press, 1994), p. 157.

8   Yong C. F., *Tan Kah Kee: The Making of an Overseas Chinese Legend* (Singapore: Oxford University Press, 1989), p. 64.

9   Interview, Yap Ee Chian, 13 August 1980, p. 46.

10 N. J. White, *Business, Government and the End of Empire-Malaya, 1942–1957* (Kuala Lumpur: Oxford University Press, 1996), p. 51.

11 Wilson, *Solid As A Rock*, p. 49.

12 See Oversea-Chinese Banking Corporation Limited, Annual Report, 1933.

13 Straits Settlements, 'Report of the Commission appointed by His Excellency the Governor of Straits Settlements to enquire into and report on the trade of the Colony, 1933–34' (Singapore: Government Printing Office, 1934), p. 26423.

14 Wilson, *Solid As A Rock*, p. 49.

15 Brown, *Capital*, p. 170.

16 Tadao Harada, *List of Lee Kong Chian Documents, vol. I* (Singapore: Nanyang University, 1979), p. vi.

17 Ibid.

18 Ibid.

19 Ibid.

20 The China Building was designed by P. H. Keys and F. Dowdeswell of the firm of Keys and Dowdeswell, who also designed the Fullerton Building (1928) and the King Edward VII School of Medicine (1927). It was built between 1931 and 1932 and was considered a major architectural accomplishment during that era. It was originally shared by the Chinese Commercial Bank and the Oversea Chinese Bank, but thereafter became the headquarters of the OCBC when the three banks merged in 1932.

21 Wilson, *Solid As A Rock*, p. 50.

CHAPTER 3

WIDENING THE HORIZON

As the OCBC operated somewhat differently from the other banks, it was not surprising that it had employees like Tan Chin Tuan who were able to work closely with the colonial government. Indeed, in the years to come, Tan would re-define the role of a Chinese banker. Previously, Chinese bankers served their banks by working within the confines of the local banking industry and meeting the parochial needs of the Chinese community. Their contacts with the government were minimal and limited to regulatory and communal matters. According to Chan, 'there was a profound suspicion of government direction, because political authority was seen as capricious, hostile, and in need of careful manipulation.'[1] This was certainly the case in Singapore, where a foreign government was in control. However, Tan Chin Tuan realised that a new channel could be created whereby the bank's interests would be advanced by working closely with the colonial government. As we shall see, his experiences in the public sector paved the way for the bank to broaden its horizons.

To understand why he felt that a banker needed to look beyond the banking industry and play an active part in public service, some knowledge of his background is necessary. Tan's roots lay firmly in the Chinese community that nurtured his early activities and moulded his personality and values. He was a member of its business elite as his father, Tan Cheng Siong, was a man of substance and status. Tan Cheng Siong owned sawmills and a rubber estate on the eastern coast of Johore and was also a banker. He had been the general manager of the Oversea-Chinese Bank. In addition, he was also the honorary president of the Po Chiak Keng (Tan clan) as well as a member of some of the most important clubs in the Chinese community like the famous millionaires' club, the Ee Hoe Hean Club. The young Tan Chin Tuan often accompanied his father to either the bank or the clubs, and grew up clued into the manners, customs and traditions of the adult world of prominent China-born businessmen. People like Tan Kah Kee got to know Tan Chin Tuan when he came with his father to visit the clubs or to his office. From an early age, Tan Chin Tuan was initiated into the world of the Chinese businessman. He was not only familiar with notions like *guan xi* (relationship) and *xin yong* (trustworthiness) but was also aware of how dialect, kin and non-kin relationships could help smoothen the path of business, by 'providing capital, credit, and access to employment and business opportunity'.[2]

Tan Chin Tuan himself benefited from the close ties that linked the Chinese community when his father passed away suddenly in 1922. He was only fourteen years old at that time. As a result of the demise of his father, earlier plans to send him to England for further studies were shelved. Instead, he completed his secondary schooling in Singapore at the Anglo-Chinese School, passing his Junior Cambridge and then the Senior Cambridge examinations. He next enrolled in the Senior Commercial class at the same school and learned book-keeping and other related subjects. English was not Tan Chin Tuan's lingua franca, and it was at the workplace that he truly grasped command of the language. After completing his secondary education at the Anglo-Chinese School, he was able to find employment because of his father's network of social and business contacts. An old friend of his late father, See Boo Ih, the managing director of the Chinese Commercial Bank, offered Tan Chin Tuan a job. At the age of seventeen, Tan joined the bank as a clerk on 1 March 1925. When the bank amalgamated with the other two Hokkien banks, he continued to work in the OCBC and became more familiar with its banking practices.

While working at the bank, Tan struggled hard to educate himself further and developed a great appetite for reading, especially the Cassell series of books on Self-Improvement and Personal Efficiency. His colleagues further encouraged him to continue learning by giving him the 1927 edition of the *Webster's Dictionary*.

Over time, Tan became increasingly self-assured and confident. Some of this confidence stemmed from his early success in business. At that young age, he not only managed a rubber estate but also succeeded in turning it into a profitable concern. In doing so, Tan made the unprecedented and novel move of appointing Europeans to manage his estate. Initially, he appointed J. W. Campbell as a visiting agent. The latter's task was to inspect the estate and report on its condition. Later, Tan Chin Tuan made Laurence Henderson the manager of his estate. At that time, few Chinese rubber estate owners appointed Europeans to run their estates. Tan also got on well with J. D. Dalley[3] who was the chief of police in Johore. Thus, unlike his colleagues in the OCBC, Tan not only had a much wider work experience in managing other business enterprises, but he was also able to handle the Europeans.

His dealings with the Europeans came in useful when he became involved in public service. Tan Chin Tuan realised that the banking industry had to find bilingual employees. As a member of the Straits Chinese British Association (SCBA) he joined lawyers Chan Sze Jin (S. J. Chan) and Wee Swee Teow when they pressed the British for certain concessions. In particular, they criticised the British for imposing a colour bar in the Malayan and Singapore Civil Service. Since 1904, there was a rule that limited entry into the Malayan Civil Service to persons of European parentage on both sides.[4]

Over time, this rule was perceived as discriminatory and Straits Chinese legislators like Tan Cheng Lock protested against it in the Legislative Council. He said that exclusion meant that Asians were prevented from participating in the government and administration of their country.[5] According to Ong, the SCBA also submitted petitions to re-open the door that had been 'banged, barred and bolted'.[6] Lee Yong Hock noted that the SCBA achieved some success in 1932 when the Government indicated that 'certain posts then normally reserved for Malayan Civil Service members would in due course be thrown open to locally-born non-European British subjects with suitable qualifications'.[7] The Governor, Sir Cecil Clementi appointed a Committee to implement the new plan. As a result, the Government created three services for Asians, each one styled with the prefix 'Straits Settlements' — the Medical Service in 1932, the Civil Service in 1934, and the Legal Service in 1937.

Despite the government's attempt to open the doors in key sectors to Asians, there was still discrimination against the Asians. This was evident in the case of the Straits Settlements Civil Service. Entry into that service was very competitive and only two Asians were selected each year. The British continued to retain their control of the Malayan Civil Service. British civil servants received higher pay and had better promotion prospects than their Asian counterparts. Furthermore, British civil servants had access to an empire-wide civil service network whilst the Asian civil servants were allowed to serve in just the one colony in which they were domiciled.

Despite discrimination in the civil service, the door had at least been opened to allow some Asians into the colonial bureaucracy and to familiarise themselves with the intricacies of government. This was no small achievement for the Straits Chinese legislators and the SCBA. The civil service issue was part of a broader campaign that the Straits Chinese had been waging for some time to exert pressure on the British to expand education in the English language. They supported their case on the grounds that Singapore would require people who could converse in English as they would have to operate in an international trading environment. Furthermore, a multi-racial society like Singapore could be united through the use of English as a common language. From the British point of view, both reasons were like double-edged swords. This was because the British differed from the Straits Chinese on the extent to which education in English was the responsibility of the government. On education as on much else, the British continued to adopt the laissez-faire approach. The Straits Chinese persisted and finally pressured the British into setting up Raffles College. Although a principal for the college, Richard O. Winstedt, was appointed in 1921, the process of setting it up was so long and protracted that the college did not open its doors to students until 1928.

Public Service — An Added Dimension

Tan Chin Tuan was impressed by the courage and conviction of the Straits Chinese gentlemen who had firmly stood up to the colonial administration in their attempts to remove discriminatory policies against Asians. He realised that many of them took time from their busy working lives as lawyers to represent the interests of Asians. They represented for him, good role models.

In August 1939, he was given an opportunity to serve when he received a letter stating that he had been appointed by the Governor of the Straits Settlements to serve on the Municipal Commission. Tan informed the chairman and the managing director of the OCBC about his appointment and they were very pleased for him. They considered it an honour for him to be selected. He had been nominated to replace Ng Sen Choy, the proprietor of Wing Loong, a well-known High Street tailor. Ng had served in the Municipal Commission for eight years before resigning. Tan was determined to do his best. Initially, he experienced difficulties with the Municipal President, William Bartley. The latter was very domineering and wanted the Asians on the Municipal Commission to be deferential. Fortunately for Tan Chin Tuan, a new President, Lazarus Rayman, took over. Tan was not only able to discuss issues with Rayman but was also able to learn from the older man. As Tan continued to impress, he was given more responsibilities. On one occasion, Tan was asked to attend a meeting with the Government as one of the representatives of the Municipal Commission. He had prepared well for the meeting with the Government representatives who included the Financial Secretary and the senior unofficial member of the legislature, Sir John Bagnall. The latter was also the chairman of Straits Trading Co. At this meeting, Tan Chin Tuan spoke on behalf of the Municipal Commission. Rayman had entrusted Tan with this important task and it was to Tan's credit that he was able to negotiate successfully with the government representatives. Thus, through his work in the Municipal Commission, Tan not only noted how government organisations were managed but also came into personal contact with key government officials and the captains of industry. These experiences and close connections were helpful when he served as a bridge between the bank and the government especially when World War Two was imminent.

Rumblings Of War

The colonial government was very concerned about the war being fought in Europe. Rayman spoke of this war at his first meeting with the Municipal Commissioners when he was appointed President on 19 October 1939. He said that 'The Empire was at war with Germany'. He was referring to the declaration of war by Britain (and France) on Germany in early September, and the start of a desperate struggle to survive the German military unleashed by Hitler. Rayman might have added that another war was being fought, since July 1937, in East Asia, as a result of Japanese aggression on Chinese soil. The international order was breaking down and this was to have a dramatic impact on Singapore.

As far as the Chinese in Singapore and Malaya were concerned, their war with Japan had already begun. Their major preoccupation was the Japanese assault on China. The Kuomintang or Nationalist Party of China and the Chinese Communist Party saw this conflict as a way of gaining more support from the overseas Chinese. Both parties had read the situation correctly. The local Chinese population in Singapore and Malaya responded to the Japanese invasion of China with great patriotic zeal and emotional frenzy.[8]

Many Chinese in Singapore rallied behind a prominent community leader: Tan Kah Kee. As Tan was not a member of either the Kuomintang or the Chinese Communist Party, he was more acceptable to the colonial authorities. They supported his attempt to raise funds for the war effort in China. The OCBC now took on a new role. It served as the treasurer of the China Relief Fund and Tan Chin Tuan was one of the members of the China Relief Fund Committee of Singapore. This fund received donations from all sectors of the Chinese community. Because of his experiences in dealing with European business leaders, Tan was approached for advice when the fund-raisers did not receive support from the European agency house, Sime Darby. The Chinese were very angry and wanted to retaliate with violence, but Tan advised them that a better way would be to hurt the pockets of the agency house. Sime Darby was the sole agent for a brand of cigarettes known as 'Black Cat', and the word went round to all Chinese not to buy this particular brand. Soon the agency house capitulated with an apology and a contribution to the fund-raising movement.

Apart from raising funds for the war effort in China, the Chinese played their part in the defence of the Colony. They were allowed to play a civilian role in Singapore and were involved in areas like air raid precaution, first aid, stretcher-bearing, nursing, and ambulance driving. All these services came under the name of Passive Defence. Some Chinese were also involved as recruits in the long-established volunteer army.

Tan Chin Tuan started as a member of the Passive Defence Council. When the Municipal Commission was asked to nominate two members to sit on this council, Rayman and Tan were chosen to represent it. The latter again criticised the discrimination against Asians when he served on this Council. He was not in favour of local men holding low ranking positions. He stressed that this was not fair and maintained that local men must be allowed to hold senior rank. Tan was subsequently appointed Assistant Commissioner and was made responsible for recruiting men and building air raid shelters. He received support from the staff of OCBC as well as from the members of the Po Chiak Keng Tan Clan Association of which he was a Trustee. Tan Kah Kee also helped him whenever he required assistance.

Though Tan Chin Tuan was busy with his work in the Passive Defence Council, he continued to have the interests of the OCBC in mind. He wanted to ensure that the bank would survive in the event of war. To this end, he worked closely with Lee Kong Chian who was also a member of the Passive Defence Council and chairman of OCBC. Whilst they could not do anything about fixed investments like property, they managed to conserve their cash and ensured that the bank did not lend excessively. Eventually, as reserves built up, their next priority was to make certain that the bank's funds would be safe. They planned to send the money to Australia and the United Kingdom.

Tan also had the foresight to suggest that the bank's documentary records be sent abroad in case of bombing in Singapore. Against this background of uncertainty, Tan wanted one set of records to be kept in his house in Cairnhill Road, another in the bank's stronghold in the China Building, Chulia Street and the third set of records was to be sent to Australia for safekeeping with the bank's agent there.

Tan was worn out by his work at the bank and the Passive Defence Council. His doctor advised him to rest, and he seized this opportunity to travel to Australia with his wife so that he could implement the plan he had worked out with OCBC Chairman, Lee Kong Chian. In Australia, he met up with the OCBC's agent, the Bank of New South Wales, and made the necessary arrangements to transfer funds and records from Singapore to Australia. Meanwhile the situation in Singapore was worsening as the Japanese were rapidly advancing down the Malay Peninsula and heading towards Singapore. When Tan Chin Tuan and his wife were in Melbourne on 19 December 1941 the Japanese bombed Singapore.[9] They returned to Singapore immediately.

Upon his return to Singapore, he made plans to send his family to Sydney as he realised that the worst had yet to come.

With his family safe in Australia, he continued to play an active role in the Passive Defence Council and helped supervise air raid drills and shelters. Despite all this activity, Tan Chin Tuan did not neglect his responsibilities to the bank. He arranged for much of the OCBC's balances to be deposited with the Treasury in England. The money was converted into pound sterling and was placed with the Midland Bank in England.

When the Japanese reached Johore Bahru on 31 January 1942, the Colonial Financial Secretary H. Weisberg informed Tan that the British had a lot of unused currency notes in the strong room at the Treasury. The British did not want the notes to get into the hands of the Japanese and decided that the notes had to be removed and burnt. Tan was entrusted with getting labourers to burn the unused notes. Once again he acted as intermediary between the government and the Chinese community. With the help of Tan Kah Kee, he obtained these labourers and the notes were incinerated. Realising that the invasion of Singapore was imminent, the OCBC and the other British banks like the Chartered Bank and the Hongkong and Shanghai Banking Corporation followed suit. An officer from the Treasury was present at the burning and copied down the serial numbers of the notes that were destroyed. Later, each bank was credited the amount it had consigned to the flames.

In addition to destroying assets which the bank could not take out of Singapore, the directors of the OCBC adopted a precedent established by corporations in Western Europe in 1940 as a means of survival against the German *blitzkrieg*. The strategy involved re-establishing their headquarters and registration in another country because the country of origin was no longer tenable. The OCBC decided to avail itself of the Defence (Companies Temporary Transfer of Registered Office) Regulations, 1942 and resolved to transfer its head office elsewhere within the British Empire in order to look after the branches still operating in the unoccupied territories, and the bank's assets abroad.

The directors of OCBC considered establishing their head office at Chungking, the Kuomintang wartime capital where the OCBC had a branch. The route to Chungking was through Rangoon, where another OCBC branch was located. From Rangoon, it was possible to go overland to Chungking by the Burma Road. The OCBC's directors decided that one of the bank's managers should leave Singapore to undertake this task.

The more senior managers like Kwa Siew Tee, Chew Hock Leong and Lim Bock Kee refused to go abroad as they did not want to leave their families behind. At first, Tan Chin Tuan also refused to go overseas because his mother and parents-in-law and other relatives were in Singapore. But he changed his mind when his mother advised him that he was putting himself and his family at risk if he were to stay put since he was so active in the Passive Defence Council.

With the Japanese advancing rapidly towards Singapore, Tan Chin Tuan was promoted to the position of Joint Managing Director on 2 February 1942, sharing the position with the then-Managing Director, Tan Ean Kiam. Tan Chin Tuan was given this position in recognition of his ability and his foresight in protecting the bank's assets and records. Armed with the power of attorney, he became the bank's external administrator-general. With the help of the Colonial Financial Secretary, Weisberg, he managed to obtain priority air passage to Rangoon, through Batavia (Jakarta), capital of the Dutch East Indies. Tan boarded a Sutherland flying boat on 4 February 1942 and was flown to Batavia in the Dutch East Indies. From there, he was to make his way to China to re-establish the OCBC's headquarters in Chungking. It was a far-sighted move as it enabled the OCBC to continue to manage its assets overseas.

By examining the responses of the OCBC to change, it is evident that the bank survived many crises. The OCBC learnt lessons from its predecessors' mistakes. Helped by people like Lee Kong Chian and Tan Chin Tuan, who were able to discern what changes were needed under new circumstances and situations, the OCBC was able to remove the blinkers imposed on its thinking by assumptions and conditions that no longer apply. Above all, it was able to formulate and adapt policies to meet the winds of change. The next chapter will focus on the bank's development during the Second World War and in the aftermath of that war, and how it survived under adverse conditions.

NOTES

1   Wellington K. K. Chan, 'Tradition and Change in the Chinese Business Enterprise', in *Chinese Business History: Interpretive Trends and Priorities for the Future,* R. Gardella, J. K. Leonard & A. McElderry, eds, *Chinese Studies in History*, vol. 31, no. 3–4 (1998): 138.

2   Wolfgang Jamann, *Chinese Traders in Singapore: Business Practices and Organisational Dynamics* (Saarbrucken, Germany: Verl. für Entwicklungspoltitik Breitenbach, 1994), p. 27.

3   J. D. Dalley was the man who later formed the Dalforce to fight the Japanese during the Occupation.

4   One possible reason for this rule was the fear that Eurasians and Indians from India might attempt to get into the Malayan Civil Service by sitting an open competitive examination held in London. Indeed, prior to 1904, some Ceylonese, Indian Muslims and Anglo-Indians had entered the service through this route.

5   Lee Yong Hock, *A History of the Straits Chinese British Association 1900–1959* (Singapore: University of Malaya, 1960), p. 53.

6   A. Ong, *Straits Chinese Politics 1890–1942* (Singapore: National University of Singapore, 1989–90), p. 22.

7   Lee, *A History of the Straits Chinese*, p. 53.

8   See Pang Wing-Seng, 'The "Double-Seventh" Incident, 1937: Singapore Chinese Response to the Outbreak of the Sino-Japanese War', *Journal of Southeast Asian Studies*, vol. 4, no. 2 (1973): 269–299.

9   The Japanese invasion of Malaya (including Singapore) began on 8 December 1941.

CHAPTER 4

IN THE FACE OF ADVERSITY

The year 1941 marked the beginning of traumatic days in colonial Singapore. Japanese aggression in China aroused the political consciousness of the Chinese in Singapore. War was not only imminent but could directly involve Singapore. However, most people believed in the British government's constant assurance that Singapore was not only an impregnable fortress but that the British would also protect the interests of the colony.

The Japanese attacked Pearl Harbor on 7 December 1941, landed troops at Singgora in southern Thailand and bombed Singapore on 8 December. The Japanese troops advanced rapidly through Malaya. It was no longer unthinkable that Singapore would fall into Japanese hands. Fear became reality when Singapore fell to the Japanese on 15 February 1942, the first day of the Chinese New Year.

For many, the familiar and comfortable way of life under the British quickly became a thing of the past. From February 1942 to August 1945, many changes were wrought under

Singapore's new Japanese masters. Though the period of Japanese rule was relatively short, its impact was significant. For a start, Singapore was re-named *Syonan-to* (Light of the South). A new order of subservience was forcefully imposed and mass screening exercises, or *Sook Ching*, were introduced to remove anti-Japanese elements, especially within the Chinese community. Chou stressed that:

> The Sook Ching operation, which lasted for two months beginning in February 1942, was but an early introduction to the arbitrary methods of persecution by the Japanese Imperial Army and its officers. Heads displayed on poles in the city, tales and experiences of torture by the much-feared Kempeitai (military police) and slappings and floggings for seemingly innocent actions initiated not only the Chinese but also our fellow countrymen of the other communities further into the brutal potential of the new regime.[1]

But more changes were to follow especially with regard to money supply. A major problem the Japanese forces faced when they occupied Singapore was the large amount of cash in circulation. Prior to the invasion, the local economy was thriving due to good tin and rubber prices and also to income derived from military projects. With the invasion, more cash went into circulation as departing British employers hurriedly paid off outstanding wages and bonuses. As the local population become increasingly aware of the inadequacies of British military defence, they began withdrawing funds from the banks. Before Singapore fell, the colonial government took measures to prevent currency notes and other valuables from getting into the hands of the Japanese. Kratoska noted that bearer bonds had been called in, converted to registered stock and finally destroyed. A total of $104 million out of the

$105 million bonds issued were processed. Currency notes worth about $75 million had been burnt and $39 million was shipped to India. Then on 14 February 1942, the Currency Commissioner further destroyed surplus currency held by the banks and even dumped stacks of coins into the sea.[2] Notwithstanding all these precautions, a large sum of money remained in the hands of the general population.

To solve the currency problem, the Japanese introduced several measures. One major initiative was to change the currency to the Japanese Malayan Dollar. These notes were initially carried into Malaya by the invaders. They were subsequently declared legal tender on 23 February 1942. Banyai stated that the value of the yen was placed on par with the Straits dollar even though the pre-war value was about half that of the Straits dollar.[3] Initially, local currency was acceptable but in May 1942, foreign currencies were declared illegal. Still, British notes continued to circulate on the black market.

Other measures adopted by the Japanese occupation force to withdraw huge amounts of currency from circulation included coercing the local community to donate to the war effort. The Chinese community was forced to form the Overseas Chinese Association (OCA) in 1942. Dr Lim Boon Keng was its first president and S. Q. Wong its vice president. The OCA was tasked with raising money for the Japanese war effort. The Japanese wanted all Chinese in Syonan-to and Malaya to donate $50 million as a gesture of loyalty. Turnbull noted that 'an organizing committee was hastily formed under Tan Ean Kiam, [former] Managing Director of the Oversea-Chinese Bank, and Singapore's liability was fixed at $10 million, with the remainder to be raised by Chinese in the Malay States.'[4] The OCA was divided along dialect lines and each dialect group was responsible for collecting money from their members. Those who could not contribute cash had to sell their properties to raise the money. According to an Archives and Oral History publication entitled *The Japanese Occupation: Singapore, 1942–1945*,[5] the OCA was unable to raise so much money in such a short period of time. The Japanese eventually agreed to provide the Chinese with a loan of $22 million. With this loan, the OCA was finally able to present a cheque for $50 million to the Japanese.[6]

However, these measures were insufficient to divert more funds to the Japanese war effort. To supplement this contribution, state lotteries, gambling and savings campaigns were introduced. In August 1943, Singapore had its first lottery and at the end of that year gambling was legalised for the first time. Many gambling dens catered to the people. Savings campaigns were initiated in February 1944 and by 1945, Singapore raised a sum of nearly $300 million for savings. Turnbull noted that

> ...the money was paid readily, since it was worth so little, but donors viewed these 'savings' as a gift to purchase peace and quiet, rather than a contribution to the Japanese war effort or a nest egg for their own future.[7]

Inflation set in and was soon spiralling out of control. The situation was not helped by the lack of economic activity in Singapore. The value of the Japanese currency dropped sharply in 1944 and 1945 and the Japanese had to print more and more notes to settle their debts. Kratoska observed that by August 1945, $1,200 million worth of banknotes had been created in Singapore.[8]

The Lean Years

The difficulties encountered by the Japanese invaders, naturally had a significant impact on the banking industry in general and on the OCBC in particular. To understand the effects of the changeover in government on the OCBC, it is essential not only to study how the bank survived in its home base in Singapore but also in its overseas headquarters.

The Japanese Occupation of Singapore dealt a mortal blow to the myth of white superiority. As the Japanese were keen to eradicate Western influence in Singapore, foreign banks like the Chartered Bank and the Hongkong and Shanghai Banking Corporation were liquidated. According to Kratoska, depositors with these banks received payments only in October 1944 from their accounts, the first $100 in full and only 20 percent of any other outstanding amounts.[9] After receiving their money, the depositors had to place their funds with approved banks.

Initially, the only banks which the Japanese authorities allowed to operate were the Yokohama Specie Bank and the Bank of Taiwan. These two Japanese banks were the first to commence operations after the Japanese invasion, starting business in March 1942. The Yokohama Specie Bank was no stranger to setting up overseas offices as it had been formed in 1880 to deal with the Japanese government's foreign businesses and to attract funds to Japan.[10] The bank expanded its Asian network of branches primarily during and after the Russo-Japanese War. According to Tamaki, the Yokohama Specie Bank accompanied the Japanese army as it advanced northwards to Manchuria.[11] This close relationship between the bank and the Japanese armed forces continued when the Japanese invaded Southeast Asia. The Yokohama Specie Bank 'was ordered to follow closely in the steps of the Japanese army and navy, and their offices opened everywhere in occupied Asia'.[12] Thus, it served as a cash and remittance office for the Japanese troops. In the case of the Bank of Taiwan, it was initially set up to fund Japanese enterprises on the island. Later and as a result of its experiences in operating outside of Japan, a branch was established in Singapore.

Kratoska pointed out that to finance economic activities and regulate the circulation of currency for the Southeast Asian countries under their rule, the Japanese also established a central bank, the Southern Regions Development Bank (SRDB), on 30 March 1942.[13] The Malayan branch of the SRDB was set up in Singapore in July 1942 and took over the duties of the Yokohama Specie Bank. According to Kratoska, from 1 April 1943, the SRDB began to issue currency to replace the unnumbered military yen that the Japanese troops had brought with them when they invaded Malaya and Singapore.[14]

However, the Japanese banks were not very successful. This was because the majority of the Chinese population were unwilling to do business with them. Therefore, the Japanese decided to allow the Chinese and Indian banks to resume their operations. The Japanese wanted the local banks not only to help circulate the new currency but also to divert funds for the war effort. The Japanese military administration agreed to allow the Chinese and Indian banks to re-open on 28 April 1942, the eve of the Emperor's birthday.[15] The first Chinese banks to re-commence operations were the OCBC, Sze Hai Tong Bank, Ban Hin Lee Bank, United Chinese Bank, and the Lee Wah Bank.[16] The China and Southern Bank resumed operations on 1 June 1942 and the Kwong Yik Bank, on 1 September 1942. The Indian Bank and the Indian Overseas Bank followed suit. Apart from re-opening in Singapore, the banks were also asked to recommence their operations overseas.

When the OCBC re-opened for business in April 1942, it had about $900,000 in Straits dollars. This was put aside and like the other banks, OCBC started lending out to the people the Japanese notes — nicknamed 'coconuts' and 'banana' notes — which were supplied by the Japanese banks.[17] Lee Choon Seng took over as OCBC's Acting Chairman as its Chairman, Lee Kong Chian was away in the United States. At the OCBC,

> the Banks' staff had to suffer most of the injustice committed against so many other innocent people and as a result the Bank lost about one tenth of its 280 Singapore staff during the Occupation. Several of the staff did not turn up for work on many days. But the Bank's offices were kept open. The Japanese wanted to create the impression that everything was going normally in the 'co-prosperity sphere'.
>
> [...] Many executives lived at the OCBC office in China Building, and one manager had his family there as well. There was an air-raid shelter and foodstuff store in the basement.[18]

An OCBC publication entitled *Twenty-one Years: Growth and Progress*[19] noted that the bank's 'branches in China and Hongkong were also ordered to re-open for business during the occupation while those in Java, in common with other Banks there, were treated as enemy concerns and placed in liquidation'.

A Changed Landscape

When the local banks re-opened for business, they operated in a changed environment. The banking system was more centralised, and the Japanese exerted much control, setting directions for local banks. For instance, Wilson observed that the local bankers had to take their instructions from the Japanese at meetings that were held at either the office of the Japanese Inspector of Banks or in the Japanese State Bank's office.[20] The directors of the local Chinese banks, for example, were ordered to sign a joint guarantee, placing their personal assets as pledge for loans from the Japanese. This enabled the Chinese banks to resume business. The amount of money that depositors could withdraw from the banks was also controlled. This measure was essential because the customers of the local banks rushed to withdraw their money when the banks re-opened. This placed a great deal of pressure on the banks. In order to help the banks, the Syonan Chinese Banks Joint Board of Control suggested to the Japanese that a scheme of blocked accounts be introduced. Under this scheme, customers with credit balances could have a certain percentage of the credit released to them at fixed intervals. Four stages were proposed, starting with 30%, then 10%, another 10% and later an additional 40%.[21] The Japanese accepted and implemented this proposal.

Apart from following the same scheme, the local banks were also told to participate in a Malayan Banking Association. Kratoska stressed that the enforcement of a common policy to be followed by all local banks was also evident when the banks offered standard interest rates of three percent on fixed deposits and two percent on normal savings accounts and in the case of loans, more controls were imposed. Limits were placed on the amount of money that could be loaned by banks and any loan exceeding this limit required prior approval from the Japanese authorities.[22] Thus, the loans that were approved by the local banks were for small sums of money and few loans were made. The banks were also required to have fixed deposit accounts with the Yokohama Specie Bank. Kratoska observed that this requirement adversely affected the local banks as their funds were returned in August and September 1945 in occupation currency that subsequently became valueless when the British de-monetised wartime currency.[23]

The banks also suffered from changes made to the currency in circulation. When the Japanese Malayan Dollar was declared legal tender, banks had only the Japanese Malayan Dollar and the local currencies to trade in. Though local currency continued to be accepted by the Japanese, Kratoska pointed out that within half a year of the occupation, the amount of local currency in circulation was reduced by 50%. As a result of the emphasis on the use of the yen, loans were in Japanese notes.[24] Such notes were not backed by real assets and when the Japanese printed more and more currency notes, the value of the yen dropped increasingly.

The banks had to cope with the changes in the value of the currency and the problem of inflation. According to Yap Siong Eu, who was a bank clerk working in the Ban Hin Lee Bank during the Japanese Occupation,

> The value of currency notes depreciated so fast that very soon...the amounts were so big you won't have the time to count. Customers just write the amount and their name outside the gunny bag and we waited for another customer to come and draw cash and push this bag to them...[25]

To survive the banks even engaged in the brokering business. Yap Siong Eu further explains that

> ...when bank customers come in to deposit or cash, we automatically ask them what goods they had to dispose or they want to buy. That's how we match them with other customers who wanted to buy or sell. It's just opportunity to keep us going, to keep us alive.[26]

It can be seen then that unlike the other Chinese banks, the Ban Hin Lee Bank played a more active role in Singapore during the Japanese Occupation. This was largely because prior to the war, Yap Chor Ee, the founder of the Ban Hin

Lee Bank, was not involved in political activities like the anti-Japanese movement or the China Relief Fund. This financial institution therefore adopted and maintained a neutral stance. Consequently, the Japanese appointed the Ban Hin Lee Bank to be the intermediary between the Japanese banks and all local Chinese banks known to have anti-Japanese attitudes. It was noted by Lee that 'the Ban Hin Lee Bank volunteered to act as a clearing house between the Japanese bank and the local banks during the Second World War.'[27] Thus, as the Ban Hin Lee Bank had established a good relationship with the Japanese, it was evident that this bank was able to play a key role in the banking sector in war-time Singapore.

In contrast, the larger and more influential OCBC played a low-key role during the Japanese occupation of Singapore. In fact, it even adopted a conservative policy. According to an OCBC memorandum dated 8 June 1946,

> ...there were no investments made by the Bank during this period in immovable properties (except in Penang in accordance with a pre-war extension plan). The lack of investments into properties was due to the question of whether titles acquired during the Occupation would be recognised. Such investments would also have been speculative in nature and not a prudent policy to follow.[28]

By following such a policy, the OCBC memorandum noted that 'during the occupation, the Bank did not suffer from any business loss'.[29] Apart from trying to reduce its risk exposure, the OCBC also had to deal with another problem. This involved a change in the leadership of the bank when Tan Ean Kiam, the Managing Director, passed away on 30 March 1943. Tan had suffered especially when he was in charge of the OCA fund-raising committee. His humiliating and terrifying meetings with the Japanese at their military head-quarters took their toll, and he died a broken man.

He was succeeded by Lee Choon Seng who held the position until the end of the Japanese Occupation of Singapore. The Japanese accepted him as the new managing director because they saw him as a pious and humble man who had been on a pilgrimage to India. As Wilson observed, 'the Japanese respected religious men'.[30] In addition, Lee Choon Seng had a low profile in the local community. Although conversant in Hokkien, Cantonese, Mandarin and Malay, he was not proficient in the English language. As he was not interested in politics, he was therefore decidedly cold to the idea of being a politician. All these factors not only made him more acceptable to the Japanese but also helped to modify the OCBC's somewhat pro-British image. The OCBC's pro-British image had been the culmination of the involvement of people like Tan Chin Tuan and Lee Kong Chian with the colonial government. The bank had also earned the displeasure of the Japanese when its assets were sent out of the country prior to the Japanese Occupation of the colony. On hindsight, the OCBC made an apt choice when it appointed Lee Choon Seng as its managing director. As Wilson noted:

> Lee's presence in the Bank and at his home only a few
> doors away must have made the lives — especially those
> of the senior executives — not so intolerable as it would
> otherwise have been.[31]

As the war progressed, the bank also found it difficult to function without a full complement of staff. According to Wilson, the bank suffered a loss of about one-tenth of its 280 Singapore staff during the Japanese Occupation. As conditions worsened in Singapore, some even failed to turn up for work.[32] Despite this shortage of staff, the Japanese insisted that the bank stay open to give the impression that life was still normal in Singapore.[33]

A Fight For Survival

Contrary to the outward semblance of normalcy, life was far from normal both in Singapore and in other occupied countries during the World War Two. Whilst the OCBC struggled to survive in Singapore under adverse conditions, it was also able to continue functioning overseas. This was largely due to the efforts of Tan Chin Tuan who was Joint Managing Director of the OCBC. He had escaped to Batavia, the capital of the Netherlands East Indies, in order to get a plane to Rangoon; from there, by travelling overland, he would continue to Chungking where he planned to establish the overseas headquarters of the OCBC. Tan waited for nearly a month in Batavia but failed to get a flight to Rangoon. Realising that the situation in Batavia was worsening as the town seemed to be rather deserted, he went to the British Consulate and insisted on knowing what was happening in Batavia. The Vice-Consul General advised him to proceed to the south of Java. Tan was enterprising and managed to make his own way to the south coast where he boarded a river steamer, the *General Verspeck*, bound not for Chungking but for Australia.

He reached Fremantle and was eventually reunited with his family in Sydney. He then established an office of the OCBC in the Bank of New South Wales and later formed close ties with the latter. Whilst he was in Australia, he interacted socially with many students from Malaya and Singapore and came to know students like Seow Eu Jin, and even assisted some whose studies were badly affected by the Japanese invasion of Malaya and Singapore. These students lacked funds to continue with their education.

One such undergraduate was Ismail bin Dato Abdul Rahman, a medical student from Johore Bahru who was studying at the University of Melbourne. When Tan Chin Tuan heard that Ismail wanted to terminate his studies to join the Royal Australian Air Force, Tan tried to dissuade him. He found out that Ismail was on a scholarship granted by the Sultan of Johore and that the money had been deposited in an account at the Bank of New South Wales' Melbourne branch. Tan then authorised the Melbourne branch to resume paying Ismail and charged the amount to the OCBC's general account. Later he approached the British government to award Ismail a scholarship. The OCBC did not have to underwrite the monthly payments for more than a year as the sum of money was later repaid by the Sultan of Johore. Ismail was grateful to Tan for his kind gesture and efforts. Later, when Ismail became a cabinet minister — in charge of, at various times, natural resources, commerce and industry, external affairs, internal security, home affairs and justice, (1955–1967; 1969–1973) — and Deputy Prime Minister (1970–1973), he always had time for Tan Chin Tuan.

By establishing these close ties with young students from different ethnic groups in Australia, Tan continued to widen his network of people on whom he could later depend on for support. The OCBC was to benefit from this network that Tan developed overseas. Apart from forming personal friendships with students, Tan also helped other members of the business community who fled to Australia from Malaya and Singapore. For instance, he assisted Lee Chee Shan when he recommended that the Bank of New South Wales extend Lee a loan of £2,000. Yeap remarked that this 'was the beginning of a life-long friendship'.[34] After the war, Lee was to become the managing director of the Chung Khiaw Bank when it was formed on 4 February 1950.

Tan Chin Tuan remained in Australia for one-and-a-half years. He then decided to make another attempt to reach Chungking. When the Japanese invaded Burma, the OCBC branch at Rangoon had been shifted northwards to Chungking, the wartime Chinese capital. The principal officers and the account books of the Rangoon branch were also transferred there.[35] Tan felt that he should proceed to China, especially since it had become the meeting place for Chinese bankers. It was therefore important for the OCBC to re-establish its headquarters there.

With East Asia and Southeast Asia under Japanese control, Tan Chin Tuan realised that the most appropriate route to Chungking was through South Asia. Accordingly, he set off on his journey accompanied by Peck Pia Jim who had been the assistant manager of the Rangoon branch. Peck had escaped with his family to Australia. Both of them arrived in India in August 1943 where they found a small community of Malayan evacuees. Most of them lived in the hill resort of Bangalore where the climate was cool; other Malayans resided in cities like Delhi, Bombay and Calcutta. In fact, due to the great number of Chinese staying in Calcutta, a Chinese consulate was set up there.

Tan Chin Tuan quickly became involved in the affairs of the Malayan community, often acting as a mediator in their arguments. For instance, he tried to resolve the dispute between the two factions of the Malayan Association of India. One group was led by John Laycock, a lawyer and pre-war Singapore Municipal Councillor, and Tunku Abu Bakar of the Johore Royal House whilst the other faction was headed by Joseph Aaron Elias[36] and H. E. Fancott. When disagreements could not be resolved, the Malayan Chinese left to form their own Overseas Chinese Association (OCA). At the OCA's inaugural meeting held in September 1943, Tan Cheng Lock[37] was elected President and Tan Chin Tuan, who had left for

Calcutta earlier in the month, was elected Vice-President in absentia. The banker was reluctant to accept the appointment and informed Tan Cheng Lock that he was prepared to work for the association, but only in the capacity of an ordinary member as he felt that Malayans should not monopolise the two top positions in the association. Eventually, Tan Cheng Lock and his son, Siew Sin, persuaded Tan Chin Tuan to remain as Vice-President in view of the latter's experience in public service in Singapore. Tan Chin Tuan acquiesced.

Using his skill as an adjudicator, Tan Chin Tuan was able to help the fledging association clear a misunderstanding with the Chinese Consul-General, Dr C. J. Pao, who was based in Calcutta. Prior to the formation of the OCA, Tan Siew Sin had spoken to Dr Pao, who advised him that the association should be registered according to Chinese regulations and laws so that the functions of the Chinese government would not be jeopardised. When Dr Pao next heard of the OCA, it was about its inauguration in Bombay. As he had not been supplied with information about the association, he was at a loss when inquiries about the organisation were directed to him. Tan Chin Tuan learnt of Dr Pao's views on the OCA and he contacted Tan Cheng Lock to find out what had happened. It turned out to be an unfortunate oversight rather than an act of discourtesy. Tan Siew Sin had in fact contacted the Consulate on numerous occasions but had not been able to meet the Consul-General. Finally, after receiving an assurance from a consular officer that Dr Pao would write fully to him on the subject, Tan Siew Sin did not proceed further. However, no such correspondence arrived. As a result, Tan presumed that Dr Pao was no longer interested and proceeded with plans to organize the OCA. Tan Chin Tuan's tact and timely mediation helped to diffuse a possible clash with Chungking.

Apart from contributing to the Malayan community, Tan Chin Tuan was also preoccupied with the law requiring 'aliens' to register in India. Unlike his father who was China-born and eventually became a naturalised British subject, Tan was a Singapore-born British subject like his mother, with the right to a British passport. On that basis, Tan refused to register himself as an 'alien'. This issue was compounded by the fact that the Chinese Nationality Law of 1929 made every Chinese, wherever born, a subject of China. Tan therefore became by default, also a Chinese subject. The dual nationality issue blurred the lines of loyalty for the Chinese and as Tan put it so succinctly, 'they used to run with the hares and hunt with the hounds'. Firmly believing that as he was loyal to the government of the country he lived in, Tan Chin Tuan expected the British Government to treat him without discrimination. Hence, he refused to budge from the view that there was no necessity for him to register.

Then, in early September 1943, shortly after his arrival in Calcutta, an Inspector Lloyd called on his assistant, Peck Pia Jim, at the Broadway Hotel where they were staying. Inspector Lloyd requested that they call at the Foreigners' Registration Office in order to be properly registered as foreign nationals in India under the Registration of Foreigners Act of 1939. Tan Chin Tuan remained adamant and even checked the ordinance and found that it defined a 'foreigner' as being 'any person who was at birth a Japanese, Chinese or Thai subject'. Though ethnically Chinese, Tan Chin Tuan was a British subject at birth. On that basis, he wrote to the Registration Office and explained that it was not necessary for him to register. But, to safeguard himself, he engaged the prominent law firm of Messrs Orr Dignam & Co. to represent him. One of its senior partners, an Irishman by the name of Irving Jones, immediately telephoned and secured the Calcutta Government's undertaking not to prosecute his client, whilst

Jones appealed to the Home Department of the Government of Bengal on the banker's behalf. Tan's case was subsequently referred to the central government at Delhi. The latter upheld the judgment of the Calcutta police to register Chinese British subjects.

Tan Chin Tuan remained steadfast and decided to fight the judgment. He mobilised the Malayan community in India and they addressed a petition to the Colonial Secretary in London, appealing to him to intervene. Tan also spoke to the British civil servants who had previously served in Malaya. They included Colonel E. V. G. Day, a Civil Affairs Officer in the South East Asia Command involved with the Malayan Planning Unit, and J. S. W. Reid, the Deputy Malayan Representative in Bangalore. These civil officers cabled a very strong protest to Delhi. Tan even approached C. D. Ahearne, the Special Representative of the Secretary of States for the Colonies in Bombay. Finally, he received a letter from Reid forwarding a cable from Ahearne to Tan stating:

> I have been informed by the Government of India that Chinese British Subjects holding British Passports issued in Malaya will not be compelled to register. Go therefore with this wire and your passport to the Registration Office and wire me the result at once.[38]

Tan Chin Tuan complied and when shown the wire, the Deputy Commissioner of Police said that anyone unwilling to register would not be compelled to do so. Eventually the Indian government amended its ruling to register 'aliens'.

Tan had won his case. There was no necessity for him to try to change the ruling because he had already been told that the war would soon end and registration would only be temporary, but the banker held a different view. To him, 'the question is not merely one of inconvenience; it is one of rights and principles'. He added: 'it matters little to me personally to register as a foreigner. I am only opposing this because of the underlying principle.' Tan further asserted that 'those who refuse to defend their rights deserve to lose them'.

He was to adopt this same stand with regard to the registration of the bank in Chungking. At the outset of the war, Tan Chin Tuan was tasked with going to China to set up the OCBC's headquarters there. But while he was in India, it came to his knowledge that the Chinese government was very short of funds. He felt rather apprehensive that the allure of the OCBC's substantial assets in London might prove too tempting for the Chinese government to resist and pressure might be exerted on him to arrange for the transfer of these funds to China. Furthermore, accounts of arbitrary executions in Chungking without trial had reached India and Tan had no desire to be on the hit list. After due deliberation, he decided that it was safer to register the bank's headquarters in India. The fact that he changed his mind in the presence of new data not only showed his flexibility and adaptability but revealed that his broad view of the situation indicated that he had to act decisively to uphold the best interests of the OCBC.

The Shape Of Things To Come

Tan Chin Tuan's determination to stand his ground and not surrender his rights without a fight won him the respect of the British. They had not come across an ethnic Chinese who was not only so staunchly loyal to them but was also willing to vigorously defend his British birthright. He gradually earned their trust and gained their confidence. Their faith in Tan's allegiance to the British Crown was to stand him in good stead. It was further enhanced when Tan himself expressed keen interest in being involved in the rehabilitation and reconstruction of post-war Singapore and in getting the OCBC back on its feet.

Prior to the Japanese Occupation, he had written a letter to S. W. Jones, the Colonial Secretary and chairman of the Passive Defence Council in Singapore offering his assistance. In his missive, Tan Chin Tuan stated:

> I feel that as I am practically the only one amongst the Chinese Unofficial Representatives on the Government Organizations in Malaya, who is luckily out of the enemies' hands, it may be my duty to place my services at the disposal of the British Government.... I am not a Military man but my experience and knowledge of Malaya, particularly Singapore may be of some use. I do not expect any remuneration since as Managing Director of the Bank, I am more or less solely respon-sible for safeguarding the assets and re-establishing the institution in Malaya and elsewhere and I can only undertake work which will still enable me to look after the Bank. On the other hand, it will be advantageous to let me retain my connection with the Bank because it had branches all over Malaya and was therefore more in touch with the population than any other organisation.[39]

In offering his services, it appears that Tan Chin Tuan was motivated by both his British loyalties as an 'unofficial representative' of the government and also by his plans for the OCBC's post-war development. He wanted the bank to play a significant role in the rebuilding of the Singapore economy, but before his plans could become reality, they had to be backed by the British government.

The British responded positively to his offer of help. This was evident in a letter that Jones wrote to Sir Edward Gent[40] of the Colonial Office on 29 December 1943. Jones strongly recommended that 'Tan Chin Tuan be given a part in the organisation for the restoration of Malaya.' Jones explained that he held Tan 'in high esteem' as he 'is one of the younger leading Chinese of Singapore and did a lot of most valuable work in connection with the preparation for the Civil Defence of Singapore'. According to Jones, Tan had played a key role in the recruitment of 'hundreds of Chinese for civil defence'. Jones explained further that he had a 'poor opinion of most of the senior Chinese public men in the Colony' and that he 'would not go out of [his] way to recommend them for any part in Malaya's future'. Apart from recognising Tan Chin Tuan's ability, Jones mentioned that the British should take into account the way in which the Chinese banks in Singapore were treated just before the invasion of the colony by the Japanese. This was because, during the evacuation, the European banks were warned and given assistance by the British while the Chinese banks were overlooked, thus leading to the heavy losses they incurred during the Occupation. As Jones pointed out in his letter 'the Chinese banks were treated very badly'. In view of this situation, Jones suggested that a 'suitable gesture of friendship and encouragement' be accorded to Tan who was the representative of the 'most important of the Chinese Banks'. Such a step would also assuage any harsh feelings residual from the shabby treatment of the Chinese banks by the British prior to the fall of Singapore.

Other British officials also shared Jones' views of Tan Chin Tuan. Colonel Patrick McKerron[41] from the War Office for example, wrote a letter dated 5 June 1944 to Edward Gent stating his opinion of Tan's opposition to the ruling that aliens must register in India. According to McKerron, 'it has been an inspiration to hear the vehemence and pride with which members of the Straits-born Chinese have spoken of their status as British subjects.' Apart from valuing Tan's loyalty,

McKerron placed great stress on his capabilities. McKerron mentioned that:

> The memorandum on War Losses Claims is the original work of Tan Chin Tuan and the realistic attitude and courageous approach to this most difficult problem is a welcome relief from the avaricious claims advocated by the Malayan Association in Bombay and of its members... It also serves to confirm my previous estimate of the worth of Tan Chin Tuan and the position he will hold as a leader of his own people.[42]

This advice was to remain in the minds of the British when they made plans for the restoration of 'economic life' in a post-war Singapore. They had misgivings about some Chinese leaders. There was no doubt that prior to the war, such leaders had helped the British maintain law and order in the local community and had even served in government bodies. Then when war was declared and the fall of the colony seemed imminent, some of these leaders had left the colony. As for those who had remained behind, a number of them had been forced to collaborate with the Japanese. The British were concerned about the ability of these people to resume their previous role in a post-war environment. Whilst the British pondered and deliberated on the right people to select for the key positions, there was no doubt in their minds that Tan Chin Tuan was a suitable candidate. It was noted that Tan was one of two Chinese the British consulted before the Colonial Office Representative in India drew up a priority list of Chinese returnees.[43]

The stage was now set for Tan to put in place his far-sighted plans for the OCBC to be at the forefront of British consideration. In particular, he had a balanced view of how it was possible to ensure that the OCBC, the largest of the

local banks in Singapore would be treated on an equal footing
with the larger European banks. He wanted the OCBC to be
allowed to recover its premises and restart its operations in
Singapore at the same time as the European banks. Unless
the OCBC could achieve these objectives, he felt that it would
entail prolonged hardship for the bank's customers and staff.

The astute banker shared his concerns with Colonel E. V.
Day and Lieutenant-Colonel Victor Purcell[44] of the South East
Asia Command in a memorandum in early 1945. They
forwarded his memorandum to the Malayan Planning Unit
in the War Office with a covering letter stating that

> Lt Col Purcell considers it politically of the utmost
> importance that some means should be found of
> enabling this large and influential bank to reopen
> for business at the same time as the British Banks.
> Col. Day supports this view and considers that failure
> to arrange accordingly will cause much unnecessary
> difficulty in re-establishing internal trade and tranquility
> on our return. It also would be a poor return for the
> foresight of the bank's officials and the co-operation of
> the S. S. Government whose actions facilitated the
> removal and conservation of so much of the bank's
> assets if it were not made possible for the bank to reopen
> without delay.[45]

These recommendations were carefully considered when
the British continued to prepare for their return to Malaya
and Singapore. Turnbull commented that 'in the months
following the collapse of British power in Malaya, the
Colonial Office began drawing up schemes for radical post-
war reorganization.'[46] Albert Lau explains that much of the
planning was done in London, especially with the creation
of a Malayan Planning Unit on 5 July 1943 with 'an initial

staff of six officers and attached to the Directorate of Civil Affairs in the War Office'.[47] After considerable deliberation, a decision was made to have a 'closer union' of the pre-war Federated and Unfederated Malay States and Straits Settlements and establish a new consolidated colonial entity, the Malayan Union.[48] According to Lau it was also decided that Singapore, because of its 'distinctive characteristics', be administered separately from the rest of Malaya.[49] This was a departure from the way in which these territories had been grouped together prior to the war. Such a plan would mean the formation of two distinct territories. However, before this plan could be implemented, the British had to get the economies of both territories functioning as normally as possible and in the shortest time.[50]

Of immediate concern to the British was the problem of the wartime currency issued by the Japanese. During the occupation, Japanese 'banana money' circulated side by side with the local currency and was on par with the latter. However, difficulties soon arose with the use of the Japanese currency. According to Turnbull:

> ...while the Japanese military offensive continued, the currency was sound, but once the fortunes of war turned against Japan, the value of paper money began to slide. Commonly known as 'bananas' or 'coconuts', because they bore designs of plants, the first notes were numbered but subsequent issues were not, and the quality was so poor that notes were easy to forge.[51]

Singapore was awash with worthless paper money. The worth of the Japanese currency declined precipitously in relation to the British Straits Settlements notes, and the local population tried to exchange it for goods. The price of goods increased and inflation spiralled out of control. The British realised that they would have to deal with this problem of inflation upon their return to Malaya and Singapore. The best solution would be to eradicate the Japanese currency when they re-occupied their colonies.

To do this, the British had to ensure that there was enough new currency for use after the war. They made preparations to exchange pre-occupation Malayan notes with new ones valued at par. Over $200 million worth of new Malayan notes and approximately $18 million in coins had been prepared. This was roughly equivalent to the amount of currency circulating in the colony before the Occupation. The British believed that in order to restore pre-war wage and price levels, the amount of currency in circulation should approximate pre-war levels. To facilitate a speedy distribution of the new currency, the British knew that it would be necessary to call on the banks for help.

While the British were making plans to return to Singapore and Malaya, the war suddenly came to an end with the surrender of the Japanese after the bombing of Hiroshima on 6 August 1945. According to Turnbull:

> ...the sudden ending of the war brought special difficulties for Singapore because no detailed plans had been made for her post-war administration. Once the sepa- ration of the island had been agreed to by the War Cabi- net, the Colonial Office concentrated on the complicated peninsular problems and virtually ignored Singapore.... The form of Singapore's constitution was still undecided when the British returned to Malaya in September 1945.[52]

As an interim measure, Singapore was made the headquarters of the British Military Administration (BMA) under the Supreme Allied Commander, Lord Louis Mountbatten.

The latter delegated control of the civil government to Ralph Hone, the Chief Civil Affairs Officer for Malaya, and Patrick McKerron became the Deputy Chief Civil Affairs Officer in charge of Singapore. The BMA controlled Singapore and Malaya for seven months from September 1945 to April 1946. Kratoska pointed out that the majority of the officers in the BMA had no experience in Malaya and they had to deal with a multitude of problems.[53] As such, they had to rely on Asians who were familiar with the local situation and who had worked closely with the colonial authorities before the war. Above all they needed people with influence and persuasive powers to set their plans in motion. One such person was Tan Chin Tuan. He had been given priority to return to Singapore. Together with his assistant, Peck Pia Jim, they were the only two Asian bankers selected to board one of the first planes bound for the island. Their other fellow passengers were the representatives of major British banks.[54] The bankers had been chosen to return to Singapore as soon as possible because they were expected to play a major role in the reconstruction of the post-war economies of Malaya and Singapore. They flew from Colombo on 13 September 1945 and reached Singapore the following day. Upon their return to Singapore, they found the colony gripped by economic stagnation and the banks closed.

Overcoming The Odds

When Tan Chin Tuan arrived in Singapore, his first commitment was to the OCBC. He attended a board meeting of the OCBC specially convened on 18 September to welcome him home. The meeting was held at the Bank's China Building in Chulia Street. The Bank's directors in Singapore were anxious to learn what the OCBC had done outside the Japanese-occupied territories during the period from 4 February 1942 to 14 September 1945. Tan described in detail the measures he adopted to protect the Bank's interests. For example, the bank had been re-registered in Bombay on 30 January 1945 and the bank had formed a Board of Directors overseas. The directors included Lee Kong Chian, Tan Cheng Lock, W. H. Chu, Lee Boon Tin and S. K. Chan.

Apart from briefing the directors on the progress of the bank overseas, Tan Chin Tuan spoke to Lee Choon Seng, the acting chairman and managing director, and requested that he be allowed to step down as the joint managing director. Lee refused and insisted that Tan take over as the sole managing director. Tan acceded to this request and resumed his position on 1 October 1945.

Tan Chin Tuan recalled that, at that time, no one in the bank wanted to be the managing director as the bank was facing many problems. For a start, the bank's vaults were filled with Japanese currency that had been declared worthless by the British, and the bank now had the difficult task of explaining to its depositors why their money had no value. Furthermore, the bank was adversely affected when customers, anticipating that the Japanese currency would lose its face value, paid off their loans using wartime notes. As these notes had lost their value, the bank incurred very heavy losses. It was therefore not surprising that the public's confidence in the bank was badly affected. Even staff of the bank tried to sell off their OCBC shares. They were concerned that the government might consider these shares invalid. Although colleagues like Chew Hock Leong advised Tan Chin Tuan not to buy OCBC shares, he went against the trend and bought more shares. He took this risk primarily because he felt that as managing director such an action on his part would help restore public confidence in the bank. As the prices of the bank shares were low, he was able to acquire a substantial amount of shares to become a major shareholder of the OCBC, joining the ranks of the owner-directors of the early Chinese banks.

However, Tan greatly differed from these directors in that he was prepared to depart from the traditional ways of operating a bank. He felt that over a period of time, these methods had become ineffective and in some cases, even unacceptable. A shake-up was therefore necessary, and he set out to change some of the bank's traditional practices. It was difficult to introduce such changes to an established bank so steeped in its own tradition, but he forged ahead. Fortunately Tan managed to gain the support of Lee Kong Chian, the bank's chairman, who had also just returned to Singapore. Just before the fall of Singapore to the Japanese, Lee had flown to Washington to attend a rubber conference as a delegate of the Singapore Rubber Millers Association and Singapore Chinese Rubber Dealers Association. His stay in the United States was unavoidably extended when the Japanese captured Singapore. When the war ended, he returned to Singapore in 1945. He too realised that the bank had to remove stifling practices in order to survive. With his enthusiastic support, Tan proceeded to modernise the bank with his innovative ideas.

Making A Difference

Tan Chin Tuan had specific thoughts about how to promote innovation and change. He realised that for the smooth and effective functioning of his administrative apparatus, he had to adopt bold and harsh measures. For a start, the bank had to change its recruitment policies to ensure that only trained and competent people were employed. Although Tan had been a beneficiary of the traditional way of hiring new staff, he set out to sweep away all the old, unprofessional practices of employment which were based mainly on dialect or kinship links. From now on, the criteria for selection of personnel would be to find the right people with ability. There would be no exceptions to the rule. In fact, he set an example for the staff and directors of the bank when he steadfastly refused to allow his son and only brother to join the bank.

Not satisfied with the enforcement of such a bold measure, Tan also instituted controls on loans that were made to relatives and friends of the directors of the bank. In the past, such loans often resulted in bad debts. Fully aware of the dangers and risks of extending loans based on kinship or friendship, he decided that all borrowings be scrutinised and approved by him. He further emphasised that any director recommending a loan would have to act as guarantor for that loan. Tan himself complied with these regulations when his friends applied for loans. Approval of loans was no longer associated with favouritism. Even Lee Kong Chian, the bank's chairman, agreed to follow these rules. To prevent conflict of interest, Tan declined offers of shares from other companies. He was of the opinion that men at the top must set good examples for those below to follow. It was not long before he established for himself a reputation for integrity.

Apart from putting into effect such stringent internal practices, Tan spurred the bank into taking on an active role in the community. During the Japanese Occupation, the OCBC adopted a low-key stance. Its close ties with the colonial government had caused the Japanese to look askance at the bank, and it remained out of favour with the invaders during the Occupation. As such, the OCBC did not work too closely with the invaders. The picture changed dramatically after the War. The factors associated with the new, bold strokes on the canvas were many. The OCBC was the only local bank to re-locate its headquarters outside of Malaya and it had the foresight to send most of its assets overseas prior to the Japanese occupation. Above all, it had Tan Chin Tuan at the helm and he had gained the trust of the British.

It was therefore not surprising that the British Military Administration delegated more responsibility to the OCBC. When the officers of the Chartered Bank were unable to return immediately to Kuala Lumpur after the cessation of war, the British asked the OCBC to act as the Treasury in the interim. It thus became the first local bank to be entrusted with the important task of distributing the new Malayan post-war currency to replace the wartime Japanese notes. According to Wilson:

> The OCBC was given as much money as it could lend out... The bank had to return all the money to the Government later. But, at that moment, it was the best way of priming the pump and distributing money to the community. The OCBC did not wish to take too much, and helped the other local banks — the Sze Hai Tong, Lee Wah and United Chinese — to get the money.[55]

Using the OCBC and later other Chinese and Indian banks which reopened on 17 September 1945, the BMA helped revive the economy. It deposited government funds of up to 5% of the individual banks' pre-war deposits. Kratoska noted that the banks paid normal interest rates and charged no more than 7% interest on loans. The banks needed such assistance as the local financial institutions had been adversely affected by the British Government's decision to make the Japanese currency worthless.[56] During the War, all Malayan currency had been removed from the banks by the Japanese and, as the invaders continued to print more and more Japanese notes to counteract inflation, local banks ended up with worthless Japanese currency. Naturally, these developments did not affect the European banks since they remained closed during the Japanese Occupation.

The urgency to distribute the new currency could also be attributed to the effects of de-monetisation of Japanese currency on the general population. Many people were affected, and some even went bankrupt. To further soften the impact of de-monetisation, the British government paid arrears in salaries and pensions, extended advances to civil servants, gave small cash payments to households, hired labourers for government works and purchased rice and rubber stocks. The success of this policy was evident. Kratoska noted that by September 1945, $8 million went into circulation and by the end of 1945, the figure reached $160 million.[57]

As the economy improved, Tan Chin Tuan considered how policy could be adapted to meet the new environment. He then took the unusual step of broadening the customer base of the OCBC beyond the confines of the Hokkien community. The bank financed businessmen from different ethnic groups and even approved loans to companies owned by members of other races. Again, Tan was the prime-mover of this initiative. He felt that when these companies prospered, OCBC would naturally benefit. Soon the bank's clientele even included former war-time internees. Many of these European civilians were penniless and, as they had no collateral, they were unable to obtain bank loans. The OCBC, keenly aware of their plight, decided that the bank should adopt a humanitarian outlook and extend them a helping hand. Civilian internees who approached the OCBC for loans were given a sum of between $500 and $1,000. Internees who had been servicemen during the war were not allowed to apply because Tan felt that it was the responsibility of the colonial government to look after their servicemen. The OCBC's fine gesture won the goodwill of those who needed it so badly in their times of distress. An Australian beneficiary who subsequently returned home to establish the Life Guard

Milk Agency to export milk to Singapore made the obvious choice of using the OCBC as his bank. A year later he died, but not before he had passed the agency to another Australian couple with the stipulation that they must continue using the OCBC as their bank.

Tan Chin Tuan also realised that it was necessary for the OCBC to follow through with its decision to make itself competitive. The bank must now compete with the European banks for clients. To achieve this objective, the OCBC offered higher interest for deposits and lower interest for borrowers. The bank also ventured into new areas of finance. Aware of how difficult it is to pump-prime the economy, the OCBC supported businessmen keen to import goods from overseas by granting letters of credit. According to a *Straits Times* report, the banks played a useful role in helping businessmen as the latter only had to deposit 25 to 30 percent of their order with the banks and the financial institutions would then forward the entire amount that was outstanding to the consignors.[58] Thus, by being able to anticipate what opportunities lay ahead and by exploiting them, the OCBC was able to grow rapidly. By the end of 1946, the bank's balance sheet listed its reserve fund at $2 million and its profit at more than $3 million.[59]

Public Service

Hitherto, we have been concerned with how Tan Chin Tuan conceived and implemented new initiatives which helped OCBC achieve sterling results. However, there is yet another dimension of Tan's career that needs to be understood if we are to gain a proper perspective of how he managed to raise the profile of OCBC. This is the public service dimension. Tan Chin Tuan came from a Chinese-educated family, but was schooled in English. His ability to move comfortably between the English colonial elite, and the Chinese-educated businessmen made him a trusted emissary on both sides. The English trusted Tan so much because he was so deeply involved in public life, serving on numerous British commissions, councils and committees. It is significant to note that Tan participated in the rehabilitation and reconstruction of Singapore during three crucial periods in its history. In this section, we examine Tan's heavy involvement in British Singapore's public life, and through this, understand why he was able to work well with both the British and the Chinese classes. This involvement also allowed him to use his considerable influence and contacts to catapult the OCBC into becoming Singapore's largest local bank.

Initially, he was a member of the Singapore Advisory Council, formed to help the BMA in its efforts to rehabilitate Singapore as quickly as possible. Then, when civil government under Governor Sir Franklin Gimson took over in 1946, Tan again served on the Advisory Council consisting of Nominated, Official and Unofficial members. Later, when the Legislative Council was formed, it was based in part on electoral seats for the Unofficial members. The Chinese Chamber of Commerce appointed Tan Chin Tuan to sit on this Council as its representative. He was to serve as a member of the first and second Legislative Councils. As he played a key role during each of these periods, it is important to examine the nature of his diversification, and to study how he extended his role as a banker to encompass these different fields.

In November 1945, the banker was one of the 17 nominated members of the Singapore Advisory Council, meeting for the first time to discuss issues ranging from repatriation of refugees and shipping, to trade, supplies of commodities and daily necessities. Tan, who served on the important

Finance Committee, became increasingly critical of the slow pace of reconstruction, the trade restrictions, shortages of commodities and hardship to the common man.

During a meeting held on 12 December 1945, he expressed his consternation at the fact that officials in London were turning a deaf ear to the needs of the people for supplies and communication with kin. He revealed that his fellow members on the Finance Committee, Brigadier Godsall and Colonel Todd, had been working very hard to get a decision from the 'Home Government' regarding the question of family remittances to China. However, they did not receive any reply to their queries. Tan Chin Tuan pointed out that since remittances to India and Australia were permitted, the delay in allowing remittances from Singapore to China was 'unnecessary and unkind.'[60]

In the case of supplies, he lambasted the government for not acting quickly enough to solve the problem of shortages of essential items. He spoke with candour and forcefulness:

> For instance, transport and estate supplies are two of our chief shortages. Therefore, the more quickly we can import trucks and, for instance, formic acid into this country, the sooner will our estates be enabled to swing into production to put forth the rubber, so badly needed by the world and which the United States are so eager to buy from us. Sir, I must confess that this apparent reluctance on the part of the Imperial authorities to delegate even a little of its powers to our Controller of Finance bewilders and disheartens me.[61]

Apart from a lack of essential goods, Tan also criticised the government for not taking appropriate measures to improve the situation. With his penchant for organisational re-finement, he explained in no uncertain terms that:

As a member of the General Reconstruction Committee which has been trying to grapple with the problem of high prices and shortages of supplies, it seems to me that in whatever direction we turn, we always find that the transport bottleneck is one of our chief ailments. One often hears that there are no ships to bring back more trucks or cars or other supplies which we badly need. One also gathers that there are not enough trucks to go up-country and bring back our supplies.... On the first problem, one cannot help wondering where all the thousands of "Liberty Ships" have gone. When Germany was defeated, we were told that all the ships available were to be diverted to repatriate the American troops and intensifying our offensive in the Pacific. Now that it is over 6 months since Germany capitulated and 3 months since Japan surrendered, we should have thought that some of those ships would have been available for bringing supplies to us.[62]

This sharp reminder clearly showed Tan to be no passive committee member; he pressed relentlessly for a decision and was not willing to accept unnecessary delays.

On the issue of law and order, he proposed the setting up of a local school for training police personnel and the introduction of an attractive remuneration scheme to draw in more recruits.[63] He also stressed that it was important for the local people to take on more responsibility for maintaining law and order.

Another bone of contention was the slow pace which Singapore was taking towards achieving self-government. Tan Chin Tuan abhorred indecision and irresolution. He complained:

All Malayans were happy and hopeful when they heard the Secretary of State for the Colonies declare not so

long ago that it is the policy of His Majesty's
Government to lead the colonies to self-government.
They thought that at long last we are to be given a little
more rope, but alas, we still appear to be tied to White-
hall's gown strings more tightly than ever. If it requires
two months for the Treasury to delegate such ordinary
discretionary powers to the Controller of Finance, one
shudders to forecast how many decades it will be before
we can ever have a semblance of self-government.[64]

By raising these issues for discussion, it was obvious that
Tan was a spokesman for the local people when he asked the
British government to account for its actions and to explain
why certain policies were not being carried out expeditiously.

The efforts of the BMA were, unfortunately, difficult to
assess since their tenure was short, and came to an end when
the civil government under Franklin Gimson took over in
1946. The short period, however, did see the beginning of
the reconstruction process. In fact, by the end of the BMA's
tenure, Turnbull noted that it was able to report that the
port was 'almost back to pre-war capacity and the supply of
water and electricity exceeded pre-war consumption'.[65]

The civil government under Gimson functioned for some
two years without a Legislative Council in place.[66] Instead,
Governor Gimson administered the colony with the help of
an Advisory Council comprising official and unofficial
nominated members. The six unofficial members were
nominated and appointed by the Governor; and of the
members, only Tan Chin Tuan was a former member of the
BMA Advisory Council. As the British were aware of his past
contributions, Tan was invited to continue offering his views
in the newly-formed Council.

This Advisory Council carried on the work of the BMA
by taking further steps to rehabilitate certain sectors of the

economy. But it was the Salaries Commission Report that attracted the most attention and the discrimination in the Colonial Service that evoked some lengthy debates. Discrimination arose because administration of the Straits Settlements was divided between the local service and the colonial service. The local officials who were sometimes better qualified than their European counterparts, resented being given lower positions and lower pay. The Straits Settlements Legal Service fought hard to gain recognition and better benefits for the local officials.

The struggle also received the support of the unofficial members of the Colony of Singapore Advisory Council. For instance, at the 25th Public Session of the Advisory Council which was held on 19 June 1947, Tan was critical of the proposed transfer of Supreme Court positions and Official Assignee positions to the Colonial Legal Service. His concern was that if the transfer was effected such positions would be beyond the reach of the local officers of the Straits Settlements Legal Service. According to Tan, this was a 'very unsatisfactory state of affairs' since there were well-qualified members of the Straits Settlements Legal Service working in the Official Assignee's Office.[67] As this question had been raised some time ago, he mocked the government's usual answer that urgent deliberation would be given to the matter. He then audaciously suggested that if the qualified officers from the Straits Settlements Legal Service were transferred to the Colonial Legal Service, there would not be a dearth of action to resolve the issue.

Tan Chin Tuan also drew attention to another issue of concern. At the 35th Public Session of the Colony of Singapore Advisory Council held on 9 October 1947, he raised the question of when the report of the Salaries Commission would be available. He noted that the Commission had already completed its deliberations some time ago even though it had not yet submitted its report.[68] At the 45th Public Session of the Advisory Council held on 19 March 1948, the Colonial Secretary finally moved that the recommendations of salaries and salary scales contained in the Report of the Public Services Commission of Malaya be accepted and adopted to effect retrospective payment to Singapore public officers.[69] Tan applauded this motion, saying that it would bring relief to the salaried section of the community who had endured financial hardship since the end of the war.[70]

One of the more controversial issues to appear before the Advisory Council was the Income Tax Bill. The Acting Financial Secretary J. D. M. Smith moved that the Bill to impose an income tax be read in the 38th Public Session of the Colony of Singapore Advisory Council on 27 November 1947.[71] He went on to explain that the purpose of the bill was to levy a tax on incomes accrued in, derived from and received in Singapore. Such a tax was a graduated tax on income which, being progressive, was the fairest of all tax systems.[72] Then at the end of 1946, it would be proposed that, to balance the budget for 1947, an income tax would be instituted.

Tan Chin Tuan pointed out that it was 'neither necessary nor advisable to introduce income tax in Singapore'.[73] His attention to detail enabled him to argue that it would be more prudent to rely on short-term borrowing to meet 'extraordinary and probable expenditure' rather than to introduce income tax'. With a clear understanding of the financial aspects of the problem at hand, he assured the Council that there would be little difficulty in raising a short-term loan of $20 to $30 million at 1% interest. He did, however, stress that such a short-term loan would only be necessary if the Malayan Union did not repay the $84 million contributed by Singapore to the Malaya (Unallocated) Account. Thus, in Tan's view, the need to introduce an income tax was not an urgent one.

He suggested that, rather than mull over when to introduce the income tax, the government should really be exercising greater economy. He pointed out that in 18 months of trading, the Joint Supply Board lost $95 million of which $19 million fell on Singapore.[74] Tan also criticised the government's excessive level of wastage, such as the high costs sustained in dredging the Singapore River — a dredging that had been unduly delayed. He emphasised that the Committees of the Singapore Chinese Chamber of Commerce and the Singapore Ratepayers' Association strongly opposed the proposed taxation.[75] Most of the other Unofficials also opposed this bill on the grounds of timing, and asked for alternative sources of income to be considered. Later, when Gimson decided to push the bill through, the unofficial members resigned en masse. It was a move indicative of a unified condemnation of the proposed Income Tax Bill. It was a gesture that clearly showed that the Advisory Council was not a rubber stamp.

The Advisory Council was also responsible for drafting the Singapore Legislative Council Elections Bill which provided the structure for the Legislative Councils in Singapore. This Bill was discussed in the 26th Public Session of the Advisory Council on 3 July 1947. According to H. P. Bryson, who was Acting Colonial Secretary when Singapore was made a Colony in April 1946, it was decided that the Colony should have a Legislative Council with equal numbers of official and unofficial members. One of the most pertinent recommendations was that there should be six elected Council members and three representatives from the Chambers of Commerce.[76]

Tan Chin Tuan was selected to represent the Chinese Chamber of Commerce: from 1947 to 1950, he was the vice-president of the executive committee of the Singapore Chinese Chamber of Commerce. The banker served at a crucial time in the Chamber's history. During his tenure, the civil war in China ended and the communist People's Republic of China came into being in 1949. This led to an adjustment in the mentality of the China-oriented Chamber whose method of dating its minutes, up till the communist victory, had been based on the Republican calendar.

Tan's background as a Straits-born Chinese, his extensive banking experience and his familiarity with the British administrators and their practices, enabled him to serve as a bridge between the Chinese Chamber of Commerce and the British government. He brought up issues of concern to the Chamber during Legislative Council meetings and explained the government's position to the Chamber when the latter met. For instance, as a member of the 25th Committee of the Chamber, he attended a meeting held on 23 September 1948 and explained that the next Legislative Council meeting had two issues of concern to the business community. The first pertained to a law that, if passed, would allow electrical companies to run electrical supply lines over private proper-ties without prior consent. It was decided by those present at that meeting to authorise Tan Chin Tuan to object to this motion in the Legislative Council. The second was the Bill to regulate a rest day for all commercial establishments. Tan sought the opinions of the directors of the chamber. His personal opinion was that while labourers needed a day of rest, the compulsory closure of commercial establishments would affect business. After lengthy discussions it was decided that businesses should be allowed freedom of choice. Tan added that enforcement of the Bill would lead to disputes.

At another meeting of the 25th Committee that was held on 29 December 1948, Tan Chin Tuan explained to the Chinese Chamber of Commerce the importance of the forthcoming Municipal elections and the ongoing electoral registration exercise. He stressed that if a person wanted to vote, it would be essential to register to be on the electoral roll. Failure to do this would deprive one of the right to vote for a candidate of one's choice. Tan urged all eligible voters to register themselves. The directors of the Chamber wholly agreed with the banker and even decided to enlist the newspapers to help in the electoral registration campaign.

At that same meeting, the members voiced their concerns about the high cost and poor quality of rice in Singapore. Tan explained that the issue of quality of rice had been raised in the Legislative Council and the government had appointed the Financial Secretary and other high-ranking officers to investigate the matter. As for the cost of rice in Singapore when compared to Hong Kong and Thailand, he assured the Committee that he would bring up this matter in the Legislative Council. This issue was eventually discussed at a meeting of the First Legislative Council held on 15 February 1949. Tan Chin Tuan not only queried the high cost of rationed rice in Singapore as compared to other British colonies, but also requested a breakdown of the cost per picul, handling charges and distribution. Above all, he wanted to know why rice 'of such low quality as to be almost unfit for human consumption' was being sold in Singapore.[77]

As the elected representative body of the people of Singapore, the First Legislative Council was vested with authority to complete the final stages of reconstruction, especially issues involving complicated financial arrangements. Issues raised included the Debtor and Creditor Bill which dealt with wartime financial transactions and arrangements; the repeal of the Moratorium Proclamation which was imposed during the BMA period; rationing of rice, petrol; foreign exchange control; war damage compensation and rent control. The Legislative Council of the Colony of Singapore appointed a Select Committee on 17 May 1949 to discuss the moratorium issue. What is interesting about the line-up of the Committee is the appointment of Tan Chin Tuan as one of its committee members. His banking expertise and refusal to be the passive figure made him an obvious choice. As noted in the Proceedings of the First Legislative Council held on 28 July 1949, the Committee was to examine and report on the Moratorium Proclamation (Repeal) Ordinance, 1949. It was further authorised to make joint deliberations with the Committee appointed by the Legislative Council of the Federation of Malaya.[78] The Bills they examined sought to repeal the Moratorium Proclamations proclaimed by the BMA on 20 and 30 August 1945. The Committees eventually presented their joint report to the Legislative Council for acceptance.

Tan Chin Tuan was also consulted by the British government. Malcolm MacDonald,[79] Commissioner-General for the United Kingdom in Southeast Asia, wrote to him on, 6 August 1949 inviting the banker to participate in an informal discussion on the international situation and foreign policy with other leaders of Singapore and Malaya. In the letter, MacDonald said:

> I feel — and the High Commissioner and Governor [agree —] that this group of responsible leaders should meet from time to time, to keep the international situation under review. The party would always be purely private and informal. The individuals attending would come in their personal capacities, without any mandate to represent any organisation or group. In fact, they would just be a group of friends having a talk. No minutes would be kept, nor would there be any record of the conversations. But I am anxious that you and our other friends should be kept in touch with our Foreign Policy as it affects Malaya.[80]

Apart from having discussions with key policy makers, he continued to be involved in the Second Legislative Council.

The latter focused more on issues that had a greater impact upon the political future of Singapore. The appointment of Tan Chin Tuan as Deputy President of the legislative on 17 April 1951 was a major step by the British towards allowing a member of the local community greater participation in the political system. This appointment made Tan, effectively Deputy Governor of Singapore. Above all, it showed recognition of his extensive experiences as a banker and his skills as a negotiator and as an intermediary for the colonial government and the local community. In both capacities, his relentless prodding and probing, his ability to make decisions and to communicate culminated in his appointment as Deputy President. Tan had indeed widened his role as a banker to include on the canvas, bolder lines and deeper hues. He paved the way by showing that it was possible for a banker to reach the pinnacle of success not only in his area of specialisation but also in other fields.

Changes in political regimes often led to profound changes in the banking sector as well. It was no different with the Oversea-Chinese Banking Corporation. During the World War Two, the bank experienced lacklustre growth but in the aftermath of the war, the rapidly gathering momentum of reconstruction and rebuilding opened up many opportunities for growth. It was a period of reconstruction, rehabilitation and political unrest. In this changing environment, the OCBC demonstrated its resilience. Realising that it was necessary to restructure some of its existing policies, those at the helm skilfully discarded the stark inadequacies of the old system and introduced new financing guidelines. This ability to adapt to changing circumstances, probably more important in the financial sector than any other, once again enabled the OCBC to survive, grow and ride on a wave of success.

NOTES

1 Cindy Chou, *Beyond the Empires: Memories Retold* (Singapore: Oral History Centre, National Archives of Singapore, National Heritage Board, 1995), p. 7.

2 Paul H. Kratoska, *The Japanese Occupation of Malaya: A Social and Economic History* (London: Hurst & Co, 1998), p. 208.

3 Richard A. Banyai, *Money and Banking in China and Southeast Asia during the Japanese Military Occupation, 1937–1945* (Taipei: Tai Wan Enterprise, 1974), p. 70.

4 C. M. Turnbull, *A History of Singapore, 1819–1988*, 2nd ed, (Singapore: Oxford University Press, 1988), p. 195.

5 See *The Japanese Occupation: Singapore, 1942–1945* (Singapore: Singapore News & Printers Limited, 1985), p. 58.

6 See Eunice Thio, 'The Syonan Years', in *A History of Singapore*, Ernest Chew and Edwin Lee, eds (Singapore: Oxford University Press, 1991), pp. 95-114. See also Tan Yeok Seng, 'History of the Oversea Chinese Association and the extortion by Japanese Military Administration of $50,000,000 from the Chinese in Malaya', *Journal of the South Seas Society*, vol. 3, no. 1 (1946):1–2.

7 See C. M. Turnbull, *A History of Singapore 1819–1988*, 2nd ed, (Singapore: Oxford University Press, 1989), pp. 200–201.

8 Kratoska, *The Japanese Occupation*, p. 213.

9 Ibid., pp. 218–219.

10 Norio Tamaki, *Japanese Banking: A History, 1859–1959* (Cambridge: Cambridge University Press, 1995), p. xx.

11 Ibid., p. 103.

12 Ibid., p. 178.

13 Kratoska, *The Japanese Ocupation*, p. 214.

14 Ibid.

15 *Growing With Singapore* (Singapore: United Overseas Bank 1985), p. 22.

16 Ibid.

17 See Dick Wilson, *Solid as a Rock* (Singapore: OCBC, 1972), p. 56.

18 Ibid, pp. 59–60.

19 OCBC, *Twenty-One Years: Growth and Progress* (Singapore: OCBC, 1953), p. 29.

20 Wilson, *Solid As A Rock*, p. 60.

21 Ibid.

22 Kratoska, *The Japanese Occupation*, p. 215.

23 Ibid.

24 Ibid., p. 210.

25 Interview, Yap Siong Eu, 1983, p. 3.

26 Ibid., p. 5.

27 Lee S. Y., *British Chinese Policy in Singapore, 1930s to Mid–1950's: With Particular Focus on the Public Service Career of Tan Chin Tuan* (Singapore: National University of Singapore, 1995), p. 115.

28 Tan Chin Tuan archives (Singapore: The Tan Foundation).

29 Ibid.

30 Wilson, *Solid As A Rock*, p. 59.

31 Ibid.

32 Ibid.

33 For more information on the Chinese anti-Japanese activities prior to and during the Occupation, see Xu Yunqiao (org. ed.), *Xinma Huaren Kangri Shiliao (1937–1945)* [A History of the Anti-Japanese Movement by the Chinese in Malaya (1937–1945)], Cai Shijun, ed (Singapore: Wenshi Publishing, 1984).

34 Yeap Joo Kim, *Far From Rangoon: Lee Chee Shan 1909–86* (Singapore: Lee Teng Lay, 1994), p. 35.

35 In 1939, a circular had been sent to all OCBC branches informing them that in preparation for the war, the branches were to be self-controlled if communications were disrupted. When Rangoon fell to the Japanese in March 1942, the officers and staff of the OCBC Rangoon branch were reported to have escaped with some of the bank's books to Chungking.

36 See Chapter 5.

37 For more information on Tan Cheng Lock, see Yeo Siew Siang, *Tan Cheng Lock: The Straits Legislator and Chinese Leader* (Malaysia: Pelanduk Publications (M) Sdn Bhd, 1990) and Alice Scott-Ross, *Tun Dato Sir Cheng Lock Tan: A Personal Profile by His Daughter* (Singapore: Kefford Press, 1990).

38 Tan Chin Tuan archives (Singapore: The Tan Foundation).

39 Tan Chin Tuan archives (Singapore: The Tan Foundation).

40 The ill-fated Gent was later to become the first Governor of the newly-formed Malayan Union.

41 PAB McKerron was later the Deputy Chief Civil Affairs Officer during the British Military Administration, then Colonial Secretary for Singapore.

42 Tan Chin Tuan archives (Singapore: The Tan Foundation).

43 Lee, *British Chinese Policy*, p. 114.

44 Victor Purcell was from the Chinese Secretariat and an authority on the Malayan Chinese.

45 Tan Chin Tuan archives (Singapore: The Tan Foundation).

46 Turnbull, *A History of Singapore*, p. 216.

47 Albert Lau, *The Malayan Union Controversy 1942–1948* (Singapore: Oxford University Press, 1990), pp. 43–44.

48 Ibid., p. 49.

49 Ibid.

50 For more information on the British plans for Malaya after the war, see A. J. Stockwell, *British Policy and Malay Politics during the Malayan Union Experiment, 1945–1948* (Singapore: Malaysian Branch of the Royal Asiatic Society, 1979); and Albert Lau, *The Malayan Union Controversy, 1942–1948* (Singapore: Oxford University Press, 1990).

51 Turnbull, *A History of Singapore*, p. 199.

52 Ibid., p. 219.

53 Kratoska, *The Japanese Occupation*, p. 324.

54 Among the British bankers on board that same plane were R. A. Stuart, who was the Singapore Branch Manager of the Hongkong & Shanghai Bank just before the War, Stanley Stocks, one of the senior members of the Mercantile Bank's staff prior to the War, and Cortwright, of whom little is known. See generally, Frank H. H. King, *The Hongkong Bank Between the Wars and the Bank Interned, 1919–1945: Return from Grandeur*, Vol. III (Cambridge: Cambridge University Press, 1988), pp. 591–593; and Edwin Green and Sara Kinsey, *The Paradise Bank: The Mercantile Bank of India, 1883–1984* (Aldershot: Ashgate, 1999), p. 95.

55 Wilson, *Solid As A Rock*, p. 63.

56 Kratoska, *The Japanese Occupation*, p. 327.

57 Ibid., p. 325.

58 *The Straits Times*, 29 November 1946.

59 Wilson, *Solid As A Rock*, p. 67.

60 Minutes, British Military Administration Advisory Council, 12 December 1945, p. 48.

61 Ibid.

62 Ibid., pp. 79–80.

63 Ibid., p. 65.

64 Ibid., p. 48.

65 Turnbull, *A History of Singapore*, p. 221.

66 The years 1947–48 saw the recovery of Malaya and Singapore from the ravages of war against the backdrop of civil and political unrest caused by the Malayan Union controversy as well as the proclamation of the Emergency. See Yeo Kim Wah, *Political Development in Singapore, 1945–1955* (Singapore: Singapore University Press, 1973).

67 Minutes, British Military Administration Advisory Council, 19 June 1947, p. 2.

68 Minutes, British Military Administration Advisory Council, 9 October 1947, p. 3.

69 Ibid.

70 Minutes, British Military Administration Advisory Council, 19 March 1948, p. 14.

71 Minutes, British Military Administration Advisory Council, 27 Nov 1947, p. 4.

72 Ibid., p. 5.

73 Ibid., p. 20.

74 Minutes, Colony of Singapore Advisory Council, 27 Nov 1947, p. 21.

75 Ibid., p. 22.

76 Minutes, Colony of Singapore Advisory Council, 3 July 1947, p. 6.

77 Minutes, First Legislative Council, 15 Feb 1949, B12.

78 The Legislative Council of Malaya was inaugurated in February 1948.

79 For more information on Malcolm MacDonald, see Clyde Sanger, *Malcolm MacDonald: Bringing an End to Empire* (Liverpool, England: Liverpool University Press, 1995).

80 Tan Chin Tuan archives (Singapore: The Tan Foundation).

CHAPTER 5

BUILDING FIRM FOUNDATIONS

The 1950s was often described as a tumultuous period in Singapore. It was a time of vibrant anti-colonial politics, when political parties campaigned vigorously for independence and the vision of a better society. Yet, the reality of poverty which enveloped the majority of the population was at clear variance with the assurance of a more equal society put forth by competing political groups.

A confluence of classical factors combined to produce what was regarded as 'intolerable' socio-economic conditions, notwithstanding the fact that the country was able to achieve modest growth in the decade of the 1950s.[1] Rapid population increase, widespread unemployment and poor housing conditions all contributed to the vicious cycle of poverty. Between 1947 and 1957, the population grew at an annual rate of 4.4% — 'a rate which (was) the highest known in the world'.[2] The rampant post-war baby boom imposed a heavy burden on the still-inadequate economic and social foundations of the country. There were simply not enough jobs created and the excess supply of labour led to much under-employment and unemployment, with 'the commonest wage between $100 and $120 a month'.[3] At a time when a minimum income of $102 was required to sustain a family of four, it was not surprising that 19% of Singapore households and 25% of individuals were found to be living in poverty in 1957.[4] Unable to afford proper housing, the indigent masses were cramped into chronically overcrowded cubicles and squatters lived in appalling squalor.

These 'intolerable' conditions were identified by the communists and pro-communists as being ripe for exploitation. Earlier in 1948, the Malayan Communist Party (MCP) under the leadership of Chin Peng had staged what was tantamount to an armed insurrection in an attempt to win power.[5] The violence that followed prompted a State of Emergency to be introduced throughout Malaya and subsequently extended to Singapore as well. The MCP was proscribed and Emergency regulations gave the authorities the power to detain suspects without trial. In order to continue its operations in the open, the MCP focused on various front organisations where a number of its members and sympathisers had already infiltrated — the trade unions and Chinese Middle schools.

Trade unions were the sinews of the communist movement and were useful instruments for fomenting unrest.[6] The communists had little problem rousing union members to undertake industrial action in spite of the fact that few union members actually understood what the communist ideology meant. The grievances over low pay, poor career prospects and unequal treatment were genuine and easily exploited by the infiltrators. A cursory look at statistics on work stoppages and man-days lost during this period highlights the extent of union militancy during the 1950s and early 1960s. At its height, nearly a million man-hours was lost through 275 strikes in 1955 alone. From 1955 to 1963, more than 2.7 million man-hours was lost through some 689 strikes.[7]

In this highly infectious strike-happy atmosphere, even those unions where communist influence was weak had few reservations about resorting to work stoppages to publicise their grievances and demands. Tan Chin Tuan and the OCBC were inevitably drawn into the uneasy politics of union militancy, becoming no small players in the dramatic confrontation with the unions.

Tackling Unionists

As the managing director of one of the largest Singapore banks and chairman of an impressive stable of blue-chip companies, Tan Chin Tuan encountered his fair share of problems with staff and their unions. The 1952 strike by the Singapore Post and Telegraph and Uniformed Staff Union provided Tan, then Deputy President of the Legislative Council, with his first experience of dealing directly with an angry and emotive group of postal workers. The staff union was incensed by the fact that a negotiated agreement drafted between their lawyer, Lee Kuan Yew, and the Director of Telecommunications was unilaterally and suddenly substituted with less favourable terms by the chairman of the government negotiating team, with no reasons given for the change.[8]

Tan watched the strike (the first since the imposition of Emergency Regulations in June 1948) with both concern and discomfort. While he was sympathetic towards the plight of the lowly-paid postal workers, he, like most people who were inconvenienced by the breakdown of an essential service, wanted the problem resolved expeditiously. Tan Chin Tuan knew the man whose words carried most weight with the Singapore Post and Telegraph and Uniformed Staff Union —

their lawyer, Lee Kuan Yew. The deputy president therefore wasted no time contacting the man whom he addressed as his 'nephew'[9], to discuss the problem.

A telephone call quickly set up a meeting. Lee Kuan Yew then brought the chairman and secretary of the union to his uncle's office for a 'friendly discussion'. Tan was able to persuade the union leadership to agree to a 'truce' to enable negotiations to resume. Governor Nicoll, apparently pleased with his Deputy President's efforts, invited Tan to join him for a leisurely Sunday lunch at his home on St. John's Island on 25 May 1952, the day before the agreed truce was to begin. However, just as Tan Chin Tuan was leaving his house for St. John's Island, he received an urgent telephone message from Lee Kuan Yew and learnt that a heated meeting was in session at the union's office at Maxwell Road. A number of postal workers were unhappy with the idea of a truce, and doubted the Government's even-handedness in dealing with the dispute.

Tan Chin Tuan rushed to Maxwell Road to intervene. This was crucial to ensure that the expected truce would be observed the following day. He was confronted by an excited group comprising largely Malay and Indian postal workers at the union's office. The air was warm and stuffy and many eyes were trained on the bespectacled banker who was invited to address the striking postmen. He spoke to them in simple and plain English. 'Give the Government a chance to prove the sincerity of its promise to settle the dispute fairly and quickly', he appealed to the crowd. For Tan Chin Tuan, it was a relief that the postmen finally consented to observe the pre-negotiated truce. The next day, all mail services were restored as representatives from the disputing parties resumed talks.

Even at the august Raffles Hotel, in which the OCBC acquired a controlling stake in the early 1950s, Tan Chin Tuan had to tackle two attempts by the union to initiate strikes. His responses in both instances were swift and decisive, typifying his no-nonsense approach.

The first incident happened shortly after Singapore achieved self-government. An 'illegal strike' (one where no notice was given to the management) took place at Raffles Hotel. Dominic Puthucheary led a group of co-workers out of the hotel and those who did not follow him were intimidated. Tan Chin Tuan's response was to bring his staff down from his own office to help keep the hotel going. He was not about to let a group of unionised employees sully the hotel's fine reputation. Meanwhile, he learnt from his contacts at the Tan Clan Association that a secret ballot would end the strike because most of the Raffles Hotel employees did not want a protracted strike. His ground information was accurate. The majority voted in favour of an end to the strike in a secret ballot conducted by the Labour Ministry.

The second incident again involved Puthucheary, who was unhappy that Raffles Hotel had engaged a housekeeper who had previously had problems with the union when she worked with the Goodwood Park Hotel. Puthucheary demanded that the housekeeper be dismissed. He repeated his demands over a period of time but these were ignored by the hotel manager who found the housekeeper's work satisfactory. Just before lunch time one day, Puthucheary called a meeting with the unionised staff to urge a walkout. The ploy was calculated to achieve maximum impact (and damage) since Raffles Hotel was (and still is) a popular lunch venue among the well-heeled. Tan Chin Tuan was informed of the union's plan by one of the hotel's directors. He immediately relayed a message to the union that he was prepared to 'close down' the hotel if staff members proceeded with the lunch-time walkout. The majority quietly returned to their work.

In the latter part of the same afternoon, Puthucheary brought a few of his union members to Tan Chin Tuan's office. The chairman listened patiently as Puthucheary explained why he had insisted on the dismissal of the housekeeper — she had 'caused trouble at Goodwood Park', and his sharp reply revealed the determined tone of one who would not tolerate the unreasonable:

> This housekeeper did wrong at Goodwood Park. You got her dismissed. She has paid the penalty. Do you mean to tell me that every time someone does wrong, he must be punished for life?

There was no further trouble from Puthucheary and his union after this episode.

Tan Chin Tuan showed the same mettle in yet another encounter with the union at Robinson and Company, an upmarket department store in which the OCBC owned a controlling stake of close to 38%. Two salesgirls were caught stealing at the store. Following consultations with Tan Chin Tuan, the general manager decided to quietly ask the salesgirls to leave after compensating them for the termination.

The union was unhappy with the dismissal. Led by Sandrasegaram Woodhull, who was known for his pro-left sympathies, the union wanted the salesgirls reinstated because 'they were not convicted in Court'. Again, Tan Chin Tuan conveyed the message that he was prepared to 'close down' Robinson's should the union go on a strike over the matter. He made clear that he was not 'bluffing'. His line of reasoning was as follows:

> Reinstating these two girls would condone, if not encourage, theft. Am I to tell the shareholders (of Robinson's) that when employees are caught stealing, the union says

we have to keep them? The whole store would be finished in no time, so we might as well wind up.

Woodhull backed down and the stop-work threat was aborted.

Not long after, on 3 February 1963, Woodhull was among the 111 left-wing politicians and trade unionists arrested during a security sweep known as Operation Cold Store. According to a statement from the Internal Security Council, the operation was necessary because the communists in Singapore had apparently intended to use the island as a 'Cuban' base for a political offensive against Malaya.[10] Following his release from prison on 28 November 1963, Woodhull proceeded to study law in London. In a surprising disclosure, Tan Chin Tuan revealed that he had provided Woodhull with financial assistance (and even bought him an overcoat!) during the latter's studies in London. He proffered the following cryptic reason for lending a helping hand to the ex-unionist who had previously crossed swords with him at Robinson's — 'because, although he was very tough and one of the extremists, he was not a communist. He was fighting a cause. We had an honest disagreement. There was no animosity'. That was Tan Chin Tuan's personal opinion and it obviously differed from the perception of the Internal Security Council which had put Woodhull behind bars precisely because he was deemed to be a communist. But the astute banker had his own sense of fair play and was a firm believer in giving others the all-important second chance.

Staff Welfarism at the OCBC

It was evident that Tan Chin Tuan also influenced the OCBC to extend the same generous attitude towards the Bank's employees. Since the end of World War Two, the OCBC had already put in place a comprehensive staff welfare package which included holidays and a bonus scheme based on results. The OCBC was one of the first private firms to award scholarships to children of past and present employees. It was also one of the first local banks to send young officers to England, the United States and Australia for training. Locally, staff who upgraded themselves by passing the Banking Diploma examination received monetary rewards. To further encourage a sense of loyalty and commitment from his staff, Tan Chin Tuan persuaded the Board of Directors to implement a scheme which gave everyone working in the OCBC a stake in the bank. This was the in-house provident fund which he adapted from the Straits Trading Company in 1956. The fund at the Straits Trading Company benefited only the European staff; locals were not allowed to join.

At the OCBC, the provident fund was open to all the employees and participation was on a voluntary basis. An interesting feature of this fund was that members could contribute $7^1/_2\%$ of their salary to the fund in the first ten years, with the Bank contributing an equal sum. Thereafter, staff members could contribute up to 10% of their salary to the fund, with the bank contributing another 10%. The fund was exempted from taxation and contributions to the fund were 'not the subject of garnishment or seizure by creditors'.[11]

Tan Chin Tuan was concerned that the in-house provident fund be properly managed to ensure that employees who participated in it would benefit. In his own estimate, all who entrusted their money to the fund reaped as much as five times in return. Available figures on the total assets of the OCBC staff provident fund as at 30 April 1978 showed that the 'book value' of the funds (which included equities, government loans and deposits in the OCBC current account) was $1,147,925 compared to a market value of $3,589,255.[12] This was certainly no paltry return.

The Singapore Bank Employees Union Episode

Notwithstanding the bank's innovative staff welfare schemes, the OCBC, like many of its counterparts in the banking and financial services industry, was not spared its share of problems with combative unions in a period teeming with labour unrest. The main union which the OCBC had to deal with was the Singapore Bank Employees Union (SBEU).

Perhaps the most significant episode of confrontation between the OCBC and the SBEU was the one which began on 22 July 1961. This dispute lasted more than a few months, created great inconvenience to the public and prompted the People's Action Party government to intervene. The consequence was the urgent introduction, in the Legislative Assembly in January 1962, of a Banking Bill which was to have considerable impact on the way banks conducted their businesses.

During the debate on the Banking Bill which was tabled on a Certificate of Urgency on 16 January 1962, the Minister for Health and Law, K. M. Byrne, explained the background of the OCBC-SBEU dispute. What started the dispute in July 1961 were differences of opinion between the bank and the union on the re-designation of all messengers as clerical assistants and on the method of converting clerks from their old scale to the new scale.'[13] Subsequently, the OCBC's offer to compensate the clerks was refused by the SBEU in September 1961. According to Byrne, 'without the knowledge of the union and against the union's stated stand',[14] the bank then paid a few of the union members and attempted to induce other members to accept payment as well. The union was apparently incensed when it discovered what the OCBC had done and demanded an apology. Instead of an apology, Byrne told the Legislative Assembly, the SBEU received a letter from the bank 'containing a series of threats'.[15] That prompted the union to go on strike.

Interestingly, it was not the strike by the SBEU, but the unique practice of the Malayan Exchange Banks Association during industrial disputes that provoked the ire of the PAP Government. As Byrne explained to members of the House:

> ...whenever there was an industrial dispute in one bank, the Malayan Exchange Banks Association [would] take concerted action to stop inter-bank clearing even if [other banks] were not in any way involved in the dispute. In this way, the association had inflicted unwarranted hardship on the public and had attempted to convert every isolated industrial dispute into a general dispute affecting all banks.' [16]

The then Prime Minister, Lee Kuan Yew, was more blunt and described the episode as 'the pigheadedness of this particular bank and the ganging up of the other banks to back this bank at the expense of the economy of Singapore'.[17] He added:

> If the banks are going to gang up on behalf of any single bank, be it the OCBC or any other bank, and stop clearing and stop the whole economic machine in the process of one industrial dispute with an individual bank, then I say, the State intervenes.... I make no apologies for that.[18]

From the thrust and tone of the Legislative Assembly debate on 16 January 1962, the Government's impatience and frustration with the OCBC as well as the Malayan Exchange Banks Association was plain. Dr Goh Keng Swee, the Minister for Finance, made no bones about where his sympathies lay:

> ...when certain members of the Exchange Banks saw me, I decided to assist in any way possible to bring the

two parties together to an early settlement. It became very clear to me that in this instance, the union was clearly in the right and the banks were in the wrong. There was absolutely no two ways about it.[19]

Such no-holds barred comments must have sounded harsh to the management team of the OCBC where Tan Chin Tuan was Managing Director. But even more perplexing to the OCBC banker was how the Prime Minister described him during the course of the debate on the Banking Bill. Tan Chin Tuan had not expected to be personally drawn into the debate and he has never forgotten Lee Kuan Yew's words:

Yes, the Managing Director. Let me tell the Member for Farrer Park the kind of gentleman we deal with. The Managing Director happens to be distantly connected with me through marriage. He told me once, when I was leading a delegation of postmen in a dispute with the Government then, that he always got his way. He was then a Member of the Executive Council, and he told me — I was then a very much younger man — that I should listen to him and settle. He said, 'You know, I always win. When I was a young chap, I kept fighting fish, and my fighting fish beat everybody's fighting fish. They asked, 'How did you do that?' I said, 'Simple.' And I said this publicly too — I think he is not feeling very well at the moment and he will not be feeling very well after he reads this. To his fighting fish every day, he added a drop of brandy. So the fish got soaked up with it. After seven drops of brandy had gone in, any other fish that entered into its bowl was out. And if it went into the other bowl, he poured half the water from his bowl into the other.[20]

Tan Chin Tuan never publicly responded to Lee Kuan Yew's remarks. When the subject was raised in a private interview, he commented in a matter-of-fact tone that the PAP Government's pro-union stance during the episode was probably related to the fact that the labour vote was crucial and it was important to win the goodwill of labour.[21] What about the story of the 'fighting fish'? In the same calm and collected tone, Tan said that he had merely shared with Lee what others did to their fighting fish, he himself 'did no such thing'.[22]

The Banking Bill was passed on the same day it was introduced. Among other things, it provided for the setting up of a Clearing House by the Government.[23] The regulation required each bank to immediately open with the Accountant-General a clearing account in the name of the Clearing House. According to the Minister for Finance, 'the inconvenience that arises out of any industrial disputes would be restricted to each bank.'[24]

It may be worth mentioning the pleasant endnote to this otherwise unhappy episode. After the dust had settled, an ex-gratia payment of 'a sizeable sum of money' was made to the SBEU for distribution to the 300 members who were involved in the 12-day strike, as compensation for their loss of pay during the strike.[25] But the payment was not made by the OCBC. The contributor was Tan Chin Tuan. A bank statement explained that the managing director had done it 'in his personal capacity (and) as a gesture of goodwill.'[26] While cynics might suspect Tan Chin Tuan's move as a less than altruistic afterthought, it was nevertheless consistent with his willingness to assist the needy and the underdog. This was his way of building up a reservoir of gratitude and goodwill for the OCBC and the companies he controlled.

The Importance of *Guanxi*

Securing the gratitude and goodwill of others was useful, even essential, to the continued growth and development of any business, and this was always at the fore of Tan Chin Tuan's instincts. He knew that earning the gratitude and goodwill of employees was likely to gain their loyalty, making them dependable, diligent and reliable. Winning the gratitude and goodwill of the influential made business sense because the returns often went beyond the calculable. Many episodes throughout Tan Chin Tuan's career would prove his instincts right.

Tan Chin Tuan's acumen for networking typified the reliance on highly personal ties which characterised many Asian, especially Chinese-owned, companies. In a study on *Tradition and Change in the Chinese Business Enterprise*, Wellington K. K. Chan observed that personal and family networking 'encourages opportunistic diversifications'.[27] He provided the example of the business operations of Thailand's CP Group which depended on 'extensive and well-placed connections (*guanxi*)' to open doors in China and elsewhere.[28] But it is not just conglomerates which foster ubiquitious *guanxi* networks to facilitate their global reach; the practice permeates all levels of enterprises in Chinese societies. Small and medium-sized firms are equally adept at crafting their own connections, often based on the goodwill established by their founders and owners.

Tan Chin Tuan also appreciated the importance of providing favours to win lasting friendships and establish strong relationships. This was the way immigrant entrepreneurs, regardless of size, conducted their businesses. Eminent entrepreneurs such as Tan Kah Kee, Lee Kong Chian and Tan Lark Sye all believed in the basic philosophy that a little goodwill could go a long way. It was part of building *guanxi* or relationships which could be counted on to further one's business empire, to enhance one's stature or even to get one out of trouble. Throughout his career, Tan Chin Tuan networked extensively and diligently and often used his personal contacts to benefit the bank and the businesses he managed. The OCBC banker did not forge friendships purely for ulterior motives. There are just too many instances when he instinctively proffered assistance — whether to a stranger, an employee or even one who had crossed him — which demonstrated his magnanimity and sincerity. He also enjoyed warm friendships with many of the rich and famous — such as Tan Cheng Lock, Lee Kong Chian, Tunku Abdul Rahman — based upon shared interests and mutual respect. Bartering of favours had no place in such close relationships. Quid pro quo relationships belonged to the pragmatic world of business contacts and acquaintances, and had no place among close friends.

One eminent businessman OCBC extended a discrete helping hand to was Aw Boon Haw, the 'Tiger Balm King'. Aw Boon Haw typified Chinese entrepreneurs of his time; he was reluctant to part with tangible assets to secure bank overdrafts since this was deemed to be a loss of 'face'. Following the Japanese Occupation, Aw began selling off his shares in the OCBC to raise funds for his businesses. Tan Chin Tuan understood his dilemma and how important 'face' was to the latter. At his own initiative, he provided Aw Boon Haw with a credit line of some $1 million, without seeking any collateral. The grateful entrepreneur used only a fraction of it to restore his business empire and repaid the money without a hitch. Years later, Lee Chee Shan, the son-in-law of Aw Boon Haw's brother, prevailed upon the 'Tiger Balm King' to transfer all his business accounts to Chung Khiaw Bank in which Aw Boon Haw himself was Chairman and owned a substantial stake. He agreed but made an exception for the Eng Aung Tong (Tiger Balm factory) account which he insisted must remain with the OCBC. The reason was simple: Aw had earlier used the credit from the OCBC to restart the Eng Aung Tong and he never forgot the source of his succour.

Networking with Midland Bank

As a banker, Tan Chin Tuan recognised the need to 'open doors' for the OCBC outside Singapore in order to increase its profile, profitability, credibility and respectability. Notwithstanding its leading role in Singapore's financial sector in the 1950s and 1960s, the OCBC was an unknown entity abroad. Tan Chin Tuan was determined to change all that. Again, the way he went about associating the OCBC with foreign banking giants validated the importance of networking in the growth of companies. As one study on corporate networks in Hong Kong and Singapore observed:

> By world standards, the Hong Kong and Singapore firms are far from gigantic. They derive their prowess not from individual size, but from mutual reinforcement. It is the strength of their networks that enables them to spread their operations globally.[29]

Like many successful entrepreneurs, Tan Chin Tuan never had to refer to business books for guidance; his decision to cultivate linkages between the OCBC and overseas banks was based purely on 'common business sense' because of the obvious advantages in globalising the OCBC name. He therefore spared no effort in making the acquaintance of the top decision makers of some of the biggest names in the industry then: the Midland Bank in England and the Chase Manhattan Bank in the United States of America (USA).

The OCBC managing director travelled to England on business every year, and made it a point to visit the Midland Bank whenever he was there. In the beginning, he could only see the assistant to the Assistant Manager of the bank. On a subsequent trip, the Assistant Manager himself attended to him. Tan Chin Tuan took the slight sportingly:

> When you are the Managing Director of a bank with a capital of $10 million, do you think that when you go to banks like the Midland Bank, they will want to see you? They treat you as a very junior person. In fact, we would be guilty in the same way...if someone from a little university visits [a big university], would [the] Vice-Chancellor see him? So one has to find ways....[30]

The OCBC banker's way was to persist, and after several more trips, he was able to meet the General Manager of the Foreign Department. Still, he was not satisfied. Soon, Tan Chin Tuan's perseverance paid off when the opportunity arose for him to apply his time-tested philosophy of doing favours to win enduring friendships. He received a request from Midland Bank to assist in booking a hotel for its Chief General Manager, W. G. Edington, who was visiting Singapore with a colleague. Tan Chin Tuan was well aware of the power and influence of this very important guest in Midland Bank and went out of his way to facilitate arrangements which would make Edington's stay comfortable. He also did something unexpected which pleased Edington thoroughly. He used his position as the Deputy President of the Legislative Council to obtain permission to personally receive Edington and his friend on the tarmac where the aeroplane landed. For the general manager of Midland Bank who needed crutches because of a wartime injury, this gesture was particularly appreciated.

Naturally, during the time Edington and his colleague were in Singapore, Tan Chin Tuan lavished them with the warmest hospitality and courtesy. The gentlemen got along famously and Edington was clearly happy with his new-found friend in Singapore. In a letter dated 6 April 1955, Edington was effusive in his acknowledgement of Tan Chin Tuan's efforts:

> Your kindnesses — which made our visit the highlight of our tour — were so numerous as almost to defy listing individually, but I must make particular mention of the magnificent reception and cocktail party which you arranged in our honour at the Raffles Hotel. This was without doubt the most impressive function of our entire tour and will have a very happy place in our memories…. For this great kindness alone I cannot find adequate words to express my thanks to you, yet this was only one of the many manifestations of your outstanding generosity.
>
> …Coupled with the pleasant and satisfying recollections we shall always have of our stay in your great and virile city will be the knowledge that our visit has done much to consolidate the inter-relation between our two institutions, which, as you so rightly pointed out, have much in common in the development of branch systems in our respective countries on conservative and sound banking principles. The various ways in which our further relationship can be made complementary will be explored with renewed vigour and the utmost goodwill.
>
> I hope — indeed I am sure — that with our business relationship further strengthened by the close personal ties which exist between our two Banks at all levels, we can look forward to a great development of our mutual business interests in the future.'[31]

It was therefore no surprise that during his next visit to Midland Bank, Tan Chin Tuan was accorded VIP treatment and Edington made it a point to invite his Singapore friend for lunch whenever the OCBC managing director was in England. Years later, Tan Chin Tuan was able to secure further goodwill and gratitude from the Midland Bank when the latter requested his assistance in persuading the newly-formed Central Bank of Malaya to open an account with it. The well-connected banker was able to do so successfully through his *guanxi* network by arranging a meeting between Midland Bank and Sir Henry Lee Hau-Shik, the then Finance Minister of Malaya. He also wrote personally to Lee Hau-Shik to request consideration of the case. Eventually, the Central Bank of Malaya opened an account with the Midland Bank in March 1959.

For Tan Chin Tuan, the ability to perform favours for his business contacts was also a measure of his personal stature and influence, aside from the store of benefits to be gained by the OCBC. Having lost his father at the young age of 14, he could count only on his own wits, instinct, acumen and diligence to achieve success. Such qualities had brought him to the highest management position in a local bank and to public office appointments in various capacities, including being Deputy President of the Legislative Council. It therefore gave him a considerable sense of pride and satisfaction to be able to accede to a request from a venerable institution such as the Midland Bank, to make a difference and earn the respect of the British bankers. The pleasure, for the Managing Director of the OCBC, was not just being in a position to do favours, but being requested to do so by the British, whom many perceived to be superior because they ruled Singapore. It felt good to be able to deal with the white man as an equal.

The Unique Role of the Raffles Hotel

To be respected as an equal of the white man, Tan Chin Tuan was always anxious that the bank's foreign guests must go away with only the fondest memories of their time spent in Singapore. Because, it was only when the guests were happily impressed could the follow-up business deals be pursued with greater interest and vigour. Thus, no effort was spared to extend to these special guests the warmest hospitality and courtesy. This meant that the VIP visitors were treated only to the best that Singapore could offer. In the colonial era, the Raffles Hotel was generally thought to be the best and was much sought after by the well-heeled white man so much so that it was nearly impossible to reserve a room at the hotel unless one spoke with a foreign accent. Not surprisingly, the OCBC staff found their attempts at making room reservations at the Raffles Hotel frustrating. On several occasions, Tan Chin Tuan even had to turn to his friend, Joseph Aaron Elias, a board member at the hotel and 'one of the richest Jews in those days', to help him reserve a room!

Tired of this tedious process of booking rooms, Tan Chin Tuan decided that the OCBC should buy sufficient shares in the Raffles Hotel to obtain a seat on its board of directors. That way, the bank's foreign guests would always be able to enjoy the hospitality of one of the finest hotels in Singapore. As early as 1947, the OCBC had already secured 50,000 shares in Raffles Hotel Limited. These shares were bought from a Dutchman who had been a prisoner-of-war in Indonesia and who decided to sell his shares before he returned home. However, the lot of 50,000 shares was insufficient to gain the OCBC a seat on the board.[32] Opportunity knocked when Joseph Elias died and his block of some 88,000 shares was offered to Tan Chin Tuan at fair market price. The shares were purchased without hesitation and the OCBC banker became the first Asian to join the Raffles Board of Directors. Years later, he even became the hotel's chairman, but not without objection from the other 'colonials' on the Board. The 'colonials' opposed his appointment on grounds that Tan Chin Tuan was unqualified because he knew nothing about hotels. To this, Tan calmly retorted: 'I know nothing about hotels but I shall employ people who know how to run a hotel.'[33]

From the start, Tan Chin Tuan saw the immense potential of using the legendary Raffles Hotel to complement the OCBC's objectives. The Raffles would become the public relations arm of the bank, offering its renowned hospitality to win the hearts of VIP guests. This was imperative because when 'important visitors' were treated well, 'personal gratitude comes in'. The Chairman elaborated on his *modus operandi*:

> We kept a suite vacant at the Raffles Hotel all the time. I even kept a private dining room all the time. No one could use it. When there were VIP guests, they were given very special treatment. That's how we made more friends. Raffles Hotel became not only an asset making money, but also a means of helping to build a Bank – the OCBC owed much to Raffles Hotel.

Management gurus might credit Tan Chin Tuan with 'helicopter vision' for his ability to tap optimum value from the companies closely associated with the OCBC. As far as the OCBC Managing Director was concerned, it was simply 'common business sense' to build goodwill with the best hospitality. This astute move turned out to be highly rewarding when it provided Tan Chin Tuan with the unanticipated chance of making the acquaintance of two top American bankers from the Chase Manhattan Bank.

Networking with Chase Manhattan Bank

George Champion and David Rockefeller, respectively chairman and president of Chase Manhattan Bank, were visiting Singapore but their aide was unable to secure rooms for them at the fully-booked Raffles Hotel. He was however told that only the Managing Director of the OCBC could arrange the requisite rooms for him, since a luxurious suite had been set aside for the bank's exclusive use. The aide went to see Tan Chin Tuan who was more than happy to welcome Champion and Rockefeller to the Raffles. For him, it was an honour to be able to extend hospitality to such important visitors. Strict instructions were quickly left with the hotel to accord VIP treatment to the two gentlemen from New York.

What Tan did not anticipate was the visit by both George Champion and David Rockefeller to his office at the China Building to thank him for his hospitality. The surprise visit made it possible for him to become personally acquainted with the American bankers and later, for Tan Chin Tuan to continue to play host to the Rockefellers in subsequent years. During this first visit, the American bankers were so impressed by the wonderful time they enjoyed at the Raffles Hotel that they persuaded the OCBC banker to let them show their appreciation by doing something for him. The urbane Tan Chin Tuan thought it crass to ask for a favour but did casually mention in their discussion that the OCBC had only a million dollar credit facility from the Chase Manhattan Bank.

Shortly after the American bankers had returned to New York, Tan Chin Tuan was pleasantly surprised to learn that the Chase Manhattan Bank had unilaterally increased the OCBC's credit facility to $5 million. This was certainly a welcome favour because the OCBC would otherwise have had to put up security for this amount. Given that OCBC's capital was only $10 million then, this would not have been possible.

David Rockefeller would return again and again to Singapore for business and each time, Tan Chin Tuan would take pleasure in playing host to him and his wife. That the Rockefellers enjoyed their visits were eloquently expressed in their letters to their Singapore friend.

Those who had the opportunity to enjoy the solicitous hospitality of the OCBC and its managing director were invariably impressed and touched. The goodwill generated not only strengthened the bank's relationship with its major foreign counterparts, it also acquainted Tan Chin Tuan with some luminaries of the banking world. All this networking made good business sense and brought the OCBC to the attention of some of the world's largest banks.

Cultivating a Local and Regional Network

While the OCBC actively pursued liaisons with major foreign banks in England and the United States, its small capital base meant that much of its activities were conducted in Singapore and the region. To facilitate its business dealings at this end, it was just as important for the bank to cultivate a strong local network of *guanxi*. The fact that Tan Chin Tuan held public office appointments in the British Military Administration Advisory Council, the Legislative Council and the Rendel Commission was helpful. It made the bank savvy to political nuances and enabled it to leverage on opportunities which its counterparts might fail to seize.

An interesting example was the Singapore City Council bond issue offered by the newly-elected Mayor, Ong Eng Guan, in 1957. The OCBC contributed $1 million towards the Council's $30 million debenture stock. In sharp contrast, the Hongkong and Shanghai Bank (HKSB) and the Chartered Bank showed their lack of confidence in the municipal issue by failing to subscribe to it. When asked what prompted the OCBC to take up such a large portion of the issue, Tan Chin Tuan explained that it was a matter of 'national duty' — a demonstration of the bank's support for the City Council.

Mayor Ong Eng Guan was furious at the apathy of the HKSB and Chartered Bank. He interpreted it as a snub from the British-controlled banks and even perceived the episode in terms of a struggle against colonialism:

> We do believe that in the fight against colonialism we should support and back enterprises which are organised and initiated by persons who are Malayans and that whenever we can, the City Council should take as a matter of principle that preference should be given to those big enterprises whose owners are local people.... We do not say that we are against foreign investment but we say wherever we can we should promote local capital vis-à-vis foreign capital.[34]

Consequently, the Singapore City Council formally approved a finance committee decision to transfer the Council's loan funds from the HKSB and the Chartered Bank to the OCBC. The funds were worth some $20 million, the bulk of which resided in the HKSB. Tan Chin Tuan recognised that a sudden withdrawal of an enormous amount of money could be damaging to the HKSB. He then quickly and quietly deposited a large sum of money in the HKSB. Some time later, when the OCBC managing director was in Hong Kong, the HKSB chief invited him for lunch to convey the bank's gratitude:

> We are very grateful that you should have helped us in this manner, and now I want to say to you that if your branch here should have any trouble, let me know and I will do the same for you.[35]

Tan Chin Tuan was glad that he had made a friend and one whom the OCBC could count upon should the need arise.

The HKSB episode underlined the macro-economic perspective guiding the OCBC in its strategic thinking. The bank was not averse to lending a helping hand to a competitor in order to avert a potentially bigger economic crisis which could arise from a sudden and drastic decline in liquidity in a major bank such as the HKSB. Mayor Ong might not have foreseen the impact of a massive withdrawal of funds on the stability of a bank, but the OCBC did. The latter would rise to the occasion again to assist the Bank of China under different circumstances in the 1960s.

A Helping Hand for the Bank of China

For 23 months between September 1963 and August 1965, Singapore was a state within the Federation of Malaysia as a result of a merger. The terms of the merger provided that all major policies, except those related to education and labour in Singapore, were to be decided by the Central Government in Kuala Lumpur. It turned out to be an unhappy union fraught with misunderstandings and suspicions between the leadership on the opposing sides of the Causeway. Wedged between was the Bank of China which had been operating in old Malaya and Singapore for a few decades. The right-wing leaders in Kuala Lumpur thought the Bank could be an instrument of the Chinese communist government and thus a security threat. The Singapore government, on the other hand, recognised the important economic role played by the Bank of China as an intermediary in the substantial trade between Beijing and Singapore. Kuala Lumpur decided that its calculations must take precedence and in December 1964, served notice to the Bank of China to close down its offices in Malaysia (including Singapore).

The public reacted anxiously to the impending closure of the Bank of China branches. Tan Chin Tuan and his colleagues at the OCBC watched the unfolding drama with growing concern. They reasoned that the situation must be contained or depositors would soon panic, especially if the Bank of China were unable to meet cash withdrawals promptly.

If that happened, it could have a knock-on effect on other banks in the country. To ease Bank of China's liquidity, the OCBC bought the latter's premises in Penang 'at market valuation' to help the Chinese convert some of their assets to cash. In addition, OCBC also extended loans to the Bank of China's offices in Singapore to provide a stream of funds to meet depositors' withdrawals. These loans were secured by the deposit of title deeds to their headquarters at Battery Road and their South Bridge Road branch with OCBC.

Subsequently, the Governor of Bank Negara (Malaysia's central bank) came down to Singapore to investigate and decided to take over the financing of Bank of China and lent the latter another $12 million. When Bank Negara learnt that the Bank of China's title deeds of its Singapore properties were in OCBC's possession, the Central Bank requested that OCBC release the deeds but Tan Chin Tuan had to decline. To confirm OCBC's rights, Tan applied for and obtained a court order stating that OCBC had first priority over the Bank of China's Singapore properties.

With the separation of Singapore from Malaysia on 9 August 1965, the Bank of China was allowed to continue operations in Singapore. When the situation stabilised, the Bank of China had sufficient funds to pay OCBC, but were in a quandary. If they repaid OCBC's loan, there was a risk that Bank Negara might stake a claim on their title deeds. It was then agreed that the Bank of China deposit a sum with OCBC which would generate sufficient interest to offset the interest OCBC was charging for the loan.

Eventually, the Bank of China not only paid off its loans to both Bank Negara and OCBC, but was able to hold onto its headquarters and branch in Singapore. The lifeline which Tan threw Bank of China proved to be a win-win solution for all. More importantly, a major banking crisis was averted.

Setback Amidst Uncertainty

Tan Chin Tuan and his board of directors exercised decisive leadership not only in the area of strengthening business networks but also in tackling unforeseen setbacks. When the situation demanded it, the board members did not flinch from making unpleasant decisions. The closure of the OCBC's branches in Indonesia in 1962 and 1963 demonstrated the swiftness and boldness which characterised the bank's response to a crisis. It was a purely financial calculation; the hefty depreciation of the Indonesian rupiah had made it unprofitable to continue operations and the OCBC had to cut its losses.

A long letter dated 18 June 1962 from the manager of an OCBC branch in Jakarta confirmed what Tan Chin Tuan had already known for some time — that 'the future outlook from the business point of view (was) not bright'.[36] All four OCBC branches in the Indonesian cities of Jakarta, Palembang, Surabaya and Jambi had been in the red for a couple of years. The state of affairs, as detailed in the letter, was bleak:

> For some time now and particularly since early 1961, the volume of our business had been so reduced that the staff had little to occupy themselves.... Since 1957, we have not been able to remit out the profit we made in Indonesia. At about this period too, we had experienced a great setback in business...it is therefore time that we should consider winding up the business of the 3 Indonesian branches and allowing Jakarta Branch only to operate on a skeleton staff.[37]

A board meeting was called on 3 July 1962 to discuss the matter. It approved Tan Chin Tuan's recommendation to shut down the Palembang and Surabaya branches before December 1962. It further agreed to wind down the Jambi branch, subject to the satisfactory liquidation of the other two branches. The Jakarta branch was spared because the OCBC wished to retain a foothold in Indonesia.

Following the board's decision, Tan Chin Tuan had to plan the evacuation of the OCBC's assets from the Indonesian cities. This was no easy task since the Jakarta government had already instituted an array of controls to prevent companies from pulling out their assets. Tan Chin Tuan hatched an ingenious plan. He converted as much of the bank's assets as possible into precious stones and jewellery and quietly had a manager bring them out to Hong Kong. He also did not forget the staff left unemployed by the closure of the bank's branches. Aside from monetary compensation, each was given a typewriter. The managing director had selected the typewriter as a parting gift because he saw the ever escalating price of typewriters as a good hedge against spiralling inflation. Staff members could thus sell their typewriters to help them tide over financial difficulties.

NOTES

1 Goh Keng Swee, 'A Socialist Economy that Works', in *Socialism that Works...The Singapore Way*, C. V. Devan Nair, ed (Singapore: Federal Publication (S) Pte Ltd, 1976), p. 77.

2 W. G. Huff, *The Economic Growth of Singapore: Trade and Development in The Twentieth Century* (Cambridge: Cambridge University Press, 1994), p. 292.

3 Ibid.

4 Ibid., p. 291.

5 Richard Clutterbuck, *Riot and Revolution in Singapore and Malaya, 1945-1963* (Singapore: Graham Brash, 1973).

6 John Drysdale, *Singapore: Struggle for Success* (Singapore: Times Publication, 1984), p. 21.

7 See *Annual Report of the Labour Department 1951* (Singapore: Government Printing Office, 1952); *Annual Report of the Labour Department 1953* (Singapore: Government Printing Office, 1954); *Annual Report of the Labour Department 1954* (Singapore: Government Printing Office, 1956); *Annual Report of the Labour Department 1960* (Singapore: Government Printing Office, 1961) and *Ministry of Labour Annual Report 1966* (Singapore, 1967).

8 *The Straits Times*, 16 May 1952.

9 Lee Kuan Yew and Tan Chin Tuan were related to each other by marriage. Lee Kuan Yew's wife, Kwa Geok Choo, also a prominent barrister, was the third daughter of Kwa Siew Tee who had married Tan's sister-in-law. The senior Kwa was a general manager in the OCBC from 1935 to 1945. Tan Chin Tuan was reasonably acquainted with his nephew and niece, both of whom were then with Laycock and Ong, the law firm used by the OCBC.

10 *The Straits Times*, 4 February 1963.

11 Personal correspondences, Tan Chin Tuan, 1956.

12 Personal correspondences, Tan Chin Tuan, 1978.

13 Proceedings, 1962.

14 Ibid.

15 Ibid.

16 Ibid.

17 Ibid.

18 Ibid.

19 Ibid.

20 Ibid.

21 Interview, Tan Chin Tuan, 18 March 1999.

22 Ibid.

23 Proceedings, 1962.

24 Ibid.

25 *The Straits Times*, 17 March 1962.

26 Ibid.

27 Wellington K. K. Chan, 'Tradition and Change in the Chinese Business Enterprise', in *Chinese Business History: Interpretive Trends and Priorities for the Future*, R. Gardella, J. K. Leonard & M. C. Elderry, eds, *Chinese Studies in History*, vol. 31, no. 3–4 (1998): 131.

28 Ibid., p. 140.

29 Wong Siu Lun, 'Business Networks, Cultural Values and the States in Hong Kong and Singapore', in *Chinese Business in Asia*, R. A. Brown, ed (London: Routledge, 1995), p. 136.

30 Interview, Tan Chin Tuan (n.d.), on file with authors.

31 Personal correspondences, Tan Chin Tuan, 1955.

32 Gretchen Liu, *Raffles Hotel* (Singapore: Landmark Books Private Limited, 1992).

33 Interview, Tan Chin Tuan (n.d.), on file with authors.
34 *Singapore Standard*, 25 September 1958.
35 Interview, Tan Chin Tuan (n.d.), on file with authors.
36 Tan Chin Tuan archives (Singapore: The Tan Foundation).
37 Personal correspondences, Tan Chin Tuan, 1962.

CHAPTER 6

EXTENDING THE OCBC FAMILY

When the OCBC celebrated its 40th anniversary on 31 October 1972, it had journeyed a long way from the bleak days of the Great Depression to become 'the largest company, in terms of assets, in Malaysia and Singapore'.[1] Indeed, at the time of its birth, following an amalgamation of three financially uncertain banks in 1932, its deposits and loans at $26.9 million and $14.8 million respectively were plainly modest by international standards. Aggregate assets stood at $38.7 million then. In a span of four decades, the OCBC had multiplied its aggregate assets over 36 times, thrusting the bank into the leading position among the top 100 companies listed in Singapore and Malaysia.[2]

It was a defining moment for Tan Chin Tuan — the OCBC's Managing Director since 1942 and concurrently, its Chairman since 1966 — who was so closely associated with the bank's progress and achievements. Tan Chin Tuan could justifiably feel a tremendous sense of satisfaction over the sizable empire he had helped the OCBC build over the decades: 41 branches (including two in Hong Kong, two in China and one in London), over 25 subsidiaries and many associates in Singapore, Malaysia, Hong Kong and London. The bank also owned stakes in the Hongkong & Shanghai Bank (now HSBC), the Midland Bank and the Bank of New South Wales (now known as the Westpac Banking Corporation). In addition, the OCBC had significant equity interests in a number of respected blue-chip companies.

Clearly, the OCBC's investments covered a wide spectrum: from banking-related businesses to unrelated industries that dealt with beverages, tin smelting, insurance, motor car distribution and general trading. Tan Chin Tuan made no apologies for his leadership in the OCBC's investment strategies. After all, the varied investment portfolio had turned out to be exceedingly profitable. Yet, profitability was not the chief concern of the savvy banker who had 'never bothered' about the total market value of all the equities controlled by the OCBC. His decisions were not encumbered by mere pecuniary interests. In an interview with *Euromoney* in 1982, Tan Chin Tuan explained why the OCBC bought stakes in foreign banks:

> The main object of buying into them is investment. For instance, I started to buy Midland Bank in 1973 when their prices were very low. I was confident that the depressed price did not reflect anything fundamental, and subsequent and current prices have justified my confidence in the Midland bank and much goodwill has resulted from this investment. We have strengthened a valuable relationship.
>
> The second objective is to establish strong ties with leading indigenous banks. In the United Kingdom, it's

the Midland Bank. In Australia, it's the Bank of New
South Wales. Because of this close relationship, our
customers can go to almost any branch of the Bank of
New South Wales in Australia or the Midland in the
UK and they will be welcomed as if they were the
banks' own customers.[3]

Tan Chin Tuan's fundamental business philosophy remained unchanged all these years. It is based on the basic
business tenets of building networks, building relationships
and building customer loyalty. Tan's unpretentious business
philosophy might not excite management school gurus, but
it had certainly worked well for the OCBC.

In retrospect, the rationale for the OCBC's investments in
related businesses is easy to discern. However, many early
observers in the 1950s and 1960s were puzzled by the bank's
substantial interests in businesses that had little or no direct
relationship with banking. In fact, the bank's total equity
interest in various blue chip companies had grown so large
by the 1980s that one interviewer actually asserted to Tan
Chin Tuan that the OCBC seemed to be 'more of an investment institution than a lending bank'.[4] The observation
invited a brisk response from the Chairman, 'I don't think so.
We are bankers in all senses of the word.'[5] What Tan Chin
Tuan had probably chosen to ignore was the backhanded
compliment accompanying that observation: that it was
precisely because of the bank's astute judgement that investments in non-related industries brought such enviable returns.

The OCBC began acquiring large blocks of shares in select
companies in different industries in the latter part of the
1940s and 1950s. At that time, such diversification was a
pioneering feat because the stock exchange was non-existent
in Singapore. It was thus impossible to buy the shares of
locally registered companies on the stock market as investors

do today. All such share transactions had to be conducted through private treaty. This meant that the OCBC had to find willing sellers among the blue-chip companies it was keen to invest in. The task was not as straightforward as it might seem because directors of the target companies had the discretion to deny registration of the share transfer if they had objections to the transferee. The OCBC did not invest in companies like Boustead and Guthries where ultimate control continued to be vested with parent companies in the United Kingdom. There were just too many imponderables in long distance negotiations. Tan Chin Tuan therefore had to be judicious in his choice of companies for the OCBC to buy into. He was justifiably proud of the pioneering lead taken by the bank:

> ...we were the first local bank to take equity interests in various industries, partly as an investment. This is now being emulated on a bigger scale by other local banks.'[6]

These decisions took on added significance in the light of the uncertain times in which the investments were made. As one historian put it, Tan Chin Tuan 'had the courage to go against the nervous tide, buying large, strategic and ultimately valuable blocks of shares in companies which were to play a large part in Singapore's economy'.[7] The 'nervous tide' was swept in by a wave of tumultuous changes in the 1950s when incipient political awakening and anti-colonialism were potently mixed with communism, communalism and union activism. Singapore was then witnessing the end of an epoch of British rule and the beginning of an era of self-rule.

The fundamental question which confronted many in the corporate world then, particularly the British companies, was a simple one: Was there money to be made in a self-governing and eventually independent Singapore? Tan Chin Tuan summarised the dilemmas aptly as he explained why the OCBC confidently took the contrary view:

> When the British Government was withdrawing, shareholders in the British companies were naturally apprehensive. I believed that those companies were sound, and that they should be preserved as going concerns. We therefore acquired their shares in the open market, and made every effort to ensure that the British executives who wished to remain were allowed to do so. People were nervous when the Labour Party came to power. After that, the People's Action Party came in, and there were fears that there would be further political instability. Consequently, the faint-hearted as well as the Britishers who preferred to return to their homeland, opted to liquidate their stakes in the companies established locally. However, I was convinced that politicians who appear radical in opposition, invariably become realistic and moderate when they are vested with responsibility. My Chairman (Lee Kong Chian) happened to share my conviction, and consequently, we started investing in well-established companies such as Straits Trading, Fraser & Neave, Malayan Breweries, Robinsons, Wearne Brothers, Raffles Hotel and Great Eastern Life Assurance.[8]

As a result of such stout-hearted decisions, the OCBC was subsequently able to extend its influence into many industries beyond banking because of the substantial stakes it held in various blue-chip companies.

But the OCBC's successful diversification had larger implications beyond dollars and cents. As Yong Pung How,[9] then a director on the OCBC Board, put it succinctly at the celebration of Tan Chin Tuan's 50 years of service at the OCBC:

> We also know of his great achievement in effecting the 'localization' of many foreign companies, which have been strengthened and had their horizons widened by the transfer of ownership and management into local hands. The resulting progress of companies like Fraser and Neave, Malayan Breweries, Straits Trading, Great Eastern Life Assurance, Oversea Assurance, Robinsons and Wearne Brothers, all of which he is Chairman, are lasting tributes in their own way to the significant contributions which he has made to them.[10]

What Tan Chin Tuan did to the established corporate names of the British empire paralleled the political developments of the 1950s which saw power being transferred gradually from the British to the local-born. By seizing opportunities to acquire sizeable stakes in well-known expatriate businesses, Tan Chin Tuan took the important step of placing the Singaporean on par with the British in the boardroom. This was not unlike his roles in the Legislative Council and Executive Council where he frequently stood up to the British and demonstrated that the local was no inferior species.

Elsewhere in Singapore and the Malay Peninsula, the more progressive among the Chinese tycoons were emulating the OCBC's moves. Nicholas White, in his book *Business and Government and the End of Empire*, observed that 'while the post-war era in Malaya was witnessing changes in the structure of share ownership.... British control over the local economy was relatively unaffected.'[11] In the rubber industry for example, he noted:

> ...the presence of even large Asian shareholdings did not guarantee control, since investors generally lacked

the expert knowledge of the investment groups. Control remained in the hands of British directors: the agency house executives, lawyers, accountants, and agricultural technologists who formed the power elite of the corporate economy, despite having only nominal holdings in their companies.[12]

This put Tan Chin Tuan and the OCBC in a unique position. Not only was the OCBC 'a substantial stakeholder in locally registered British firms',[13] Tan Chin Tuan actually sat on the boards of many of these erstwhile British-controlled companies. He would again and again display his acumen and wisdom, borne of years of experience, in the boardrooms and earned himself the chairmanship in a number of these illustrious companies. The OCBC banker was not one to tolerate a puppet's role — as chairman, he had de facto control — a situation which 'greatly alarmed established British investors.'[14] But the alarm was unnecessary because Tan Chin Tuan was no zealous anti-British nationalist. He recognised the importance of retaining in the companies he controlled, those whose specialist knowledge was essential to the smooth functioning of the organisation, and 'made every effort to ensure that the British executives who wished to remain were allowed to do so'.[15]

The OCBC's major share-holdings, coupled with Tan Chin Tuan's personal involvement and management in these companies, made them synonymous with the OCBC marque. Indeed, they are today still referred to as the OCBC group of companies. To understand the intertwining effect of OCBC's stake-holding and Tan Chin Tuan's role in the companies, it is necessary to examine in some detail how this situation came about.

Overseas Assurance Corporation

One of the earliest companies to which Tan Chin Tuan became affiliated was the Overseas Assurance Corporation (OAC). The underwriting company had been established by a group of prominent businessmen including Lim Boon Keng, Lim Nee Soon, Ong Boon Tat and Tan Ean Kiam in February 1920, and was the first locally-owned composite insurance company which provided both general and life insurance. In 1976, OCBC and its related companies controlled a total of 16.5% in OAC.

Tan's association with the OAC dated back to 1937 when he was co-opted onto its Board of Directors. He witnessed the steady growth of the company in the early years, based on the principle that growth should 'never (be) too [sic] rapid as to involve risk'.[16] It was a principle which accorded with his own philosophy of prudence. Still, the 'never too rapid growth' cut impressive figures by industry standards. The OAC's average growth rate after World War Two amoun- ted to approximately 300% every decade.[17] Translated into tangible sums, the amount of premium less insurance covered by the OAC climbed from $103,000 in 1921 to $424,000 in 1940 and in the post-war years, reached $1.68 million in 1950 and $5.97 million in 1960.[18]

The company's fortunes essentially paralleled the economic health of Singapore, which in turn was vulnerable to the ups and downs of the international economy. On the flip side, global slowdowns too were similarly mirrored in the OAC's balance sheets. One such crisis occurred when Tan Chin Tuan was chairman of the company. The OCBC banker had to deal with the 'most crucial single event of the decade' — the sudden sharp rise in oil prices in 1973.

This crisis caused the global economy to simultaneously suffer both steep inflation and recession! The general insurance department of the OAC was badly hit and was saved from a worse fate by the culture of prudence imposed under Tan Chin Tuan's stewardship. When the crisis was over, the company's underwriting activities rebounded robustly. In fact, the gross premium income of the general insurance department registered a three-and-a-half time increase during the period of his chairmanship from 1969 to 1981. At the same time, the OAC's shareholders' funds jumped a healthy 6.6 times from $7.286 million to $48.427 million and the paid-up capital climbed from $1.95 million to $11.7 million between 1969 and 1981.[19]

Fraser & Neave Limited

In Singapore, Fraser & Neave, or F&N, is synonymous with soft drinks. Originally established by John Fraser and David Chalmers Neave in September 1883, it was then known as The Singapore and Straits Aerated Water Company and operated from modest premises at Battery Road where it manufactured 'soda water, seltzer water, potass water, lemonade, tonic, ginger ale, ginger beer, etc., of the first quality'.[20] As its business grew in tandem with societal affluence, Fraser & Neave Limited was established as a new public company in 1898. By the turn of the century, F&N was already one of the largest companies in Singapore with branches in Kuala Lumpur, Malacca, Seremban, Ipoh, Penang, Bangkok and Saigon.[21]

The fortunes of F&N were further enhanced when it diversified into the brewing business through a joint venture with the well-known Dutch brewery, Heineken NV. As a result, Malayan Breweries Ltd was born in 1931. The taste of Tiger Beer, produced by Malayan Breweries, became a familiar part of Singapore life. Subsequently, F&N also acquired the Archipelago Brewery Company which produced Anchor Beer. In 1936, F&N successfully secured a much sought-after franchise for Singapore and Malaysia — the Coca-Cola franchise. This development, together with the company's joint venture with Heineken, was singled out by F&N, as crucial to 'ensur(ing) the company's place among the major companies in the region.' [22]

F&N was not only the market leader in the aerated drinks industry, its status as a public company allowed investors an opportunity to buy a stake in its operations. Its competitors, Phoenix and Framroz, were family-run concerns and the families were reluctant to relinquish their shares in the companies. Tan Chin Tuan watched the aerated drinks scene with keen interest. His calculations showed him the enormous potential in the local drinks market. He explained why:

> Drinks are bulky and very expensive to transport. That means locally produced drinks stand a good chance in competition with imported drinks. Besides, all the raw materials for producing drinks are available in Singapore. We only had to buy sugar and essence and these were cheaply sourced from Malaysia and the region. So, if we can manufacture our drinks cheaply, we can compete.[23]

Tan Chin Tuan therefore started buying F&N shares for himself, and later, for the OCBC. By 1950, the OCBC stake was substantial enough for its managing director to join F&N's board of directors. He took over the chairmanship in 1957 and remained in the position of control until his retirement in 1983. The accumulation of shares over the years has resulted in the OCBC holding some 22% of F&N's total shares today (1999)[23a].

Throughout his involvement with F&N, the banker surprised many with his easy familiarity with the technical know-how of factory floor production and was responsible for pushing F&N towards mechanisation. He was on a constant lookout for new and better production techniques. In 1963, new bottling lines were installed in F&N factories in Malaysia and Singapore to increase production and by 1967, the beverage giant introduced the 'first aerated water canning line in South East Asia'[24] at its River Valley Road plant in Singapore. The rapid expansion in production volume as a consequence of mechanisation in turn enabled F&N to price its drinks competitively. Tan Chin Tuan was particularly proud of the fact that the post-war prices of F&N drinks were kept unchanged for 27 years! This feat was accomplished because:

> We were able to acquire everything cheap. We bought most of the sugar from Robert Kuok's plantations and got a good price. Our glass bottles were imported from the Australian Consolidated Industry, so I bought shares in the Australian company to ensure that the bottles were sold to us at a cheap price. Later, I even bought a glass bottle factory in Johore to produce our own bottles and acquired equity in Metal Box to manufacture cans for our own drinks and for sale to other customers.[25]

Tan Chin Tuan practised simple economics — keep costs low to keep prices low to enlarge market share. Part of the strategy involved exercising a considerable degree of control over backward linkages to ensure quality and competitive pricing from suppliers. That was why Tan Chin Tuan led the F&N into buying substantial stakes in Malayan Glass Factory Bhd in Malaysia in 1972 and in Metal Box (Singapore) in 1979.

Tan Chin Tuan played a major role in diversifying the OCBC's interests, and saw the incorporation of more products as the way to enlarge F&N. A joint venture with Beatrice Foods of Chicago made this possible and in 1961, the company ventured into milk products. A multi-million dollar milk condensery was set up in Petaling Jaya, Malaysia and recombined sweetened condensed milk was produced in Southeast Asia for the first time.[26] Subsequently, Carnation International of Los Angeles was included in the joint venture in 1966, enabling F&N to process evaporated milk and manufacture its own cans as well.

The 1960s was a period of rapid expansion by F&N, notwithstanding the political flux which saw Singapore become a part of Malaysia in 1963 followed by the separation of Singapore from Malaysia in August 1965. Tan Chin Tuan's confidence was not shaken by the severing of ties between the two territories — he steered F&N to establish even more plants across the Causeway, in Kuching, Johor Bahru, Ipoh, Kota Kinabalu and Sandakan. The reason, as the F&N Chairman put it, was 'obvious' because 'bottled and canned drinks were very bulky items and it was both cheaper and easier to have manufacturing plants in Malaysia to produce drinks for direct distribution there.'[27]

Growth in the F&N group continued unabated in the 1970s with the securing of more franchises and the launch of a greater variety of drink products. Fanta, Sunkist, Zappel, multi-flavours of Daisy milk and Meadow Gold ice-cream were all introduced in the 1970s. By the time Tan Chin Tuan retired, he was satisfied that his 33 years as director and then chairman had yielded positive results with shareholders' funds having risen from $10.5 million in 1950 to $300 million in June 1983.[28] It is noteworthy that such growth had been achieved 'without any recourse to shareholders and despite always keeping the prices of its products at levels which only yield a reasonable return when sales volume is high'.[29] Many would be keen to fathom the secret of his success at F&N, but Tan Chin Tuan was dismissive of attempts to credit him:

> I knew nothing about banking when I started, but I
> always believe that you can bring in people with the
> expertise. So, in F&N, I feel all those people, being the
> experts, must know the business. The only thing I con-
> tributed was common sense.[30]

Malayan Breweries Limited

Malayan Breweries Limited (MBL) was established in 1931 as a result of a joint venture between F&N and Dutch brewery, Heineken NV. Its new brew, appropriately named Tiger Beer to connote the strength and vigour associated with the beast, was an immediate success. MBL would later include rival brand, Anchor Beer, in its line, when F&N bought over the German-owned Archipelago Brewery Company for MBL at the outbreak of World War Two.

As a result of the OCBC's sizeable stake in F&N, Tan Chin Tuan joined the Board of Directors at MBL in 1951 and became its chairman in 1957, the year he assumed the same post at F&N. The path to the most powerful position in MBL was not an easy one. Prior to his assumption of directorship in 1951, the chairman and all other MBL board members were all Europeans. Eventually, the board members had to defer to the OCBC Managing Director who shrewdly used the OCBC, Great Eastern Life and other companies in the OCBC stable to buy a majority stake in MBL.

Tan Chin Tuan replicated in MBL the same strategy of diversification through acquisition and boldly globalised the local brewery's reach with the purchase of the South Pacific Brewery of Papua New Guinea in 1955 and the Leopard Brewery of New Zealand in 1956. These were gutsy moves because few local companies had the confidence to venture beyond the familiar Southeast Asian region in those days. The responsibility thus fell on the OCBC banker, particularly after he became chairman, to ensure the profitability of these overseas investments.

Initially, sales from the South Pacific Brewery plant in Port Moresby were slow. A ban on drinking by the indigenous people had stalled the growth of the brewery. But Tan Chin Tuan had placed his bets on an imminent lifting of the ban which was expected to send the sales of South Pacific Brewery soaring since the latter was the sole local producer of beer. He was right. The lifting of the ban in November 1962 pushed sales of beer up by 50%. Later, a second brewery was opened in Lae to meet the strong demand for beer in Papua New Guinea. Even with the setting up of a rival brewery in 1971, South Pacific Brewery continued to enjoy strong profitability, to the delight of the chairman.

The story of MBL's investment in the Leopard Brewery of New Zealand was less upbeat. From the start, a series of unexpected problems aggravated the situation. Competition proved much tougher than Tan Chin Tuan had imagined and Leopard Brewery faced an uphill task keeping pace with bigger breweries in the market. The banker was also surprised by New Zealand's peculiar regulation which required breweries to be involved in hotel development in order to get outlets for their beer. Eventually, the multifarious problems compelled Tan Chin Tuan to agree to a merger between Leopard Brewery and New Zealand Brewery (the largest in the country) in 1966. While the merger enabled Leopard Brewery to gain access to its partner's outlets, the bottom-line figures remained unimpressive. In 1982, Tan Chin Tuan sold off MBL's remaining shares in Leopard Brewery.

In contrast, MBL flourished in its home ground of Singapore and Malaysia. In 1962, he helped reorganise Malayan Breweries and Archipelago Brewery Company into a single organisation: Malayan Breweries Limited. Among the subsidiaries of MBL were Malayan Breweries (Singapore) Limited and Malayan Breweries (Malaya) Limited. Even after the dramatic political separation of Singapore from Malaysia in 1965, both subsidiaries continued to record strong growth in their respective territories.

Robinson and Company Limited

One of Singapore's most venerable retailers, Robinson & Company Limited, began life as Spicer & Robinson back in 1858.[31] Established by Philip Robinson and James Spicer, the store was 'replete with a well selected stock which they are determined to offer at the lowest renumerating rates, in order to ensure a large amount of public support'.[32] Like the fine range available at its competitor, John Little and Company, Spicer & Robinson sold goods such as fancy wine biscuits, Gloucester cheese, preserved meats, English jams, Martell's brandy, fashionable bonnets and perfumery which were found affordable only among the well-heeled.

When the partnership of Spicer and Robinson ended in 1859, the store was renamed Robinson and Company. To extend its business into the Malay Archipelago and Borneo, Robinson's employed travelling sales representatives to promote its wares. The store counted most of the Malay Sultans and even King Mongkut of Siam among its regular customers. Business prospered. The Great Depression of the 1930s altered the fortunes of Robinson's when the store suffered consecutive losses from 1931 to 1935. This was not surprising since the value of Malayan exports fell by 65% and trade was, as the chairman of the Chartered Bank put it, '(in) utter stagnation'.[33] Further misfortune befell the company when Japanese bombs blew up parts of the store twice during World War Two.

The physical and fiscal damage suffered by Robinson's did not distract Tan Chin Tuan from the company's intrinsic worth. That Robinson's was a well-managed store with a loyal team of faithful employees impressed the astute banker. He thus decided that the OCBC should invest substantially in Robinson's, a stake which in 1998 amounted to a sizeable 37.8% of total share-holdings.[33a] As the department store recovered to become a leading shopping destination in post-war Singapore, Tan Chin Tuan joined the board of directors in 1950 and became its first local chairman in 1957.

Among the significant decisions made by the Robinson's directors in the 1950s was the acquisition of the rival John Little department store in 1955. It was a triumph for the younger Robinson's to become sole owner of the bigger and older John Little. Under Tan Chin Tuan's chairmanship, Robinson's gradually moved away from its early image as a European store and established a reputation as a store which offered quality merchandise and good service to 'people of all communities'. He tackled, with panache, problems involving personnel and unions and guided the company through a tough period following the disastrous fire of 1972 which reduced the store to ugly ruins. Still, Robinson's triumphed in spite of the difficulties and shareholders' funds leapt 485.29% during Tan Chin Tuan's term as chairman while paid-up capital correspondingly rose 546.9% to $30.59 million in 1976 from $4.73 million in 1957.[34]

Straits Trading Company Limited

In 1887, two friends, Herman Muhlinghaus and James Sword incorporated the Straits Trading Company (STC) with a capital of $150,000 because they saw the 'smelting of tin in a more efficient way could be a profitable business'.[35] The quiet beginnings of the Straits Trading Company gave no hint of the distinguished status it would subsequently achieve by the turn of the 20th century. At its height, the company was handling one-third of the world's supply of tin, making it the largest tin smelting company in the world.[36]

Business flourished from the start. With superior technology and methods, the STC was able to produce tin ingots (all stamped with the name 'Straits Tin') that were pure in quality and competitive in price. The company's phenomenal growth was interrupted during the two World Wars and the Great Depression in between. In particular, the Japanese Occupation of Malaya and Singapore inflicted heavy losses with the total destruction of the Butterworth plant in Malaya and the extensive damage of the Pulau Brani smelter in Singapore.

The road to recovery following World War Two was led by newly-installed Chairman Sir Ewen Fergusson who was a member of the Legislative Council. This period of rehabilitation saw the transfer of substantial lots of STC shares into the hands of Singaporeans who purchased them. The OCBC was among the biggest local investors in the company, with its stake approximating 33% of total shares today (December 1999). It was Tan Chin Tuan who urged Lee Kong Chian and the OCBC to buy STC shares. He himself invested money in the company too. He was keen to acquire control of STC because the latter was able to fix the price of tin in the market. It was a powerful position and Tan Chin Tuan wanted the OCBC to be in command of that position.

In 1954, Tan Chin Tuan found himself invited onto the STC's board of directors because of his acquaintance with chairman Fergusson as well as the OCBC's stake in the tin smelting company. His association with the STC was a long and challenging one which lasted 38 years, of which 27 were spent as chairman from 1965 to 1992. Interestingly, Fergusson had invited the OCBC managing director onto the STC board because of his prominence — there was no intention of allowing an Asian to eventually lead such an influential company. That Fergusson had clearly intended Tan Chin Tuan to be a figurehead director was apparent from the fact that Fergusson had minutes of meetings written before the meetings! But time was on Tan Chin Tuan's side and he waited for his opportunity to act when the Europeans retired.

Following Fergusson's retirement, Tan Chin Tuan became chairman of one of the most renowned companies in Singapore and Malaysia. During his term, significant changes had to be effected to preserve profitability in the face of inevitable decline of ore available for smelting and rising costs. To offset the lower yields of Malaysian mines, he imported ore from other sources for smelting. The shrewd banker also trimmed costs by employing more efficient technology and writing off a loss-incurring mining subsidiary in Tanzania. At the same time, he steered the STC into diverse global investments which included plywood manufacturing, property development, plantations and breweries. In 1982, a restructuring saw the company transfer its smelting business and related assets to a subsidiary, Malaysia Smelting Corporation Berhad, leaving the STC to focus on its new interests.

In Singapore, the STC was also involved in the property sector from the latter part of the 1960s. The company left its mark in the redevelopment of a historic site in the prime business district in 1969 and the 21-storey Straits Trading Building, completed in 1972, was a landmark structure in Singapore.[37] Notwithstanding the unavoidable troughs in business cycles, the company's vast portfolio of worldwide investments helped it weather fluctuating commodity prices, collapse of tin support prices and the mid-1980s recession. Stacked side by side, the plusses more than compensated for the minuses. As Tan Chin Tuan pointed out, if a stockholder had bought 1,000 shares in 1954 when the former first joined the STC Board, the number would have multiplied to 329,750 shares by the time the OCBC banker retired as chairman in

1992. In monetary terms, this translated to an astronomical 60 times increase from an outlay of $24,000 to $1,440,790![37a]

The Great Eastern Life Assurance Company Limited

Incorporated in August 1908, the Great Eastern Life Assurance Company is unanimously regarded as the doyen of the life insurance industry in the region. Its first office in Winchester House at Collyer Quay in Singapore was a modest operation comprising 15 staff members and assets of $70,000. Founder A. H. Fair, a Canadian, initially concentrated his business on Singapore and the more populous towns of Malaya. That niche expanded rapidly and soon, Great Eastern Life was offering life insurance plans throughout Malaya and Borneo and to clients in Java, Sumatra, Ceylon, India, Burma, Thailand and Hong Kong.

The first Asian to become the Chairman of Great Eastern Life was Dato S. Q. Wong who held that position from 1950 to 1969. In a report in 1956, Wong observed that the growth of the life assurance business in Southeast Asia was still very much lower than in Western countries. This problem corrected itself during the tenure of Tan Chin Tuan who succeeded Wong on the board. His term as Chairman from 1969 until his retirement in 1992 coincided with a period of buoyant growth and prosperity in the region. During this time, Singapore was enjoying an average growth of nearly 8% and a per capita income which rose from US$2,457 in 1969 to US$17,000 in 1992.[38] Similarly, the Malaysian economy expanded at an average rate of 8.3% between 1969 and 1992 and household incomes rose concurrently.[39] Greater affluence among the new middle class generated greater awareness and interest in protection against all possible contingencies. Life assurance boomed.

Under Tan Chin Tuan's leadership, Great Eastern Life established itself firmly as the largest life insurance company in the region. Its book value assets reached $500 million in 1977, doubled to $1 billion in 1982 and by 1985 had tripled to $1.5 billion.[40] The 1980s was only the start of the billion dollar decade for Great Eastern Life whose business figures scaled even higher in 1990 to reach $6.9 billion that year.

Beyond these impressive revenues, the experienced banker infused into Great Eastern Life a fundamental philosophy which had anchored the OCBC over the years — prudence. He introduced his own rules, in addition to the laws which already regulated the industry, to augment the integrity of the company's assets. He insisted on a good spread of sound investments and more importantly, insisted that the market value of assets must greatly exceed their book value. The golden rule proved to be a prescient practice when Great Eas- tern Life survived the global stock market crash of October 1987, unscathed. Not surprisingly, the shareholders' funds rose from $16,929,443 to $225,603,000 between 1969 and 1992 when he was chairman and the paid-up capital of the company correspondingly increased almost 16 times from $6,134,840 to $97,176,000.[41] The OCBC's substantial holdings in Great Eastern Life, at about 40.35% of total shares at the end of 1999, is continued manifestation of its confidence in the insurance company[41a].

Wearne Brothers Limited

In 1906, two brothers from Australia, C. F. F. Wearne and T. J. B. Wearne, formed a partnership in Singapore to sell and service cars. Wearne Brothers was initially the sole distributor of Ford motor cars and as its operations expanded, it acquired the Morris franchise as well. Soon, Wearne Brothers opened motorcar showrooms in cities outside Singapore such as Kuala Lumpur, Penang and Rangoon.

The Japanese Occupation of Malaya and Singapore interrupted Wearne Brothers' business plans and almost ruined the company. Fortunately, its fortunes were ably restored by W. J. Wearne and A. J. Sampson after the war. Sampson, who was company chairman from 1952 to 1967, established more branches in various Malaysian towns and spearheaded the diversification drive of Wearne Brothers into the trading of heavy equipment like tractors and marine engines. During the chairmanship of Sampson's successor, W. J. Wearne, two assembly plants were set up in Malaysia and Singapore which saw the local assembly of motor vehicles represented by Wearne Brothers. The assembly plants brought 'satisfactory returns' despite the tendency of the Singapore Government to exact a myriad of taxes on motor vehicles as a means to curb motorcar ownership.

Following the unexpected demise of W. J. Wearne in 1974, Tan Chin Tuan took over as chairman by virtue of the sub-stantial stake the OCBC had acquired over the years. Tan himself owned a 1.02% stake in the company.[42] It was the worst of times for the automobile industry as the world was reeling from a hefty hike in oil prices following an oil embargo imposed by the Arab states in October 1973. The business of Wearne Brothers was badly hit. As consumers delayed or even aborted their plans to buy cars and as smaller, energy-efficient cars gained popularity, Wearne Brothers found its inventory stagnating. This imposed tremendous costs on the company because market interest rates were high and financing was therefore expensive. The situation was described by Tan Chin Tuan as 'a most difficult one in the history of the company'.

The OCBC banker moved quickly to implement his tough brand of prudence and discipline in Wearne Brothers. He bit the bullet and liquidated stocks 'at marginal or no profit', trimmed operating expenditure and retrenched redundant manpower. Eventually, he divested the automobile assembly plants and returned Wearne Brothers to its previous car distribution activities. Notwithstanding the difficulties which confronted the company in the 1970s, he skilfully engineered a soft landing. By the time of his retirement from Wearne Brothers in 1982, Tan Chin Tuan could take pride in the value he had added to the company in the 9 years he was its chairman. The paid up capital of Wearne Brothers jumped 50% from $45.08 million in 1974 to $67.62 million in 1983 while shareholders' funds increased 131 percent in the same period, from $108.8 million to $251.2 million.[43]

Sime Darby

The history of the Sime Darby conglomerate began in 1910 when Scottish adventurer William Middleton Sime and English banker Henry Darby teamed up to form a company to manage 500 acres of rubber estates in Malacca. Malacca was chosen as their first base 'because it was accessible by sea, a prime consideration then as land transportation was by slow bullock carts'.[44] The company enjoyed immediate success by exploiting the opportunities made available by the rising global demand for rubber. It joined other major plantation agencies such as Harrisons & Crosfield, Boustead-Buttery, Guthries and REA-Cumberbatch to become the 'big five' which together 'controlled more than 60% of the total estate acreage in Malaya owned by Europeans'.[45]

Sime Darby's propitious start can also be attributed to the unique relationship between its founders and the Chinese tycoons of Malacca like Sir Tan Cheng Lock and Lee Chim Tuan.[46] While Sime Darby was not the only European-controlled company which conducted win-win commercial relationships with Chinese compradors and entrepreneurs, its appointment of non-Europeans onto its board — albeit in non-executive capacities — was unconventional. The few European-controlled companies which invited prominent Chinese businessmen onboard generally installed them as figureheads. These figureheads were there to bolster the positions of their European friends and associates who had appointed them in the first instance. The exact role played by Tan Cheng Lock and Lee Chim Tuan in Sime Darby is uncertain, but many decades later, Tan Cheng Lock's only son, Tun Tan Siew Sin, would become the Chairman of the Sime Darby Group (1976–1987), wielding much power.

The expansion path of Sime Darby typified those trodden by other European investment groups in Malaya. From rubber estates, the company moved rapidly into general trading, engineering, manufacturing, insurance, shipping operations, property development, motor franchises, travel, leasing and computer equipment and software. Ironically, as the Group extended its branches throughout Southeast Asia and more than a dozen other countries, it became increasingly Malaysianised. This was because, in the 1970s, the Malaysian Government bought a large number of Sime Darby shares, through its trading corporation in London and 'eventually emerged its most powerful shareholder.'[47] The bulk of the remaining shares were held by Asian investors, including the OCBC, effectively making Sime Darby a predominantly Asian conglomerate.

For a conglomerate the size of Sime Darby, the application of a system of checks and balances to safeguard the integrity of its operations is no simple task. Indeed, it was found in 1973 that the Group's chairman and managing director had himself misapplied funds. D. W. Pinder was dismissed, along with Pinder's predecessor, A. W. Scott. Amidst the scandal, the company auditor, Walter Bowman Bellam was found dead in his bathtub with stab wounds in the abdomen.

It was under these unfortunate circumstances that Tan Chin Tuan was invited to assume the chairmanship of the troubled Sime Darby. For the OCBC banker, the already thankless task was further exacerbated by demands from Malay nationalists for a Malay Chairman for Sime Darby. But the intrepid banker was not one to bow readily to such demands because he saw it as his 'duty' to steer the Group out of troubled waters. In a letter to the then-Prime Minister, Tun Abdul Razak, Tan Chin Tuan outlined his strategic thinking for Sime Darby and explained that he would be acting in the interest of shareholders in both Malaysia and Singapore to ensure that Sime Darby did not 'fall into the control of foreigners' or even 'unscrupulous hands'.[48] The reply from Tun Razak made clear the Prime Minister's approval of Tan Chin Tuan's candidacy.

As Chairman of Sime Darby, Tan Chin Tuan's first task was to clean up Sime Darby's own backyard. He made himself a non-executive chairman and appointed a chief executive to manage the huge conglomerate. The post went to J. E. Bywater, previously with the Ford company and according to Tan Chin Tuan, 'a very experienced and capable corporate organizer'.[49] Next, the board of directors was reconstituted to attain an equal number of executive and non-executive directors. As a number of British expatriates arrived to take up posts as executive directors, the chairman appointed Yong Pung How, Chan Chin Cheung and Tan Siew Sin as non-executive directors to provide the balance. He also co-opted bumiputras such as Tan Sri Taib bin Haji Andak to the Board to further offset the British elements. To ensure a credible new start for the Group, Tan Chin Tuan and Bywater jointly recruited a new top management team to replace some 30 executives who had left as a result of the restructuring.

A significant systemic reform which Tan Chin Tuan entrenched in Sime Darby during his two-year chairmanship was the concept of separation of powers. To forestall a repetition of the Pinder scandal, the OCBC banker emphasised the need to separate the powers of the chief executive and the chairman. Consequently, following his departure, chief executive Bywater only acted as Chairman for a year until a successor was found. The appointment of Tan Siew Sin as non-executive chairman in November 1976 and James Reid Scott as the new chief executive restored the Sime Darby Group to its stable balance.

Lessons from Colonial Capitalism

Long before Tan Chin Tuan skilfully steered the OCBC into a concerted acquisition of substantial stakes in European-controlled companies, the overarching economic structure in Malaya and Singapore was dominated by a few well-established agency houses. Those were the years of colonial capitalism. Nicholas J. White in *Business, Government and the End of Empire* described the pervasiveness of colonial capitalism:

> ...colonial capitalism in Malaya was highly incestuous. By the Second World War an almost impenetrable mass of cross-holdings not only linked the rubber and tin companies, but also bound together several of the agency houses. Through strategic interlocking directorships and shareholdings, companies with vast estate and mining assets could be controlled with minimal capital. Thus no more than two dozen directors in London, often agency house executives, sat on the boards of nearly two hundred rubber companies which owned close to a million acres of rubber in Malaya.... In turn, the British houses were linked to the British banks, and the investment groups continued to handle huge volumes of import-export, shipping and insurance busi-

ness. What appears, on the surface, as a cluster of competing 'free-standing' firms was, in reality, a closely knit and highly concentrated system of operating units managed by a few powerful organisations and individuals.[50]

That so few could control so much and wield such immense influence was due to the fact that the elite monopolised the resources, expert knowledge and business acumen. By acquiring stakes in so many companies, the colonial elite generated much visibility for themselves and created an aura of power from their numerous cross-holdings. Tan Chin Tuan observed the manoeuvrings of the 'gentlemanly capitalist' elite with keen interest. After World War Two, when opportunities presented themselves, the astute banker did not hesitate to seize them and applied the lessons he had learnt from the colonialists themselves.

Opportunities in Malaya and Singapore arose as a result of significant changes which reshaped the political and economic structures of both colonies in the late 1940s and 1950s. White noted the emerging importance of Chinese capital, much of which were accumulated during the Korean War boom when many Chinese rubber estate owners earned large profits from the export of rubber. Instead of investing most of their profits in property whose returns were declining, the Chinese tycoons, including the likes of Lee Kong Chian and Tan Chin Tuan, turned their attention to the potential provided by well-managed European-controlled firms. Where previously the prospect of gaining a foothold in exclusively European-controlled and European-run companies was bleak, the post-war period opened up new possibilities for the locals who had the resources and the foresight.

How did the opportunities arise? White explained the developments in the 1950s which led the faint-hearted among the British to withdraw from the Malay Archipelago:

> ...following the problems of reconstruction, low rubber prices, increasing wage costs, and political anxieties, the colossal profits of 1950–2 provided a good opportunity for Britons to withdraw their investments. This tendency was reinforced in the later 1950s when declining demand for Malaya's principal exports directed British investors to other more renumerative fields.... Chinese interests bought up shares or even whole estates (and mines) from established British companies, manoeuvres far cheaper than floating fresh enterprises.[51]

Among the Chinese who recognised the excellent value of the erstwhile British-controlled firms were Tan Chin Tuan and Lee Kong Chian. In the immediate post-war period, Tan Chin Tuan, with the approval of his chairman, launched into a buying spree with the OCBC's considerable resources. The fact that the OCBC survived the Second World War with its resources practically intact certainly placed the bank in an advantageous position. In the 1950s, no local bank had ventured so extensively beyond familiar or related businesses. In that context, the OCBC's considerable acquisitions in companies and industries with little or no link to banking was both innovative and revolutionary. As White observed:

> ...by the mid-1950s OCBC was on par with the European banks, holding two-thirds of the total deposits of the Chinese banks in Malaya.... Additionally, OCBC had become a key player on the Singapore stock market, and was a substantial stakeholder in locally registered British firms.[52]

The OCBC was thus among the pioneers who initiated the process of localisation in many European-controlled companies by investing a substantial portion of its capital within Malaya and Singapore. That the OCBC's confidence in the Malay Archipelago was also upheld by other local businessmen, particularly those in the rubber and tin industries, was reflected in the relevant statistics:

> In 1948, 55% of capital invested in locally registered rubber companies came from outside Malaya and Singapore, 76% being held by Europeans. By 1958, 69% of local rubber company capital was invested from within Malaya and Singapore, 75% being owned by Chinese entrepreneurs and local institutions. In 1954, 78% of shares in locally incorporated tin dredging companies were held outside Malaya compared with just 36% 10 years later.[53]

For most Chinese enterprises which bought stakes in various European-controlled companies, their investments often took the form of 'sleeping partnerships' allowing the Europeans to continue to exercise executive control. What distinguished the OCBC from the rest was the active role the bank sought in the companies in which it had acquired substantial stakes. The Europeans had shown the way in an earlier period. Tan Chin Tuan saw the extent of power wielded by a few individuals and organisations 'through strategic interlocking directorships and shareholdings'. The power could only be exercised with a presence on the board of directors. That was why Tan, notwithstanding his multiple portfolios, was always ready to maintain a presence on so many boards on behalf of the OCBC. His pervasive visibility as director or chairman of a diverse group of blue-chip companies gave him greater power which, in turn, strengthened the bank he represented.

Synergies from Interlocking Directorships and Share-holdings

Like a patriarch who casts a benign yet watchful eye over his extended family, Tan Chin Tuan devoted much attention to the well-diversified business empire which he helped the OCBC build over several decades. In particular, he took deep pride in his acquisition strategy which focused on synergies and continuity, as opposed to popular latter day corporate raider practices of takeovers and disintegration. He took pains to explain his philosophy:

> I believe in mergers, not takeovers. The big difference is that in the former, you are prepared to work together and create goodwill, whereas in the latter you take over by force and create resentment. For instance, Fraser and Neave had a merger with a glass factory in Johor Bahru so that we could manufacture the glass bottles for our beer and aerated waters and we could also send the bottles from Johor to Singapore.[54]

Tan Chin Tuan clearly practised what he preached. In the companies he had carefully selected to form part of the OCBC's vast investment portfolio, he played the role of an institutional builder, improving and even diversifying their businesses. The emphasis was always on how the companies in dissimilar industries could work together and complement one another to achieve synergies that would strengthen the entire group. In this respect, the OCBC managing director was quick to adapt the strategies of the agency houses in the colonial era.

What Tan Chin Tuan borrowed from the European capitalist elite was the system of interlocking directorships in which he personally exercised extensive control and power by virtue of his position on the boards of the public companies closely associated with the OCBC. He ensured that each company actively supported the business of others in the group and in turn, the entire group benefitted from the network of mutual co-operation and collaboration:

> When I got control of these companies, I insisted they bring their business to OCBC. F&N had to buy foreign exchange to pay for raw materials. Give OCBC the business but only if OCBC's quote is better or equal to other banks. If our quote is high, F&N is free to go elsewhere. I told OCBC to quote as good if not better than other banks. That kept the OCBC competitive. Therefore both sides were told to do their best for their companies.... The same with insurance, Great Eastern Life and OAC would try to get owners of insured properties to borrow from OCBC and when people came to OCBC to obtain mortgage, the bank would recommend these clients to Great Eastern Life or OAC for insurance. It's a two-way street.[55]

Tan Chin Tuan was acutely aware of the dangers of conducting transactions within an extended family; familiarity had a tendency to breed inefficiency, even corruption. He therefore deemed it imperative for the flow of business between the OCBC group and the companies controlled by the group to be conducted in a fair and transparent manner without fear or favour. Above all, he instituted a culture of meritocracy and professionalism to keep the companies competitive. These were the foundations Tan Chin Tuan laid in all the companies in which he was a major player. Without exception, the paid-up capital and shareholders' funds, in every one of the public companies he steered increased many-fold during his tenure as director and chairman of the boards.

How was Tan Chin Tuan able to achieve such an unbroken record of success? Like legendary entrepreneurs such as

Tan Kah Kee and Lee Kong Chian, the feisty banker was also reputed to possess uncanny business instincts balanced with a sharp far-sightedness. A firm believer in attracting, cultivating and retaining talents, he was always ready to 'bring in people with the expertise' and amply reward deserving individuals. Furthermore, the fact that Tan Chin Tuan was a public figure of considerable influence was undoubtedly an invaluable asset to the blue chip companies associated with him. Whether directly or indirectly, his far-reaching network of excellent connections and his prominent stature in the eyes of the government and the community must have added value to the companies he guided. But the indefatigable banker, who had survived and triumphed over many challenges, preferred to attribute his achievements to luck:

> Luck is a big factor. It creates opportunities, finds you friends, finds new people who will help and support you. We Chinese have a saying 'kui jin' which means 'saviour' — when you are fortunate, at the right moment, someone will come to your rescue. I am a great believer in that. It has happened to me in my life many times.[56]

Luck had certainly smiled favourably on Tan Chin Tuan and rubbed onto the many companies he had managed. It probably pleased him to note that they have all continued to thrive, even after his retirement.

NOTES

1   Personal correspondences, Tan Chin Tuan, 1972.
2   *The Straits Times*, 1972.
3   P. Fallon, 'The Tide in the Life of Tan Chin Tuan', *Euromoney*, October 1982, p. 143.
4   Ibid.

5   Ibid.

6   Ibid.

7   Melanie Chew, *Leaders of Singapore* (Singapore: Resource Press, 1996), p. 218.

8   Fallon, 'The Tide in the Life of Tan Chin Tuan', *Euromoney*, October 1982, p. 147.

9   Yong Pung How became one of the youngest directors of the OCBC in 1972. Educated at Victoria Institution, Kuala Lumpur, and then at Cambridge University where he obtained a law degree, he became Chairman of the Malayan Airways (later to become the Malaysia-Singapore Airlines or MSA) in 1964. From 1964 to 1969, he steered MSA through some of its most difficult years. He also became director in a number of other companies, like Guinness Malaysia, the Chemical Company of Malaysia, Harrisons and Crosfield (Malaysia), Malaysian Industrial Development Finance and the Southeast Asia Development Corporation. In 1970, he gave up his legal practice and became, in 1971, Chairman and Managing Director of the OCBC's Singapore International Merchant Bankers (SIMBL). Yong subsequently became Chief Executive of the Government of Singapore Investment Corporation (GIC), and then Managing Director of the Monetary Authority of Singapore (MAS). In 1989, after spending 18 years in the business sector, Yong was appointed Judge of the Supreme Court of Singapore, and in 1990, became independent Singapore's second Chief Justice, a post he continues to hold today.

10 'Tan Chin Tuan-OCBC-50', *Berita OCBC*, vol. 6, no. 2a (March 1975).

11 N. J. White, *Business, Government and the End of Empire — Malaya, 1942–1957* (Kuala Lumpur: Oxford University Press, 1996), p. 52.

12 Ibid., pp. 52–53.

13 Ibid., p. 52.

14 Ibid.

15 Fallon, 'The Tide in the Life of Tan Chin Tuan', *Euromoney*, October 1982, p. 147.

16 Overseas Assurance Corporation, *Fifty-One Years of Progress: The Overseas Assurance Corporation Limited.* (Singapore, 1971).

17 Ibid.

18 Overseas Assurance Corporation Limited, *The 51st Year Souvenir: 51 Years of Progress* (Singapore: OAC, 1972)

19 Overseas Assurance Corporation Limited, Annual Reports, 1969 & 1981.

20 Fraser and Neave, *Fraser and Neave: 1883-1983: The Great Years* (Singapore: Ho Printing, 1983), p. 8.

21 Ibid., p. 9.

22   Ibid., p. 13.

23   Interview, Tan Chin Tuan, 8 March 1999.

23a Fraser and Neave Limited, *Annual Report 1999*, p. 117.

24   Fraser and Neave, *Fraser and Neave*, p. 19.

25   Interview, Tan Chin Tuan, 8 March 1999.

26   Fraser and Neave, *Fraser and Neave*, p. 16.

27   Interview, Tan Chin Tuan, 8 March 1999.

28   Fraser and Neave Limited, *Annual Report 1983*, p. 14.

29   Fraser and Neave, *Fraser and Neave*, p. 3.

30   Interview, Tan Foundation Files.

31   Robinson and Company Limited, *The Story of Robinson* (Singapore: S.N.,1958).

32   Ibid.

33   Ibid.

33a Robinson and Company Limited, *Annual Report 1998*, p. 38.

34   Robinson and Company Limited, *Annual Report 1976.*

35   Ibid., p. 4.

36   Straits Trading, *The Straits Trading Company Limited: 100 Years of Growth 1887–1987* (Straits Trading Singapore, 1987), p. 5.

37   Ibid., p. 16.

37a Interview with Tan Chin Tuan, 8 March 1999.

38   *Singapore National Accounts, 1960–1973* (Singapore, Department of Statistics, 1975); EMF Foundation, *World Competitiveness Report 1995* (Geneva, Switzerland: The Foundation, 1995), p. 366.

39   EMF Foundation, *World Competitiveness Report 1995* (Geneva, Switzerland: The Foundation, 1995), p. 366.

40   See Great Eastern Life website.

41   The Great Eastern Life Assurance Company Limited 1997 company figures.

41a The Great Eastern Life Assurance Company Limited, *Annual Report 1999*, p. 42.

42   Wearne Brothers Limited, *Annual Report 1996* (Singapore: Wearne Brothers Corporation Limited, 1997), p. 97.

43   Wearne Brothers Limited 1997 group figures.

44   Sime Darby, *Sime Darby 75th Anniversary* (Kuala Lumpur: Sime Darby Communication Department, 1985), p. 4.

45   J. J. Puthucheary, *Ownership and Control in the Malayan Economy* (Singapore: Eastern Universities Press Ltd, 1960), p. 28.

46   Sime Darby, *Sime Darby*, p. 6.

47   Ibid., p. 12.

48   Personal correspondences, Tan Chin Tuan, 1973.

49   Interview, Tan Foundation Files.

50   Ibid.

Indian Chettiar moneylender, plying his trade along the five-foot way (pavement) at the turn of the century (c. 1900). *Source: National Archives Singapore (NAS)*

The long-established Heng Fatt Yong Kee Pawnshop at South Bridge Road (c. 1950). *Source: NAS*

The Four Seas Communications Bank, founded in 1906, is the oldest surviving Chinese bank in Singapore. It was subsequently absorbed as a wholly-owned subsidiary of the OCBC in 1973. This picture shows its Board of Directors in 1927. *Source: NAS*

The Mercantile Bank, originally known as the Chartered Mercantile Bank of India, opened branches in 1856. This building, which was located at Raffles Place, was completed in 1930. It was later demolished to facilitate the construction of the Raffles Place MRT Station. *Source: NAS*

The Chartered Bank, originally, the Chartered Bank of India, Australia and China was incorporated by Royal Charter in 1853. It opened its first branch in Singapore in 1855 with Walter Ormiston as Manager. The bank moved to Battery Road in 1905. This building was later demolished to be replaced by the Standard Chartered Building. *Source: NAS*

The Hongkong & Shanghai Bank, c.1910. This building, which housed the bank, was built in 1892, and became a prominent landmark. It was, however, demolished in 1919 to make way for a larger and more modern structure. *Source: NAS*

Chee Swee Cheng, first
Chairman of the OCBC.
He served as Chairman
from 1932 to 1937.
*Source: Tan Chin Tuan
collection (TCT)*

Tan Ean Kiam became Joint
Managing Director (with Yap Twee)
of OCBC at its inception, sole
Managing Director from 1933 to
1942, and then Joint Managing
Director (with Tan Chin Tuan) till
his death in 1943. *Source: Mr Tan
Tock San*

Yap Twee, Joint Managing Director
(with Tan Ean Kiam) at the OCBC's
inception. He later served as
Vice-Chairman of OCBC under
Tan Chin Tuan from 1966 to 1973.
Source: Mr Peter Yap

Lee Kong Chian, Singapore's most famous rubber magnate, was OCBC's Vice-Chairman from 1932 to 1938, and Chairman from 1938 to 1964. *Source: Mr Lee Seng Wee*

An Agreement

An Agreement made this *14th* day of *December* 1932 Between **The Chinese Commercial Bank Limited** incorporated in Singapore and having its registered office at China Building, Chulia Street, Singapore of the first part, **The Ho Hong Bank Limited** incorporated in Singapore and having its registered office at Meyer Chambers, Raffles Place, Singapore of the second part, **The Oversea-Chinese Bank Limited** incorporated in Singapore and having its registered office at China Building, Chulia Street, Singapore of the third part and **Oversea-Chinese Banking Corporation Limited** incorporated in Singapore and having its registered office at China Building, Chulia Street, Singapore (hereinafter called "the New Company") of the fourth part.

WHEREAS The Chinese Commercial Bank Limited was incorporated in Singapore in the year 1912 under the Companies Ordinance 1889 with a nominal capital of $4,000,000 divided into 40,000 shares of $100 each, of which 20,000 shares have been issued and the sum of $50 per share stands credited in the books of the Company as having been paid up thereon.

AND WHEREAS The Ho Hong Bank Limited was incorporated in Singapore in the year 1917 under the Companies Ordinance 1915 with a nominal capital of $20,000,000 divided into 200,000 shares of $100 each, of which 80,000 shares have been issued and the sum of $50 per share stands credited in the books of the Company as having been paid up thereon.

AND WHEREAS The Oversea-Chinese Bank Limited was incorporated in Singapore in the year 1919 under the Companies Ordinance 1915 with a nominal capital of $2,000,000 divided into 200,000 shares of $100 each, of which 105,000 shares have been issued and the sum of $50 per share stands credited in the books of the Company as having been paid up thereon.

AND WHEREAS at an Extraordinary General Meeting of The Chinese Commercial Bank Limited held on the 14th day of September 1932 it was resolved (1.) That it was expedient to effect an amalgamation of The Chinese Commercial Bank Limited, The Ho Hong Bank Limited and The Oversea-Chinese Bank Limited on the terms indicated in the Scheme of Amalgamation submitted to the meeting and (2.) That, provided that resolutions similar to the resolutions now being recited were on or before the 1st day of October 1932 passed by the shareholders of the other two Companies concerned, the Directors be and were thereby authorised to carry out such amalgamation with or without modification, and for that purpose, after the incorporation of the New Company to be formed in accordance with the said Scheme of Amalgamation, to enter into an agreement substantially in the terms of the draft agreement submitted to the Meeting and expressed to be made between The Chinese Commercial Bank Limited of the first part, The Ho Hong Bank Limited of the second part, The Oversea-Chinese Bank Limited of the third part, and the new Company to be incorporated as aforesaid of the fourth part.

AND WHEREAS at an Extraordinary General Meeting of The Ho Hong Bank Limited held on the 12th day of September 1932 similar resolutions were passed and at an Extraordinary General Meeting of The Oversea-Chinese Bank Limited held on the 13th day of September 1932 similar resolutions were also passed.

AND WHEREAS the New Company being the New Company referred to in the above recited resolution has been duly incorporated under Ordinance No. 155 (Companies) with a nominal capital of $40,000,000 divided into 1,000,000 shares of $40 each and for the following amongst other objects namely to acquire, take over, amalgamate and carry on as going concerns the undertakings of The Chinese Commercial Bank Limited, The Ho Hong Bank Limited and the Oversea-Chinese Bank Limited (hereinafter called "The Vendor Companies"), and with a view thereto to enter into the agreement referred to in Clause 3 of the Company's Articles of Association and to carry the same into effect with or without modification.

AND WHEREAS these presents are a copy of the agreement referred to in the above recited resolutions of the Vendor Companies.

AND WHEREAS by Clause 3 of the Articles of Association of the New Company it is provided that the New Company shall forthwith enter into an agreement therein referred to, being these presents.

NOW IT IS HEREBY AGREED between the Vendor Companies each with the others and other of them and by the Vendor Companies and each of them with the New Company and by the New Company with the Vendor Companies and each of them as follows:—

1. Each of the Vendor Companies shall sell and transfer to the New Company and the New Company shall purchase and take over all and singular the lands, buildings, goods, chattels, moneys, credits, debts, bills, notes, things in action of such Vendor Company and the undertaking, business (including accrued and accruing profits) and goodwill thereof with the full benefit of all contracts and agreements and of all securities in

Merger Agreement signed between the Chinese Commercial Bank, the Oversea-Chinese Bank and the Ho Hong Bank in September 1932.
Source: SAAR

Wee Theam Seng, General Manager of the Chinese Commercial Bank, at the time of the merger.
Source: Ms Yeo Kheng Sian

Seow Poh Leng, General Manager of the Ho Hong Bank, at the time of the merger.
Source: Ms Lim Sing Yuen

Ong Pia Teng, General Manager of the Oversea-Chinese Bank, at the time of the merger.
Source: SAAR

Kwa Siew Tee, General Manager of the OCBC from 1935 to 1946.
Source: Dr Kwa Soon Bee

The China Building at Chulia Street, c. 1969. This building was designed by P. H. Keys and F. Dowdeswell of the firm of Keys and Dowdeswell and was considered a major architectural accomplishment during that era. It was originally shared by the Chinese Commercial Bank and the Oversea Chinese Bank, but thereafter became the headquarters of the OCBC when the three banks merged in 1932. It was demolished in 1970 to make way for the OCBC Centre. *Source: TCT*

Oversea-Chinese Banking Corporation Limited.

(Established in 1932)

Successors to

**THE CHINESE COMMERCIAL BANK LTD., THE HO HONG BANK LTD.,
and THE OVERSEA-CHINESE BANK LTD.**

HEAD OFFICE:

China Building, Chulia Street, Singapore.
Local Branch: 458, North Bridge Road, Singapore.

CAPITAL:

AUTHORISED	...	...	...	$40,000,000.00
PAID UP	...	...	...	$10,000,000.00

BOARD OF DIRECTORS:

CHEE SWEE CHENG, Esq., *Chairman.*
LEE KONG CHIAN, Esq., *Vice-Chairman.*

Tan Ean Kiam, Esq.	S. Q. Wong, Esq.
Lee Choon Seng, Esq.	Gan Say Hong, Esq.
Aw Boon Par, Esq.	Lim Keng Lian, Esq.
Lee Choon Poh, Esq.	Chan Kang Swi, Esq.
Dr. H. T. Wee.	Hon. Mr. Tan Cheng Lock, C.B.E.
Lim Liat Boon, Esq.	Tan Swee Hoe, Esq.
Oh Sian Guan, Esq.	Tan Sew Aik. Esq.
Parkcane C. Hwang, Esq.	Yeap Chor Ee, Esq.

Tan Ean Kiam, Esq	Lim Bock Kee, Esq.
Managing Director.	*Manager in Charge of Branches.*
Ong Pia Teng, Esq.	Kwa Siew Tee, Esq.
Manager (Head Office).	*Exchange Manager.*
Chew Hock Leong, Esq.	Lim Kho Leng, Esq.
General Inspector.	*Inspector.*

BRANCHES:

Hongkong, Shanghai, Amoy, Penang, Malacca, Kuala Lumpur, Seremban, Ipoh, Batu Pahat, Muar, Kota Bahru, Rangoon, Batavia, Palembang and Djambi.

CORRESPONDENTS:

Aberdeen, Alexandria, Amsterdam, Bandjermasin, Bangkok, Basle, Berlin, Bombay, Cairo, Calcutta, Canton, Cheribon, Edinburgh, Foochow, Glasgow, Hamburg, Hangchow, Hankow, Harbin, Jesselton, Kuching, Lisbon, London, Lyons, Madrid, Manila, Marseilles, Medan, Menado, Milan, Nanking, New York, Padang, Pekalongan, Paris, Peiping, Pontianak, Port Said, Samarinda, San Francisco, Semarang, Sibu, Sourabaya, Swatow, Tientsin, Tsinan, Tsingtao and Vienna

---

REPORT OF THE DIRECTORS OF

Oversea-Chinese Banking Corporation Limited

For the Year Ended 31st December, 1933.

To be submitted to the Shareholders at the Ordinary General Meeting to be held at China Building, Chulia Street, Singapore, on Friday, 25th day of May, 1934, at 12 o'clock noon.

The Directors have pleasure in submitting to the Shareholders the Balance Sheet and Statement of Profit & Loss Account for the year ended 31st December, 1933.

The Net Profits for the year after deducting all current expenses amounted to $608,979-46.

The Directors recommend that this amount be dealt with in the following manner :-

To Provision for Doubtful Debts.	$500,000-00
To Directors' Fees.	12,000-00
To Staff Pension & Provident Fund.	12,000-00
Balance to be carried forward.	84,979-46
	$608,979-46

The Directors wish to point out that they have made the above recommendation for the appropriation of $500,000/- for Doubtful Debts Reserve in pursuance of the sound policy of building up as early as possible an ample Reserve adequate to meet even remote contingencies.

During the year, Messrs. Chua Kah Cheong and Yap Twee resigned from the Board, and Messrs. Tan Sew Aik and Yeap Chor Ee were elected to fill the vacancies.

The retiring Directors are Messrs. Tan Sew Aik, Yeap Chor Ee, Lim Liat Boon, Chee Swee Cheng, S. Q. Wong and Dr. H. T. Wee, but being eligible, they offer themselves for re-election.

The Auditors, Messrs. Evatt & Co., also retire and offer themselves for re-appointment.

By Order of the Board,
CHEE SWEE CHENG,
Chairman.

China Building, Chulia Street,
Singapore, 15th May 1934.

The first annual report of the OCBC, 1933. At its inauguration, the OCBC was the largest and strongest local bank in the Straits Settlements with capital and reserves exceeding $12 million, and deposits totalling $22 million. *Source: TCT*

Name plate of the OCBC at the China Building, c. 1969. *Source: TCT*

Malcolm MacDonald flanked by two OCBC bankers who served on various Post-War government councils, among them the Governor's Advisory Council. *Left to Right:* Tan Chin Tuan (Managing Director, OCBC), Malcolm MacDonald (Commissioner-General, Southeast Asia), and Lee Kong Chian (Chairman, OCBC). This photograph is a personally inscribed copy from MacDonald to Tan. *Source: TCT*

Officials of the first post-War Legislative Council of Singapore 1948–51.

Front Row L–R: Mrs Vilasini Menon; John Laycock; T. P. F. McNeice; E. J. Davies, W. L. Blythe; Sir Franklin Gimson, Tan Chin Tuan, W. C. Taylor, R. Jumabhoy, C. C. Tan & Elizabeth Choy.
Back Row L–R: H. J. C. Kulasingha, C. R. Dasaratha Raj, A. Gilmour, Lim Yew Hock, J. A. Harvey, N. A. Mallal, Dr W. J. Vickers, L. W. Donough, L. Rayman, Thio Chan Bee, C. H. Butterfield, A. McLellan, Dr C. J. P. Paglar, Ahmad bin Mohamed Ibrahim & E. M. F. Fergusson.
Source: TCT

Tan Chin Tuan taking his oath of office as Deputy President of the Singapore Legislative Council, 23 April 1951. *L–R:* William Blythe (Colonial Secretary), Tan Chin Tuan (Deputy President, Legislative Council) and Sir Franklin Gimson (Governor). *Source: TCT*

Tan Chin Tuan, Deputy President of the Singapore Legislative Council, chairing a session of the Council's proceedings, 1951. *Source: TCT*

Official opening of the OCBC's Raffles Place Branch, 1955. *L–R:* Tan Hong Ghim (Manager, OCBC Raffles Place Branch), Chew Hock Leong (General Manager, OCBC) and Tan Chin Tuan (Managing Director, OCBC). *Source: TCT*

Official opening of the Hong Kong Branch of the OCBC, 1960. *L–R:* K. C. Chen (Manager, OCBC Hong Kong Branch), Tan Chin Tuan (Managing Director, OCBC), Lee Kong Chian (Chairman, OCBC) and Chew Chin Bee (Sub-Manager, OCBC Hong Kong Branch). *Source: TCT*

Tan Chin Tuan, Managing Director of OCBC, 1942 to 1972 & Chairman, 1966 to 1983. *Source: TCT*

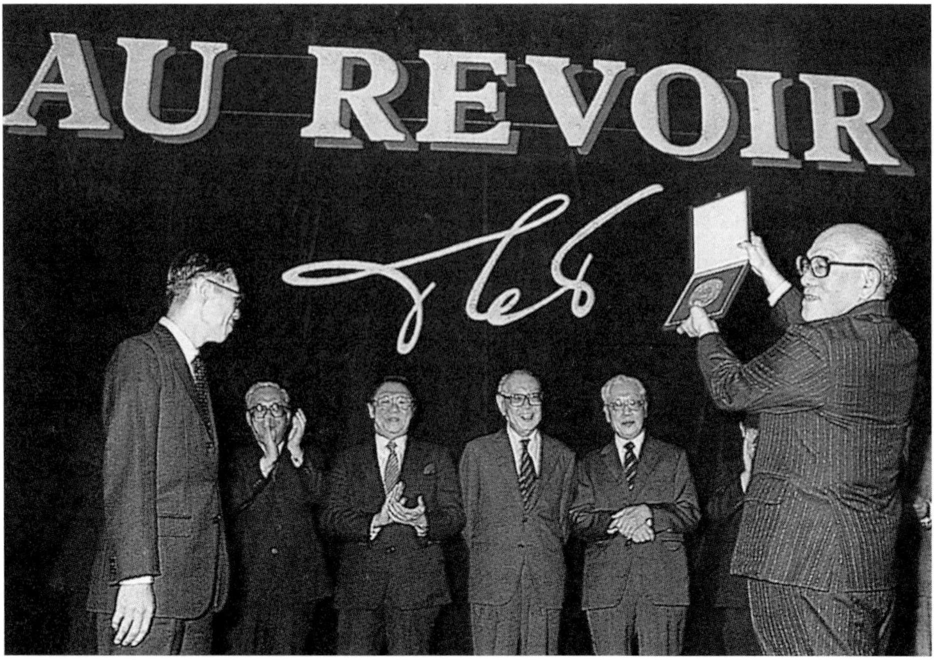

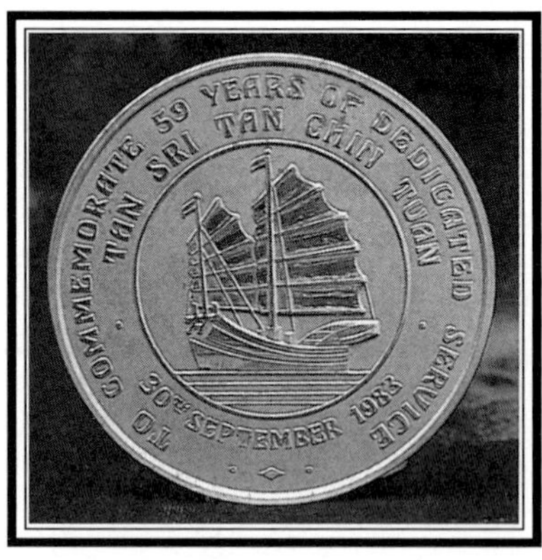

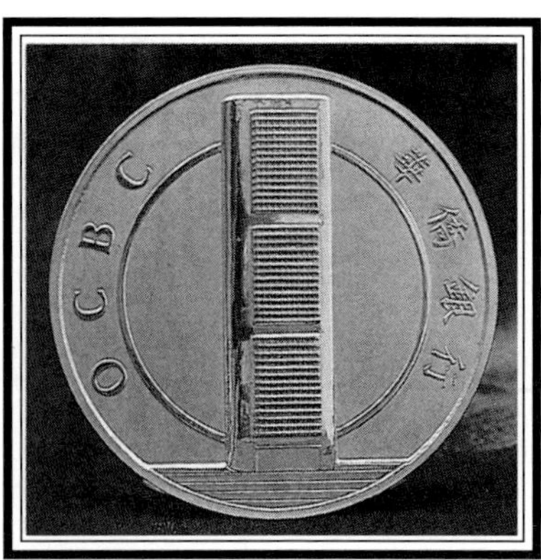

Tan Chin Tuan holding up the gold medallion presented to him on his retirement from OCBC. *Source: TCT*

A Gift of Gold...

Close-up of the gold medallion presented to Tan Chin Tuan by the Board of Directors of OCBC on the occasion of his retirement on 30 September 1983. The 22-carat gold medallion, which measures 11.5 cm in diameter, is cast in 1,000 grammes of fine gold. *Source: TCT*

Yong Pung How, Chairman of OCBC, 1983 to 1988. *Source: TCT*

Teo Cheng Guan, Chairman of OCBC, 1989 to 1991. *Source: Mr Teo Cheng Guan*

OCBC Board of Directors, 1987

L–R: Teo Cheng Guan, Tan Puay Yong, Tan Hoon Siang, Yong Pung How (Chairman and Chief Executive Officer), Lee Seng Wee, Tan Tock San, Peter Yap Ee Kaw and Lee Hiok Siang. *Source: TCT*

Dr Tony Tan, Chairman of OCBC, 1991 to 1995. *Source: Dr Tony Tan*

Lee Seng Wee, Chairman and Chief Executive Officer of OCBC since 1995. *Source: TCT*

OCBC Board of Directors, 1993
Front Row L–R: Lee Seng Wee, Tony Tan Keng Yam (Chairman), Teo Cheng Guan
Back Row L–R: Tan Puay Yong, Peter Yap Ee Kaw, Choi Siew Hong, Michael Wong Pakshong, Tan Tock San & Tang I-Fang. *Source: TCT*

Chairman Tan Chin Tuan speaking at the 80th Anniversary of Great
Eastern Life, 26 August 1988. *Source: Mr Allen Pathmarajah*

The Great Eastern Life Board of Directors at the 80th Anniversary Dinner.
L–R: C. C. Tan, Shaw Vee Meng, Allen Pathmarajah, Michael Wong Pakshong,
Lee Seng Wee & Tan Chin Tuan (Chairman). Absent: Dato Dr Yahya Ismail.
Source: Mr Allen Pathmarajah

A view of Raffles Hotel from Beach Road, c. 1950. *Source: NAS*

The world-famous Palm Court of Raffles Hotel, c. 1920. *Source: NAS*

Sculpture of the Fraser & Neave crest by famous Italian sculptor Rudolfo Nolli. *Source: NAS*

Early advertisement for Fraser & Neave. *Source: NAS*

Workers of Fraser & Neave working overtime for the National Defence Fund, 1968. *Source: NAS*

An early exterior view of John Little Co. at Raffles Place, c. 1920.
Source: NAS

The main stairway of John Little Co., 1906. *Source: NAS*

An exterior view of Robinsons Department Store at Raffles Place, 1956.
Source: TCT

The men's-wear department of Robinsons Department Store in 1960.
Source: TCT

The Straits Trading Company's tin smelting headquarters at Pulau Brani, c. 1900. *Source: NAS*

Chairman Tan Chin Tuan cutting the birthday cake at the Straits Trading Company's centenary celebrations on 7 November 1987. Straits Trading Board of Directors L–R (in suits): Michael Wong Pakshong, I. F. Tang, Lee Kok Chee, Tan Chin Tuan (Chairman), C. C. Tan, and General Tan Sri Ibrahim bin Ismail. Not in picture: C. W. Tresise. *Source: TCT*

Tin smelting in progress at the Straits Trading smelting plant. *Source: Straits Trading Co.*

Straits Trading tin ingots ready for shipment. *Source: Straits Trading Co.*

At the height of its influence, the Straits Trading Company was smelting one-third of all the the world's tin. *Source: Straits Trading Co.*

Chairman Tan
Chin Tuan (in dark
suit) inspecting the
new canning line
of Malayan
Breweries Ltd, 14
August 1965.
Source: TCT

Chairman Tan Chin Tuan's visit to Lion Breweries, New Zealand, 1984.
L–R: Robert B. Young (Director, Malayan Breweries Limited), Robert
Muldoon (Prime Minister, New Zealand), Tan Chin Tuan (Chairman,
Malayan Breweries Limited) and Ralph Thompson (Chairman, Lion
Breweries). *Source: TCT*

Wearne Brothers Limited was founded in 1906 by two Australian brothers C. F. F. Wearne and T. J. B. Wearne. *Source: Wearne Brothers Limited*

Dr Goh Keng Swee, Minister for Finance, touring the Associated Motor Industries (AMI) Limited assembly line. AMI was formed by the two leading motor industry groups: Wearne Brothers Limited and Motor Investments Berhad. Accompanying Dr Goh is B. H. F. Henry, Assembly Plant Manager. In the background (in glasses) is Tan Sri Tan Chin Tuan, who was to become Chairman of Wearne Brothers Limited in 1974. *Source: Wearne Brothers Limited*

The Singapore headquarters of United Engineers Limited at River Valley Road, c. 1930. The building was demolished in the early 1990s to make way for the United Engineers (UE) Square. *Source: NAS*

United Engineers workers fabricating stone chute at their factory on River Valley Road, c. 1938. United Engineers Ltd. *Source: United Engineers Ltd.*

Part of the banking hall of the OCBC at China Building occupied by the International Division of the bank, 1969. *Source: TCT*

Bills Division, OCBC at China Building, 1969. *Source: TCT*

Customer service section of the OCBC banking hall at China Building, 1969. *Source: TCT*

The OCBC office in Xiamen, China, 1986. *Source: TCT*

Chairman Tan Chin Tuan chatting with David Rockefeller, Chairman of the Chase Manhattan Bank during the latter's visit to Singapore in 1981. *Source: TCT*

The OCBC Board of Directors, 1969–70. *L–R:* Lin Jo Yan (General Manager), Raja Tun Uda bin Raja Muhammad, Tan Hoon Siang, Tan Lark Sye, Yap Twee (Vice-Chairman), Tan Sri Tan Chin Tuan (Chairman), Dato S. Q. Wong, Tan Sri Runme Shaw, Lee Seng Wee, Tan Tock San & Cheah Heng Sin (Secretary). *Source: TCT*

Celebrating the OCBC's 50th year in 1972. *L–R:* Tan Tock San (Director), Lee Seng Wee (Director), Tan Sri Tan Chin Tuan (Chairman and Managing Director) and Lee Hiok Siang (side to camera). *Source: Mr Tan Tock San*

Architect Ong Eng Hung (Project Architect, BEP Architects) explaining the structural design of the new OCBC Centre, 1974. Looking on are *L–R:* Tio Seng Chin (Property Department Manager, OCBC), H. C. H'ng (M & E Engineer, Preece Cardew & Rider Consultants), Tan Tock San (OCBC Director, 3rd from left), David Glanville-Williams (Management Consultant, PA Management), Goh Sin Tub (Executive Director, OCBC Centre Pte Ltd), Ong Eng Hung, Alex Foo (Assistant Project Architect, BEP Architects), Bill Seah (Quantity Surveyor, Langdon Every & Seah) and Joseph Huang (Structural Engineer, Ove Arup & Partners). *Source: Mr Tan Tock San*

Henry Moore's sculpture, 'Reclining Woman', situated outside the OCBC Centre. *Source: NAS*

The OCBC Centre, designed by world-renowned architect I. M. Pei. At the building's inauguration in 1976, it was the tallest building in Asia outside Japan, and boasted what was probably the world's largest banking hall. *Source: TCT*

51 Ibid., p. 51.
52 Ibid.
53 Ibid.
54 Interview, Tan Foundation Files.
55 Interview, Tan Foundation Files.
56 Interview, Tan Foundation Files.

EXPANSION THROUGH PRUDENT CONSERVATISM

Separation from Malaysia in 1965 brought relief to the communal tensions that threatened to tear Singapore and Malaysia asunder. Even so, many people within Singapore as well as foreign observers were skeptical that a small island without natural resources could remain economically viable. From the start the new Republic rose like a phoenix from the ashes. Separation from Malaysia and the subsequent announcement that the British military forces were hastening their withdrawal from Singapore created a heightened sense of urgency. Fuelled by the ruling People's Action Party's pragmatic ideology, it led to a wave of economic nationalism unprecedented in Singapore history.

The 1970s marked a new epoch in Singapore's economy. Economic development now depended less and less on staples and shifted increasingly towards the export of manufactured products. There was also a gradual shift towards higher value-added investments by foreign investors as more sophisticated technology was imported into Singapore. The

nation's open-door policy successfully established an industrial base, albeit one characterised by the dominating power
of foreign enterprises. In spite of the oil crisis of 1973 which
led to sluggish industrial production, widespread retrench-
ment and even closures of local and medium local firms, the
Singapore economy performed well throughout the 1970s,
registering an average growth rate of 8.7% for the period 1973
to 1979. This period also witnessed the transformation of
Singapore's banking and financial sector into one of Asia's
most competitive and open financial hubs.

The central idea running through this part of the book is
that the 1970s marked a decade of expansion for OCBC, both
domestically and internationally, and its achievements sym-
bolically encapsulated in the magnificent skyscraper: the
OCBC Centre. As we have seen, the Bank's premier position
in the 1970s was largely the result of decades of steady and
purposeful changes initiated by Tan Chin Tuan and his group
of trusted leaders. The Bank had successfully evolved from
a communally and locally-based commercial bank into a
multinational banking organisation with a regional and international network of branches and subsidiaries.

One important point must be noted. Although OCBC's
'family' includes a range of non-banking subsidiaries, its
primary strength lies in the role the Bank plays in Singapore's
financial and tertiary sector. The rationale is obvious. The
popular business culture that developed since Singapore's
colonial days was one which supported trading, financial
and brokerage services. Enhanced by a stable political climate
and an efficient civil-service, businessmen and entrepreneurs
honed their management and inter-personal skills creating
wide-ranging business connections or *guanxi*. These intangible assets are deeply rooted in the historical development
of Singapore as a trading and brokerage emporium in Southeast Asia. The OCBC continued to play this historic role

when working to expand and diversify the tertiary sector, and especially in helping Singapore fulfil its aspiration of becoming the region's financial centre. In response to the changing political and economic climate after 1965, the Bank, under Tan Chin Tuan's chairmanship, initiated structural and institutional changes to transform itself from a regional bank to an international financial giant.

Role of Banks in Latecomer Industrialization: The Case of Singapore

Historically, banks played a significant role in the rise of industrial capitalism in the West. Britain's economic transformation as the 'first industrial nation' during the 18th and early 19th centuries was made possible by the development of banking institutions which provided funds for industrial entrepreneurs and mercantilists. Economic historians have pointed to the burgeoning of banks during the 'take-off' period of 1780 to 1830.[1] At the heart of this financial revolution stood the Bank of England which emerged as the central institution in the management of state finance. For 'late-comers' to the industrialisation process, bank finance of commerce and industry was crucial. For example, before World One, Germany not only had an industrial economy of the first rank, but also a highly developed and efficient financial system. During the inter-war period, stronger banks in Berlin such as Deutsche Bank and Dresdner Bank, consolidated their positions through takeovers and mergers. These 'great banks' provided the essential capital for the rise of big industry.

In East Asia, banking institutions had a central role in the transformation of the 'tiger' economies of Japan, Taiwan, South Korea, Hong Kong and Singapore. The miraculous reconstruction and high growth of the Japanese economy after the Pacific War was made possible by the activities of banks headed by the Bank of Japan (BOJ). The BOJ supplied the strategic industries and the Yokohama Specie Bank with the so-called growth money abundantly, especially during two key periods — from 1888 to 1910 when Japan was experiencing its own industrial revolution, and 1941 to 1979 when the country launched itself into war, the post-war economic reconstruction and the high economic growth.[2]

As former colonies of Imperial Japan, both Taiwan and South Korea had in place a modern banking system and highly-developed commercial market network. By the 1970s both newly-industrialising economies had developed a dense, inter-connected system of banks, insurance companies and security houses. Under close supervision of government bureaucrats, commercial banks in Taiwan and South Korea played an active part in providing loan and venture capital to industrialists and budding entrepreneurs.[3] In South Korea, for example, the government owned the banking institutions, set their interest rates, and directed a substantial portion of their loans. Although this policy could inhibit the development of an efficient banking system, 'it was the government surveillance over the banking system and how it was used as an industrial policy instrument to effect corporate governance that contributed to rapid industrialisation and growth'.[4]

In the case of Singapore, the growth of banking prior to 1965 cannot be interpreted simply as a reaction to the needs of an industrialising economy. Before this period, Singapore was still an entrepot centre and its banking mechanism was only marginally attuned to the needs of a manufacturing sector. Banks concentrated largely on commercial firms either engaged in the export of raw materials or the import and domestic marketing of consumer goods. They focused on these commercial firms because commercial transactions were short term and reaped profit directly, in contrast to investments with a longer-term gestation period which were seen as extremely risky business.

After 1965, however, the environment changed dramatically. Singapore's commercial banks had to adapt quickly to the new challenges facing a fully-independent republic. The bank's response would determine the direction and the rate of progress of Singapore's economic growth. This change of circumstances can be attributed to the aftermath of the separation from Malaysia. Political independence stimulated local commercial banks to take over from foreign banks, an ever-increasing volume of financing Singapore's domestic commerce, industry and foreign trade. Currency independence meant that the government and people had now to rely on their own resources to provide and regulate money supply, the life-blood of economic health. Commercial banks were the channels through which this life-blood circulated.

It became obvious to Singapore's commercial banks that they now had a vital role to play in the various facets of the country's national economy — industrialisation, diversification of export markets, export promotion, balance of payment, foreign exchange and national income. A bank's lending policies had to be directed towards financing productive enterprises, instead of individuals. To play this role well, the policies, functions and structures of commercial banks had to be drastically revised and completely re-oriented. It became important for banks to operate as a group, in harmony and in close association with one another. In this context, the Association of Banks in Singapore was established in 1973 with rules to regulate banking procedures and practices. From its inception right up to 1981, the OCBC was the 'chairman bank'. The Bank also had the honour of having one of its senior executives, Teo Cheng Guan, a banker with more than 25 years' experience in OCBC, elected chairman of the Institute of Bankers (Singapore centre) in 1973, a post previously held only by expatriate bankers.

No longer would the success of local banks be judged by their annual balance sheets and shareholders' annual dividends. In addition to these traditional indicators, commercial banks would be assessed on their contribution to the economic activities and growth of the country, the spread of their loans, advances and investments, the quality of their services, the efficiency of their allocation and utilisation of their resources, and their role in community development.

Becoming a Regional Financial Centre

Perhaps the single greatest change in the world economy since the end of World War Two has been the extent to which national financial systems were driven by the power of international markets. Unlike the early decades of the twentieth century, trade barriers and exchange controls have either been abandoned or become ineffective. Exchange rates and long-term interest rates were determined principally by market forces, rather than government decisions. This new-found freedom allowed the financial services industry to create a vast array of products which enabled borrowers and savers to take advantage of financial conditions around the world. In Asia, the rapid rise of Japan as a world economic power in the 1960s and 1970s gave further impetus to the internationalisation of financial markets. Tokyo became a significant player within the world's financial community. The effect of internationalisation on national economies was particularly important since enormous amounts of money were freely available for projects deemed by the markets to be commercially attractive. This in turn gave developing countries the opportunity to grow much more rapidly than they otherwise would.

Indeed, these international flows of funds spurred the rise of the tiger economies of Taiwan, Hong Kong, South Korea and Singapore. South Korea, for example, achieved its economic take-off to sustained growth in the early 1970s through the use of foreign bank loans to finance economic development. The 1970s was also a period during which a country's national wealth was increasingly used as a benchmark of its international status in the community of nations. In the days of the Cold War, wealth was used largely to develop armed forces. In the post-Cold War world, sustainable economic growth (and political influence) is largely determined by the accumulation of national savings and overseas assets. The savings ratios in the Asian tiger economies were double that of the established industrial countries.

The 1970s was also a watershed period in Singapore's business and financial history. Before 1970 there was no Monetary Authority of Singapore (MAS), no significant Asian Dollar market and no Securities Industry Council. There were no merchant banks, no discount houses and no offshore banks. By the end of the 1970s, all these institutions were in place, exchange controls were loosened and regulations on foreign bank licences were selectively liberalised.

It was to their credit that the Singapore Government decided to give renewed emphasis to one of the Island's time-tested, historical vocations. This was the traditional role of the port-city as a brokering, trading and business centre. As one of Britain's premier ports in the East, Singapore was able to attract traders and business houses with its open, laissez-faire economic system. Similarly, after gaining independence in 1965, the concept of free, competitive market remained the cornerstone of Singapore's economic revival and subsequent take-off. Ironically, Singapore's separation from Malaysia, the hastening of the British troop withdrawal, and the total split between the Singapore and Malaysian currencies in 1973, freed the hands of the Singapore leaders to initiate a range of measures to promote Singapore as an international financial centre of major significance.

In 1968, at the initiative of the local branch of the Bank of America, and after some meticulous planning and consultation with international banks, the Singapore Government committed itself to the development of an off-shore banking system — the Asian Dollar Market and, a few years later, the Asian Bond Market. This move opened an epoch of a new and more competitive banking system as distinct from ordinary commercial banking.[5] Local bankers welcomed the creation of the Asian Dollar market and saw it as a springboard for Singapore to diversify into more sophisticated financial services that were offered by great financial centres in the industrialised West. Immediately, the Government adopted strategies, such as the abolition of taxes on interest earned from deposits made by Asian Currency Units and lower taxes on loan interest and off-shore income, to ensure a successful entry.

By early 1971, the Asian Dollar market had attracted an estimated US$250 million in deposits, and 12 banks (nine foreign and three incorporated in Singapore) were licensed by the Ministry of Finance to participate. The uncertainties of post-war political changes and inflationary trends in Southeast Asia and East Asia caused many entrepreneurs, mostly overseas Chinese, to look for a safe domicile where they could liquidate and deposit their holdings. Before 1969, such nervous capital landing in Singapore usually found its way to the Eurodollar market (usually in London) for the attraction it offered in the way of tax exemption and high interest rates. With the establishment of the Asian Dollar market to facilitate the flow of new capital into Asia, Singapore now became a significant player in international financing. Indeed, its initial success had given rise to two other Asian dollar centres in the region, in Bangkok and Manila.

The gold bullion market enjoyed a similar success. In April 1969, the Government established a Gold market to allow non-residents to purchase gold, and the Republic moved nearer to its objective of becoming the financial centre of Southeast Asia. The Singapore Government's levy of US$1 on one fine ounce of gold was US$0.50 less than Hong Kong's. Coupled with lower transport costs and generally lower dealers' profit margins, the price of gold was relatively cheaper in Singapore than in Hong Kong. Prospective buyers of gold would be attracted to exploit the Singapore market and hence ensured its future growth. By mid 1970, it was estimated that total export of gold bullion exceeded $100 million. Gold became a real market commodity.

Leading the Financial Revolution

The OCBC played a significant part in the rapid transformation of Singapore into a regional banking and financial hub. Undaunted by the economic uncertainties during the merger-separation years (1963–65), the Bank embarked on a policy of diversification and expansion. Since 1965, OCBC had been assisting the Government to woo foreign capital. It cooperated with well-established foreign banks to set up local financial institutions and gave guidance and assistance to various commercial activities in industry. In short, OCBC played a proactive role in developing the national economy under the PAP's leadership.

(a) Formation of the Asian Dollar Market

The OCBC was one of the most active participants in the Asian Dollar market. Indeed, its success could be attributed largely to the fact that the Bank's Asian Currency Unit was headed by Tjio Kay Loen, a Singapore-educated mathematician. He succeeded in uplifting the Bank from an insignificant position in the market to number three in the space of six months.[6] In December 1971, the leaders in the Asian dollar market were the Bank of America (estimated total deposit of US$320 million), First National City Bank (US$250 million) and the OCBC (US$100 million) respectively.

The Bank's gold trading business also took off with the establishment of Singmas Limited in July 1976. But it was not an easy decision for the management and indeed the Singmas episode ended on a sour note. By the early 1970s, the glitter had gone out of the Singapore gold market.[7] Gold sales had been declining and reached an estimated 209,000 oz. for the first half of 1972, as against 4.5 million oz for the whole of 1970. Regionally, Indonesia, Singapore's major buyer, purchased less gold. The Indonesians reduced their gold hoarding activities and instead opted for monetary deposits in banks in Singapore (and Malaysia) to earn higher interest. Internationally, there were currency uncertainties, especially the US dollar crisis, in mid-1971, followed by the upward trend of the free market gold price.

Despite the risks involved in gold business, OCBC's entry into the trade was stimulated by a proposal by John Curran, a chartered accountant who was then Managing Director of New Court Merchant Bankers Limited (NCMB). He proposed setting up a company in Singapore jointly with OCBC and his two gold dealers, to deal exclusively in gold. Prior to making the final decision, the OCBC carried out a detailed investigation of the prospective partners and the feasibility of the venture. The three employees of NCMB had excellent track records. The report stated that 'in less than 18 months this team of 3 people has brought NCMB to the position of what is believed to be the largest gold dealing operation in Singapore [and that] all three have learnt the bullion business from scratch and are now familiar with all aspects of the trade'.[8] Therefore, 'the joint venture, if successful, will enable OCBC to have the lion's share of the gold business'.[9]

In July 1976, Singmas Limited, with OCBC taking up 40% of the shareholding, the Singapore International Merchant Bankers Limited (SIMBL), the merchant banking arm of OCBC, 20%, and John Curran and colleagues another 40%, went into operation. The new company came under the wings of SIMBL. Security for OCBC was provided by the full-time presence of an OCBC officer, seconded from SIMBL, who would monitor all gold deliveries and payments. Singmas traded profitably but greed soon overcame one of its young directors. He started trading for himself and committed the company to a substantial trading position. Singmas Limited lost all its capital. Tan Chin Tuan remained calm over the matter. 'Bad luck,' he said, 'we have to honour our commitments even though substantial loss [was incurred].' The Bank then bought all the worthless shares and paid off the loans. Singmas Limited became dormant and gold trading was taken over by the Bank itself. The Singmas episode illustrates the point that while the decision-making process involves a study of detailed reports of risk management, profitability, and of the background and credentials of prospective partners, trust and honesty are still traits which the OCBC culture have cultivated and expected in all its loyal employees.

In 1979, a wholly-owned subsidiary, OCBC Bullion Limited, was formed to help promote the fledgling gold futures market. It became one of the five dealer members of the Gold Exchange of Singapore. The Bank took 20% equity in the Singapore Gold Clearing House Private Limited, and was authorised to issue Gold Certificates. It introduced the one-kilobar gold certificate which proved to be more popular than the alternative three-kilobar certificate. Continuing its innovative approach to the gold market, encouraging results of its one kilo and three-kilo gold certificates prompted the Bank to become the first institution to sell 100 and 500 gram denominations in November 1981. Besides the general popularity of the metal, these smaller denominations were introduced because they could be used as gifts during festive occasions, such as the Chinese New Year.[10]

(b) Leasing and Industrial Financing

In line with the Singapore Government's pragmatic industrialisation policy during the 1970s, OCBC was one of the first local banks to offer leasing and industrial financing services. It was a bold move because, unlike the financing of trade and commercial activities, the financing of industry — such as construction of plant and acquisition of equipment and machinery — on a large scale by banks was hitherto unheard of in Singapore. Indeed, the whole process of heavy equipment lease operations was very complex and required a range of expertise. The Bank reckoned that it could offer a valuable service to an industry which was handicapped by under-capitalisation, through lease finance. This was particularly true in the context of Singapore's industrial scene in the early 1970s where some industries were under-capitalised. Essentially, the prospective lessee need not tie down its funds nor pay a deposit or down payment. Hence, lease finance was a marked departure from the more traditional types of finance based on pledged securities. OCBC thus adopted a forward-looking attitude in order to consolidate its position as the premier local bank.

The Bank teamed up with First National City Overseas Investment Corporation, a US-registered corporation specialising in leasing and industrial financing to form the First Oversea Credit Limited (FOCL) on 16 February 1970. This was OCBC's first venture with a foreign bank. The portfolios included factoring, leasing of all types of equipment and merchandise, and engaging in all forms of financing operations. FOCL's tasks of selecting prospective lessees and ensuring the availability of business and funds were made easier by the management expertise, credit information and technical staff offered by its two major partners. With its formation, under-capitalised companies in Singapore could now seek the capital to start operations. During the early years, much of FOCL's asset portfolio was taken up by timber, construction and marine services equipment. By the mid-1970s and in the context of Singapore's rapid industrialisation, priorities gradually shifted to industrial equipment financing.

The FOCL was one of the many companies with foreign partners that became 'localised', whereby ownership and management was transferred to local directors. OCBC was entitled to appoint three directors and First National two directors. The Chairman of the Board of Directors was also a nominee of the OCBC Group. This illustrates Tan Chin Tuan's 'localisation' strategy, mentioned in the previous chapter. It not only widened OCBC's network of subsidiaries but also ensured that the Bank had the final say in decision-making.

(c) Merchant Banking

By the early 1970s, Singapore was home to 31 banks incorporated in countries like Malaysia, Britain, India, the United States, Japan, Italy, West Germany, Russia, Pakistan, Thailand, Indonesia and France. This was clear testimony to the Republic's economic success and to the pivotal intermediary position it had achieved as the financial metropolis of Southeast Asia. These banks not only introduced financial and managerial expertise and money, they also brought along their important clients — traders, investors and industrialists — to open up ventures in Singapore. In addition, the Singapore economy was on the upward trend during the late 1970s. Considerable progress was made towards creating a large industrial-based and service-oriented economy. Consequently, as financing of businesses became more complex, there was an urgent need for special institutions to raise, manage and utilize monetary funds for corporate clients. The local banking and financial sector saw the rapid rise of merchant banking. These banks had the expertise in financial matters and intimate knowledge of the capital markets of the world.

The OCBC was quick to respond to the rising importance of merchant banking in Singapore. In 1970, Tan Chin Tuan continued his strategy of entering new markets and establishing long-term connections through joint ventures with prominent local and overseas partners. The creation of the Singapore International Merchant Bankers Limited (SIMBL), under the chairmanship of Yong Pung How, was OCBC's second joint-venture with foreign financial institutions.

Interestingly, the full name of the institution was rarely used by business associates and even its own staff. Some said it was too long and pompous and preferred the acronym. The joke was that too many could not remember what it stood for. But all those familiar with the name recognised the acronym as a symbolic reference to how merchant banking started in Singapore. Today SIMBL stands for Schroder International Merchant Bankers Ltd. It was one of the first merchant banks to be given a licence for an Asian Currency Unit by the MAS. The Bank's partners were the Crown Agents, Continental Illinois National Bank of Chicago and Alexanders Discount and Yong Pung How — hence the five petals in SIMBL's logo. Through the trials and errors of involvement in various types of financial activities suitable for a merchant bank, SIMBL soon built up a reputation based on traditional merchant banking services — corporate finance, banking investment, advisory and corporate secretariat, share registration and nominee services. The achievements during the early years included the flotation of Eu Yan Sang Holdings and Metro. Both were then small family companies. As a member of the OCBC Group, SIMBL's corporate philosophy was also the inculcation of excellent relationship with clients and an emphasis on the building up of talents within the organisation.

Despite some scaling down of its operations in the light of the international banking crisis and the accompanying recession in the mid-1970s, SIMBL was one of Singapore's most well-known merchant banks and it attracted the interest of one of London's oldest and most important merchant banks, Schroders Limited. Recognising that the Pacific Basin was experiencing rapid economic growth, Schroders devoted a lot of effort to making its presence felt in the region. A series of alliances were formed and subsidiaries established in Tokyo, Hong Kong, Singapore and Australia.[11] The British merchant bank's entry into the Singapore domestic scene coincided with SIMBL's reconstruction resulting from the Crown Agents' decision to leave the partnership. They recommended Schroders which, subsequently, was admitted into the partnership through the purchase of a 24.5% shareholding in SIMBL. Michael Gleeson-White, a director of J. Henry Schroder Wagg & Co. Limited, became its Managing Director.

In 1977, institutional and management changes occurred within SIMBL. Yong Pung How left to become Vice-Chairman of OCBC and Schroders did a comprehensive review of the business outlook in the Far East. Its Chairman, David Airlie, felt that SIMBL could be 'developed as an investment banking operation to augment and support our existing activities in Hong Kong, Tokyo and Sydney [and that] we are prepared to take responsibility for providing the leadership of such an instrument and the necessary senior management'.[12] Two months later, on 27 July 1981, it was publicly announced that Schroders had increased its stake in SIMBL to 49% by purchasing Continental Bank's interest and Nicholas E. H. Ferguson, a director of J. Henry Schroder Wagg & Co. Limited, was appointed as the new managing director of SIMBL.

Expansion through strategic alliances continued when two officials, Charles Tresise and Tjio Kay Loen, went to Tokyo to negotiate the formation of a merchant bank in Singapore. The Bank had earlier (on 12 May 1973) received a joint venture proposal from the directors of Yamaichi Securities Company Limited (represented by Masayoshi Katsuta) and the Bank of Tokyo (represented by Keikichi Honda). The initiative taken by the Japanese was a clear indication of the reputation and financial strength of OCBC. Although SIMBL was already well established, the 'Japanese parties were not in favour of this [association with SIMBL], regarding it as important that they should be seen to have a direct connection with OCBC'.[13] In 1973, Yamaichi Securities were the largest underwriters, brokers and dealers in Japan with 83 domestic and overseas branches and subsidiaries in seven major cities abroad. Similarly, the Bank of Tokyo had a wide range of connections with Japanese companies operating in South-east Asia. The Japanese negotiators did a meticulous feasibility study and this impressed the prospective Singapore partner. It was thorough and based on a review of Bank of Tokyo's clients who may be in need of merchant banking services within the next few years.

The 1970s was generally a time when Japanese intitutions, companies and investments were forming strategic business alliances and making their presence felt in South-east Asia. In March 1973, there were some 164 Singapore-Japanese joint-venture companies, Japanese wholly-owned subsidiaries and branches of Japanese companies registered in Singapore, the majority of which were in the manufacturing and commerce sectors. The proposed merchant bank the Singapore-Japan Merchant Bank would specialise in financing Japanese joint ventures in the region and participating in the Asian Dollar bond market. However, cultural differences soon forced OCBC to move out of the partnership. OCBC sold its shares to the Japanese partners and made good profits.

Crossing Borders

Modern corporate multinational banking had its roots in the nineteenth century when Western imperial merchants and entrepreneurs set up banks in their conquered colonies. Dramatic changes in the world economy since 1945 saw an intensification of multinational banking led by American, British and Japanese banking institutions. In Singapore's banking and financial history, the 1970s saw the rise of multinational banking initiated by big players like OCBC. It was a period of expansion by Singapore banks to own and control branches and affiliates in more than one country. In the case of OCBC, the internalisation of its banking facilities had its roots as far back as the mid-1920s when the Oversea-Chinese Bank opened branches in Rangoon, Jambi and Amoy. At the OCBC's 50th Anniversary celebration in 1982, Tan Chin Tuan remarked:

> One of the greatest satisfactions to me is that over the last three decades OCBC has managed to develop into the leading bank in Singapore with branches in a number of capital cities and a complete network of international ramifications.

By that time, many OCBC overseas branches were established in Malaysia, China, Hong Kong, Britain, and Japan. They embraced a wide range of commercial, industrial and trading activities closely associated with the rapid economic develop- pment of the countries. More significantly, these branches spearheaded Singapore's economic thrust abroad by creating in their cities of operation greater awareness of the opportunities and capabilities that were unique to Singapore.

(a) In Malaysia

The OCBC had an indirect hand in shaping the economic development of Malaysia. In 1963, OCBC bought over 97% of the shares of the Batu Pahat Bank Limited and subsequently incorporated The Pacific Bank Berhad on 30 May that year. As a result of Singapore's separation from Malaysia, the bank suffered from a 'split personality'. Although the registered office of the bank was at Batu Pahat, it was a Singapore, and hence, foreign bank. With the Malaysian Government's implementation of the New Economic Policy (NEP) in the early 1970s, *bumiputras*, as 'sons of the soil', were given equity participation and employment in the economy. It was a period of intense economic nationalism, stimulated by the economic downturn brought about by the Oil Crisis of 1973. When the First Malaysian Plan was announced in 1970, it was revealed that foreigners held 63% of corporate assets in the country. By contrast, *bumiputras* held a mere 2%, and the remaining 35% were split between Chinese and other Malaysians.

To achieve the NEP's social and economic objectives, a number of financial measures were introduced. In July 1972, a Credit Guarantee Corporation was established with equity participation from Bank Negara Malaysia as well as commer-

cial banks. It was to provide guarantee cover to the banks
designated loans to small-scale enterprises. More significantly, in 1976, selective guidelines were issued to both
commercial banks and finance companies. The *bumiputra*
community, housing, manufacturing and agricultural
production was specified as priority sectors. In short, these
measures were aimed primarily at re-distributing the wealth
of non-*bumiputra* community, even though it was at the
expense of interfering with market forces and producing
economic uncertainties. A proposal to restructure the Pacific
Bank's paid–up capital (which allowed for not less than
30% of *bumiputra* control) was approved by the Malaysian
Government in August 1976. The move meant that
Malaysians, and not OCBC, now controlled The Pacific Bank
Berhad, even though the close association 'was considered
desirable to enable The Pacific Bank Berhad to have access
to ample back-up funds when the need arose'.[14]

The implementation of the NEP created some tension
between OCBC's Malaysian operations and the Bank Negara
Malaysia. In a meeting with the deputy governor of Bank
Negara Malaysia in August 1976, OCBC was requested to
take the lead in achieving the 10% target ratio of *bumiputra*
loans.[15] It was mentioned that smaller foreign banks such as
the Chartered Bank, the Hongkong and Shanghai Bank and
Chung Khiaw Bank were close to or had already met the set
target. In addition, OCBC was asked to make greater effort
in recruiting *bumiputra* staff, especially in supervisory and
clerical levels. While the Bank subscribed fully to Malaysia's
policy of uplifting the economic status of *bumiputras*, the
bottom-line was, in the words of Choi Siew Hong, the
general manager in charge of the Malaysian division, 'finding viable projects, and willing borrowers who can make
efficient use of the funds [and] in this connection, safety of
depositors' funds is a very important factor'.[16] It was a stand

which strongly reflected Tan Chin Tuan's personal conviction that OCBC must look after the depositors' money at all times.

A few years later, in 1982, the 'Bumiputra Napoleon' and former Governor of Bank Negara, Tun Ismail bin Mohamed Ali, commented:

> Now that I am no longer governor of Bank Negara, I think I can say this — that I'd like the foreign banks to restructure and incorporate locally, as Malaysian entities. Not just Hongkong and Shanghai and Chartered Bank: It should apply to all, including Overseas Chinese Banking Corporation.[17]

Rumours that branches of the Singapore-based bank were hiving off their operations spread quickly. The broking and financial community pointed to the Bank's decreasing stakes in The Pacific Bank Berhad, from 97% of the equity of the bank in 1975 to 75% in 1976 and only 29% in 1977. At the same time, after the retirement of Lin Jo Yan, OCBC's general manager in 1977, separate general managers for Malaysia and Singapore operations were appointed. Although Tan Chin Tuan had his own reservations about the NEP and the eventual 'loss' of The Pacific Bank Berhad, OCBC was still among the top five banks in Malaysia, with 25 branches within the peninsula, Sabah and Sarawak. Indeed, the conglomerate of companies under Tan Chin Tuan's chairmanship, as one journalist puts it, 'has a far wider net over the Malaysian economy than many would have expected.'[18]

(b) In China and Britain

Just after World War Two, OCBC sent Yeo Tiam Siew to China to explore the possibility of opening up branches in Peking,

Nanking, Hanchow and Tientsin. Yeo reported that it was not the right time to increase OCBC's network of branches there. The country was embroiled in a civil war between Mao Tse-tung and Chiang Kai-shek and if 'Mao won and China became communist then it was possible that any branches OCBC had in China might be nationalized'.[19] Yeo recommended the shelving of the expansion plan and that time and resources be concentrated on the three existing branches at Hong Kong, Amoy (now Xiamen, established in 1925) and Shanghai (established in 1927). It was a sensible decision and Yeo was assigned the task of consolidating the branches between 1946 and 1949, spending about six months of the year at the three branches. In retrospect, the decision and subsequent consolidation of the two China branches augured well for the Bank — some 30 years later.

After Mao's death in 1976, China gradually opened its doors to foreign investors. The country and its people were experiencing a new lease of economic life under the leadership of Deng Xiaoping. Of all the local banks, OCBC had the upper hand by virtue of the fact that it was the only Singapore bank with two long-established branches in China. Both branches had invaluable experience in dealing with provincial officials and were able to provide insightful reports on business opportunities within the economic zone. Between 1979 and 1984, Singapore investors ploughed $400 million into China's industrial and real estate ventures. OCBC was then the most active Singapore bank in China. In 1985, the State General Administration of foreign exchange control in China permitted the Shanghai branch (and three other foreign banks) to expand their business scope. The overall objective was to develop the city into a major financial centre. OCBC was the only Singapore bank to be given the privilege. The other three were Standard Chartered Bank, Bank of East Asia and Hongkong and Shanghai Banking Corporation.[20]

In 1967, Yeo Tiam Siew was once again given the task of opening an overseas branch. This time it was in the political and business centre of Britain, London. He was the obvious choice as he was a frequent visitor to the city and because of his *guanxi* with people within and outside banking circles. Without delay, he entered into a protracted negotiation with the Swiss Reinsurance Company at 108 Cannon Street for an office space on the latter's ground floor. The lease was eventually signed. Yeo's next task was to recruit a number of senior officers and, more importantly, a good dealer in foreign exchange. Personal contacts gave him the edge and an exchange dealer who 'had been a foreign exchange comptroller in Singapore in the colonial days' was recruited.[21] It was a timely move. As Yeo explained:

> This man was very useful as he was very quickly able to obtain a licence from the Bank of England for the branch to deal in foreign exchange. Usually branches of foreign banks had to wait a long time before such licences were granted; two other Singaporean banks who had established branches in the City a few years previous to OCBC's were still waiting for theirs.[22]

On 4 August 1969, the door to OCBC's first direct link with London opened for business. The London branch was the Bank's 13th branch office outside Singapore. In 1976, OCBC began negotiations with the Bank of China to purchase its historic London Stone House in Cannon Street, about 100 metres from the leased building. The asking price was more than $13 million but the building eventually changed hands for about $11.7 million.[23] The branch, as one of the principal arms of the International Division in OCBC, was now in a much better position to expand its business in Britain and in Western Europe via the London connection.

(c) In Japan

One major factor accounting for Singapore's successful export-oriented industrialisation strategy during the 1970s was the influx of international capital into the city-state. Notwithstanding the recession of 1975, foreign net investments in the manufacturing sector during the period 1974–1978 increased from $168.8 million to $765.7 million. Although investment of US-based capital in the 1970s was the heaviest, Japanese-based investment expanded at twice the US rate during this period. This resurgence of interest by Japanese investors in Singapore can be explained by the erosion of manufacturing competitiveness in Japan. Singapore was thus viewed as an excellent off-shore production site.

It did not take long for OCBC to recognise the potential of linking up directly with the source of Japanese investment. Reading the changing environment correctly, Tan Chin Tuan wrote to the Japanese Minister of Finance in June 1972 to seek permission to open an OCBC branch in the heart of Japan's financial district, Tokyo. As stated in the letter, the main objective was 'to provide better facilities to our customers who have dealings with Japan [and] to develop further the trade and investment between Singapore and Japan'.[24] Within two weeks, the Japanese Government replied positively and senior officers from OCBC were invited to Tokyo for further discussions. Subsequently, in August, Tjio Kay Loen, one of the Bank's senior officers, went to Japan. The Tokyo branch, the Bank's sixth in its overseas network, was opened on 23 April 1973. With Singapore in the middle and Tokyo in the north of the Pacific Basin, which had been identified as the growth area of the 1970s, OCBC was now in an enviable position to make important contributions to the development of this area.

Prudent Acquisitions and Diversification

Besides crossing national boundaries, the 1970s was also a busy decade during which OCBC expanded its stable of sub-sidiaries, most of which were wholly owned and based in Singapore. In early months of 1973, the OCBC Group acquired the oldest surviving bank in Singapore — the Four Seas Communications Bank or Sze Hai Tong Bank (founded in 1906). It was not an aggressive takeover because in Tan Chin Tuan's view, 'people are important and in takeovers, people often get hurt'. The agreed merger of Four Seas was a mutually beneficial arrangement and, more significantly, 'the same people still run the bank'.[25] Under the stewardship of OCBC (which controlled 99% of its shareholdings), the Four Seas group shareholders' fund increased from $32.3 million in 1972 to $65 million in 1981. Another noteworthy subsidiary was the Bank of Singapore, in which OCBC had a 89% stake. The acquisition of the two banks and their subsidiary finance companies allowed the OCBC to strengthen its retail network within Singapore.

The OCBC continued its expansion programme by participating in the establishment of the International Bank of Singapore (IBS) in 1973. The other partners were the Development Bank of Singapore (DBS), Overseas Union Bank (OUB) and the United Overseas Bank (UOB), each with a 25% stake. The primary objective of IBS was to establish branches in important financial centres of the world where the 'Big Four' — OCBC, DBS, UOB and OUB — were not represented. After several years, the consortium failed to take off profitably. In May 1983, the four joint owners decided that it was in the best interest of everyone to have IBS owned and managed by a sole party. Each of the partners bid for the shares of the rest. OUB made a successful bid of $3.11 per share and gained total ownership of IBS for a consideration of $116 million.

To put the episode in its proper perspective, the timing of IBS's formation was not quite right. During the late 1970s, the Singapore Government was pushing hard to restructure the economy by placing strong emphasis on developing a capital-intensive industrialisation programme. One significant consideration was that local banks, through such services as industrial financing, now had an even greater role to play in supporting the Government's effort. Hence, resources were channelled to developments at home and took precedence over expansion overseas. Indeed, the early years of the '70s saw the opening of more foreign banks tapping new opportunities arising from the influx of multinational corporations into Singapore. By 1976, there was a total of 70 banks, 36 finance companies, 21 merchant banks and 38 representative offices. The small city-state was on her way to becoming a major regional financial hub.

In response to the changing scenario, OCBC opened two more branches — the Jalan Sultan Branch and the Balestier Branch — in 1975. Four years later, in 1979, the fully 'on-line' Bedok branch opened and became OCBC's 20th full-service branch in Singapore and the 51st in its international network. Apart from its 25 branches in Malaysia, the Bank had branches in Tokyo, London, Kowloon, Amoy and Shanghai. As part of the move to strengthen the group's banking services, OCBC acquired Bankers Trust Company in July 1979. The Bank's association with the group extended back to 1938. As previously mentioned, it was formed under the Trust Companies Act to operate as trustees, executors, administrators, guardians, attorneys and agents.

This restructuring allowed the OCBC Group to have a greater share of the growing trustee business in Singapore. Besides these local acquisitions, Tan Chin Tuan also bought into Midland Bank and the Bank of New South Wales when their prices were low. Although the objective was primarily investment for long-term gains, there was also much to gain in terms of establishing close relationship with leading indigenous banks. OCBC could tap on their large network of branches. In his own words, '[b]ecause of this close relationship, our customers can go to almost any branch of the Bank of New South Wales in Australia or the Midland in the UK and they will be welcomed as if they were the banks' own customers.'[26] While Tan Chin Tuan would have liked OCBC to expand internationally, the problem lay in the 'difficulty in finding competent and trustworthy officers who are willing to work abroad.' Nevertheless, by the end of 1983, OCBC was ranked 173rd among the world's top 500 banks by the reputable financial magazine, *Euromoney*, as shown in Table 1.

Table 1. Ranked by Equity of the Four Major Local Banks (in 1983)

Rank 1984	Rank 1983	Bank	Total group shareholders funds(US$mm)	Growth in shareholders funds 1983–4(%)	Net Income ($mm)	Growth In net income 1983–4(%)	Total assets %	Growth in assets 1983–4	Total number of employees
178	173	OCBC	443.31	2.34	44.46	15.53	2.36	12.78	2646
128	129	UOB	588.30	5.79	63.04	-12.81	4.90	0.01	4019
111	121	DBS	234.76	1.45	19.83	-9.85	3.01	9.23	1991
315	307	OUB	718.02	22.87	46.76	-9.23	5.27	-1.40	2948

Note: Figures for the year 1984 are unaudited.
Source: 'The Euromoney Five Hundred', Euromoney, March 1985, pp. 54–211.

To reward its more than 14,000 registered shareholders in 1982 for their unstinting support, OCBC had six bonus and two rights issues, the last one being made for the year ending 1981 to commemorate the 50th anniversary of the Bank. From an issued capital of $10 million, shareholders' funds had gone up to $70.4 million by 1966, a year after a tumultuous road towards gaining independence for Singapore.

In 1982 the shareholders' fund went beyond $1 billion while net profit rose to $126 million, compared to $5.3 million in 1966. Between 1966 and 1982, total assets too increased from $665 million to $ 8.7 billion.[27]

In the midst of this expansionary programme, OCBC did not forget that the continuous innovation of new products and services was important in a service-oriented and customer-focused industry. In February 1981, OCBC joined the credit card market when it became a principal member of Singapore MasterCard International Incorporated. In September that year, travellers cheques in Singapore dollars, for use within the nations under the Association of Southeast Asian Nations (ASEAN), were introduced to the public. The move did not contradict the Government's policy of limiting the international role of the Singapore currency because the dollar value of the travellers cheques issued was considered too marginal to trouble the authorities. On the contrary, the new cheques were seen to provide a boost to the country's tourist industry since 42% of the tourists who came to Singapore in the first half of 1981 were from the neighbouring countries.[28] Fully backed by OCBC, the signature of the Bank's Chairman, Tan Chin Tuan, appeared on all the cheques which also showed the OCBC Centre and the Bank's logo in front and the Merlion vignette behind. The design was carefully conceptualised to reflect the organisation's familiar but reputable symbols and imagery.

Management educators, such as Charles Fombrun, have suggested that good reputations create wealth. By developing strong and consistent images, well-regarded companies generate hidden assets or what Fombrun termed as 'reputational' capital, which gave them a distinct advantage over their competitors.[29] In the banking industry, branding is used as a 'pull' strategy to bring in customers into a bank. Branding, according to David Neenan, is 'primarily concerned with identification — where a customer can distinguish a product or service by its name, design features, and/or logo attributing certain qualities to that product or service based on past experience'.[30] The OCBC travellers cheques were used as a product to promote corporate identity with the Bank's large customer base.

In line with the Singapore concept of banks functioning as multi-purpose engines of growth, OCBC further developed its interest in property development and industry in the 1970s. It is a well-known fact that besides the Government, OCBC was the biggest land and property owner in Singapore. Its reputation as a canny real estate investor may be traced to the fable of one director. Chee Swee Cheng, OCBC's first Chairman who was known for his thriftiness, and who was considered eccentric enough to buy houses with the number 13 at low prices because no one wanted to live in a house with the unlucky number. He lived in a house and worked in an office with the same number: 13. The legacy that was passed on by the Chairman is this: It is easy to make money if you can seize the opportunity but it is equally easy to lose money if you are not careful. Taking the cue from his predecessors, Tan Chin Tuan was quick to recognise the business opportunities available as a result of the British withdrawal of its military forces in Singapore in 1971. He took over Robinson's and John Little department stores which he felt should focus on serving the local population rather than expatriates. His venture into real estate and retail industry – the first by a local bank — was marked by the construction of the Specialists' Centre.

In July 1972, the 25-storey, $20 million Specialists' Centre in Orchard Road designed by B. E. P. Akitek was declared open. It was fully capitalised and solidly backed by the OCBC and housed what was then the Bank's newest and biggest branch (including more than 4,000 safe deposit boxes and night safe) and offices for its associate, the Great Eastern Life Assurance Company. The design and layout of the branch and convenience of its location illustrates the important business strategy of making branch banking truly customer-orientated. It added value to the public perception of banking with OCBC. Two months later, in August, the 300-room Hotel Phoenix was ready for occupation and it was advertised as 'a luxury hotel in everything but price'. As part of the Bank's contribution to Singapore's declared aim of becoming a regional medical centre, three floors were assigned as a medical centre. In the 1970s, the Specialists' Centre complex was considered a unique building as it offered a number of amenities within easy reach of each other. Sadly, 1972 ended with the destruction of the landmark Robinson's department store at Raffles Place as a result of a fire that killed nine employees on 21 November.

While the Specialists' Centre project was initiated and completed by the Bank itself, Tan Chin Tuan's favourite strategy was to take a majority stake in those projects launched by others if he is convinced of the long-term gains. A well-known but unusual example was the Raffles City Project in which OCBC and associated companies took up 17.55% stake or 43 million shares. The major shareholder of Raffles City was Raffles Holdings, a joint-venture between DBS and Temasek Holdings (a wholly-owned government subsidiary), which held 60% of the stake. It cost the OCBC Group $250 million but according to the Chairman who was originally reluctant to get involved with the project, 'spreading the risk and putting yourself in a strong position' was worth the investment in the long run. Nevertheless, the OCBC Group's involvement in the $900 million Raffles City signalled the willingness and flexibility of the Chairman and his Board to depart from traditional business policy and practices. Rarely did the Bank commit itself to a project the size of Raffles City.

The gestation period was very long and shareholders would not see any dividends until about 1990. It was also 'out of the ordinary' for the Group to take a minority stake in major and prestigious projects because partial stakes in companies in the past had been the exception rather than the rule. The project also marked the first time OCBC had teamed up with DBS on a large scale.

Perhaps the common factor — at least to Tan Chin Tuan — that brought the two banks together was I. M. Pei, the architect of the OCBC Centre who was also entrusted with the basic design of Raffles City. Notwithstanding the unusual circumstances, the bottom-line for OCBC's participation was the need to be seen in the front line of business expansion in Singapore. Situated in close proximity to the future Raffles City was the site of another new mega-project: the $700 million Marina Centre. UOB, OUB and the Post Office Savings Bank (POSB) were the major local banks involved in financing the Marina Centre. Hence, strategically speaking, OCBC must be seen to be contributing to the development of Singapore's futuristic complexes that would bring in the shoppers and tourists once fully completed by the mid-1980s.

As we saw in the previous chapter, Tan Chin Tuan adopted the unprecedented strategy of using the Bank's reserves, not the depositors' money, to buy shares of other companies. It is not easy to provide an accurate total of the number of companies that come under the OCBC Group in one way or another. By the end of the 1970s, the net had spread to 60-odd companies. The term 'OCBC company' was often taken in local corporate circles to mean a 'blue-chip' company like Great Eastern Life Assurance, Fraser and Neave, Wearne Brothers, Malayan Breweries, Straits Trading, Raffles Hotel and Robinson.

Interestingly, besides financial operations, Tan Chin Tuan did not know much about the technicalities of manufacturing concerns. For example, he hardly knew about brewery operations, but he saw the prospect in the industry in the long run. He knew the importance of branded and packaged goods in a competitive world. Brand names could only be established by companies capable of exploiting economies of scale and scope in marketing. The companies owning them must be relatively large and must stick around long enough for consumers to develop an awareness of the quality and distinctiveness of their products. Names like Kodak, Sears, Sanyo, Shiseido, and Panasonic have a long history and were created by very large, well-institutionalised corporations.

Collectively, the OCBC Group consisted of one of the largest insurers in the region, the largest soft drink bottler, one of the biggest car distributors in both Singapore and Malaya, the largest brewery in the region, the oldest hotel and the department store that considered itself the Harrods of Singapore. In addition to this powerful core of commercial and industrial giants, Tan Chin Tuan also bought stakes in newspapers, supermarkets, and engineering companies. It became clear that the influence of the OCBC Group was (and is) indeed very pervasive. Table 2 indicates the strength of the major companies within the OCBC network as in 1976.

Behind this very successful investment game was Tan Chin Tuan, the undisputed expert. His phenomenal grasp of details — Yong Pung How called him a 'walking encyclopaedia of knowledge and experience' – and his ability to pick winners is near legendary. It is known that he is interested in only taking over companies at bargain prices. In his own words:

> I did no private business, either in partnership or with
> private companies. The only thing I did was to buy

Table 7.2 The OCBC 'Family' of Companies as in 1976

HOLDING COMPANIES	MAIN BUSINESS	BALANCE SHEET ($ Million)			PERCENTAGE HELD BY HOLDING COMPANIES										NO. OF EMPLOYEES
		Share Capital	Net Worth	Total Assets	OCBC	GEL	OAC	F&N	MBL	Str. Trading	Robinson	Wearnes	Raffles Hotel	Bankers Trust	
OCBC & Subsidiaries	Banking and finance	114	373	3,188		41.5	46.3	11.1	6.1	11.6	20.8	6.9	52.7	34.9	1,900
Great Eastern Life	Insurance	9	26	387	5.0		12.8	13.0	3.0	14.0	15.4	13.0			175
Overseas Assurance Corp	Insurance	8	20	77	0.5	2.8		2.1	0.9	2.7	4.9	2.6			140
Fraser & Neave	Soft drinks manufacturer	45	119	154	2.1				35.1						3,430
Malayan Breweries	Brewer	36	99	139				2.4							729
Straits Trading	Tin smelting, plantations	45	125	159											630
Robinsons	Department store	31	53	54	0.2	0.3									457
Wearnes	Motor vehicles	45	109	166											3,000
Raffles Hotel	Hotelier	1	5	5	0.5			0.3	0.1		2.5	0.3			280
Tan Chin Tuan, family & investment companies		-	-	-	5.8	3.1	5.3	1.5	0.4	1.4	5.7	0.6	12.1	6.1	-
Bankers Trust Co. Ltd	Investments holding co.	-	-	-	0.6	4.4		1.6	0.3	1.2	1.9	0.5	0.8		-
Totals		334	929	4,329	14.8	52.1	64.4	32.0	45.9	30.9	51.2	23.9	65.5	47.7	10,741

Source: *The Business Times*, 14 October 1976.

> shares in public companies... I bought shares. Then I
> worked to make companies successful. In so doing I
> formed a group to ensure the companies can't be taken
> over. I bought companies, all these. I was Managing
> Director first, then I became a Director. When the time
> came and senior directors moved on, I became Chair-
> man. I used my luck and skill.[31]

In his opinion, the OCBC Group expanded steadily because his major role was to oversee and ensure 'their sure
and steady growth'. He continued: 'For instance, when it is
cloudy and threatening, I would counsel fishing nearer the
shore, until the sky is clear and blue. I would also urge watch-
ing the economic tides and taking advantage of their fluctuations instead of plunging in impatiently.'[32] But once the
companies had built up their reserves and the 'sky is clear
and blue,' Tan Chin Tuan would venture afar to look for new
opportunities to strengthen OCBC's economic empire.

As Chairman of Malayan Breweries, Tan Chin Tuan went
to New Zealand and bought the Leopard Brewery which was
described by the Chairman as 'small and broken down'. It
was rebuilt and Malayan Breweries went on to acquire shares
in Lion Breweries Limited (then called New Zealand Breweries) which also held shares in Leopard Breweries. In the
meantime, Tan Chin Tuan's buying spree sent uneasy signals
to the people who controlled the brewery business in New
Zealand. They knew that they were up against a reputable
and, more often than not, successful international investor.
Bruce Judge, a close associate of Ron Brierley, head of
Brierley Investment Limited (BIL), one of New Zealand's
largest companies, came to Singapore and attempted to negotiate with the OCBC Chairman. Judge was interested in
acquiring New Zealand Breweries and 'committed a rash of
ideas,' promising BIL's full support in the venture to Malayan

Breweries chief executive Desmond Neill.[33] Neill was a long-time trusted employee and friend of the Chairman who knew him 'as a callow youth and inducted him into the group's service, in which he has remained, faithfully ever since'.[34] Tan Chin Tuan disliked such bullying tactics and refused to see Judge. Instead, he continued to jack up investment in New Zealand Breweries to 18%. Bruce Judge had failed to read Malayan Breweries' or Tan Chin Tuan's move accurately. It was a pure investment decision, with no intention of a takeover. Moreover, as a foreign investor, Malayan Breweries was aware that it was not welcomed anyway and hence did not want to contribute to any sense of uncertainty.

Nevertheless, the increased stakes did cause apprehension in the New Zealand Breweries' board headed by Clifford Plimmer. In the words of Tan Chin Tuan: 'They did not like me but feared me.' In January 1978, Plimmer decided to form an anti-takeover, 'paper company' called Androcles Corporation Limited that held 50 million shares in the breweries or 27% of the voting rights. The Singaporean banker did nothing. But not Ron Brierley, who was perturbed by the tactics used by Plimmer. The focus then shifted to BIL's action against Plimmer for making use of paper companies to thwart hostile takeovers. Androcles was actually up against the business community and was eventually dismantled.

In March 1984, Ron Brierley arrived in Singapore and requested to see the man who had thwarted his takeover plan. According to Brierley's biographer, van Dongen, Brierley 'was probably motivated by a mixture of awe and curiosity, for [he] loves meeting the rich, famous or powerful'.[35] Although Tan Chin Tuan had misgivings about the activities of BIL, especially after Bruce Judge's ill-thought-through letter to Malayan Breweries, he agreed to the meeting. The OCBC patriarch was fair in his judgement and after the meeting commented that Brierley was not such a bad guy after all. Ten years later, in October 1995, Tan Chin Tuan received a complimentary copy of the book, *Brierley: The Man Behind the Corporate Legend*, with a short hand-written note by Brierley himself, which reads, 'Like most of history, this book is partly fact and partly fiction. I well remember our meeting in Singapore in March 1984. With regards and best wishes.' Tan Chin Tuan reflected: 'He knows not to disturb me. In spite of my repudiating him he paid me tribute in the book. It's not easy to be spurned. I frustrated his (and Judge's) plans, yet he still wanted to see me.'[36] Brierley was pleased with the meeting in 1984 and paid tribute to the 75-year old retired Chairman of OCBC: 'I have met the great man at last.'[37]

NOTES

1   L. S. Pressnell, *Country Banking in the Industrial Revolution* (Oxford University Press, 1956); R. E. Cameron, *Banking in the Early Stages of Industrialisation* (New York: Oxford University Press, 1967); P. L. Cottrell, *Industrial Finance 1830–1914: The Finance and Organisation of English Manufacturing Industry* (London: Methuen, 1980).

2   K. Ishii, ' The Role of Banking in Japan, 1882–1973', in *Banking, Trade and Industry: Europe, America and Asia from the Thirteenth to the Twentieth Century*, A. Teichova, G. K. Van Hentenryk and D. Ziegler, eds (Cambridge: Cambridge University Press, 1997).

3   Ezra Felvel Vogel, *The Four Little Dragons: The Spread of Industralisation in East Asia* (Cambridge, Mass: Harvard University Press, 1991); Jon Woronoff, *Asia's 'Miracle' economies*, 2nd ed (Armonk, New York: M. E. Sharpe, 1992).

4   Cho Yoon Je and Kim Joon-Kyung, *Credit Policies and the Industralisation of Korea* (Seoul: Korea Development Institute, 1997), pp 99–100.

5   Lee Sheng Yi, *The Monetary and Banking Development of Singapore and Malaysia*, 3rd ed (Singapore: Singapore University Press, 1990), p. 4.

6   *OCBC Journal*, vol. 2 (1972): 28–29.

7   *The Straits Times*, 21 July 1972.

8　Report on 'Gold Business', 19 May 1976 (Singapore: The Tan Foundation).

9　Correspondence between Tony Tan and Tan Chin Tuan, 19 May 1976.

10　*The Business Times*, 29 November 1980.

11　Richard Roberts, *Schroders: Merchants & Bankers* (London: Macmillan Press, 1992), pp. 495–496.

12　Correspondence between David Airlie and Charles Tresise, 12 May 1981 (Singapore: The Tan Foundation).

13　Correspondence between Charles Tresise and Tan Chin Tuan, 3 July 1973 (Singapore: The Tan Foundation).

14　The Pacific Bank Berhad, *Seventy-Five Years of Service to the Community, 1919–1994* (Malaysia: Percetakan Kum Sdn. Bhd., 1994), p. 41.

15　Notes of Meeting, 24 August 1976 (Singapore: The Tan Foundation).

16　Ibid.

17　*Institutional Investor*, May 1982, p. 222.

18　*The Star*, 25 May 1978.

19　Yeo Tiam Siew, *Destined to Survive: The Story of My Life* (Singapore: Toppan Printing, 1993), p. 149.

20　*Euromoney*, March 1985, p. 179.

21　Yeo, *Destined to Survive*, p. 173.

22　Ibid.

23　*The Straits Times*, 22 May 1976.

24　Correspondence between Tan Chin Tuan and Japan's Minister of Finance, 30 June 1972 (Singapore: The Tan Foundation).

25　Quoted in *The Sunday Times*, 31 October 1982.

26　Interview, *Euromoney*, October 1982.

27　Director's tribute, *OCBC Annual Report*, 1982.

28　*The Straits Times*, 12 September 1981.

29　Charles J. Fombrun, *Reputation: Realising Value from the Corporate Image* (Boston, Mass: Harvard Business School Press, c1996).

30　David Neenan, *Added Value Banking: Recruitment and Retaining Customers, Maximising Sales* (Ireland: Lafferty Publication, 1993), p 147.

31　Interview, Tan Chin Tuan (n.d.), on file with the authors.

32　Interview, *Euromoney*, October 1982.

33　Y. van Dongen, *Brierley: The Man Behind the Corporate Legend* (Auckland: Viking, 1990), p. 155.

34　Speech at F & N Farewell Dinner, 20 December 1983.

35　van Dongen, *Brierley*, p. 156.

36　Interview, Tan Chin Tuan (n.d.), on file with the authors.

37　van Dongen, *Brierley*, p. 156.

CHAPTER 8

THE LOGIC OF OCBC's FAMILY NETWORK

In Asian societies, businesses that expanded beyond the individual enterprise framework are often re-structured into 'network organisations'. In Japan, the *keiretsu*, which consists of alliances of companies revolving around a bank, is the dominant type of network organisation. Mitsubishi, Sakura, Sumitomo, Fuji, Sanwa and Dai-Ichi Kangyo banks all control *keiretsu* that are composed of the country's leading firms in automobiles, electronics and heavy industries. Although the members of this network organisation may have different structures and management styles, they have one thing in common: they receive strategic direction and long-term financial support from a bank. Similarly in Britain, the banking *keiretsu* are led by the clearing banks of Barclays, Lloyds, Midland and National Westminster. These institutions have merchant bank and investment bank subsidiaries that enable them to offer universal banking services. The Korean version of the network organisation is known as the *chaebol*, among which are well-known names like Hyundai, Daewoo and Samsung. Hong Kong and Taiwan also have their own network organisations but they are much smaller in size, they are not centred on a bank or some other financial institutions, and they are (as in the Korean *chaebol*) largely based on family kinship.

In essence, Tan Chin Tuan created a hybrid form of network organisation that contains features of a Japanese *keiretsu* and a Korean *chaebol*. The OCBC network organisation is a horizontal *keiretsu*-type of corporate structure, with the family-controlled bank at its heart. However, unlike Japanese banking *keiretsu*, the Bank itself does not, in the OCBC family network, operate as the 'main bank' and the subsidiaries have the autonomy to borrow from any financial institutions. The OCBC banking *keiretsu* is illustrated in the figure below:

Figure 8.1   A Model of Linkages within the OCBC 'Family of Companies'

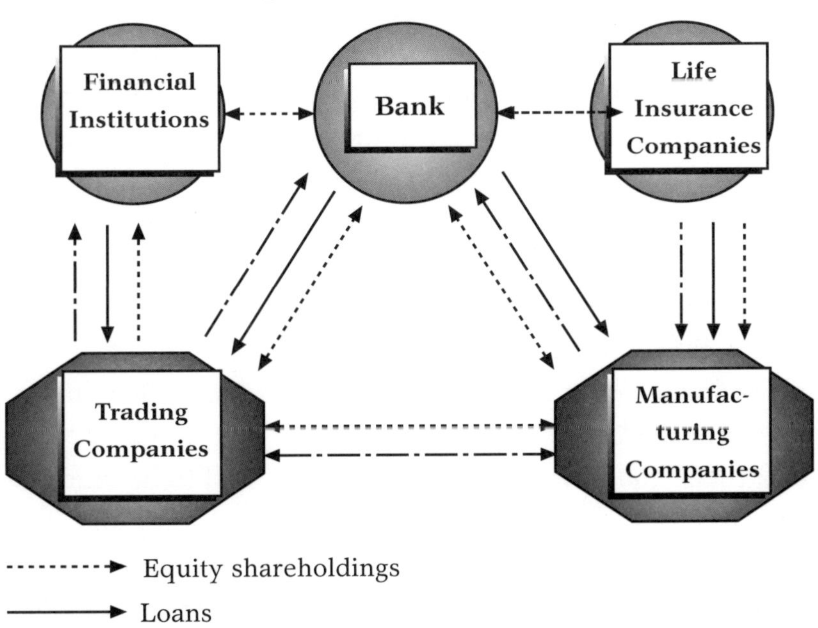

- - - - - - - -► Equity shareholdings

————————► Loans

— - — - —·► Trade (supplies, finished goods, bank deposits, life insurance policies)

Member firms in OCBC's network organisation are legally independent and do not operate within the framework of a hierarchy directed by the Bank, or as autonomously self-regulating and impersonal units. Rather, the 'family' members function as companies interlocked in complex networks of formal and informal inter-firm relationships. They are bound by a set of tangible and intangible commitments, including cross-shareholding, interlocking directorates, intra-group trade, and capital, technology, and personnel transfers. Co-operation within the OCBC 'family' is maintained through regular formal and informal meetings of key personnel to discuss employment, production and marketing issues. As a result of information exchange, affiliated firms felt confident in making joint investments. Policy decisions were made after careful collective deliberations and business risks were reduced.

Why did Tan Chin Tuan decide to form a *keiretsu*-type structure? The impact of historical experience is significant here. As we saw in the earlier chapters, the three local Hokkien banks — the Chinese Commercial Bank, the Ho Hong Bank and the Oversea-Chinese Bank — were severely affected by the economic upheaval of the Great Depression of 1929–1932. As the situation worsened, the directors, who were closely associated with each other, with family roots being traced back to China's coastal Fukien province, entered into a gentlemen's agreement to help each other out by merging the banks into a single entity. To Tan Chin Tuan the lesson of the Great Depression era was that, to be 'as solid as a rock', the new organisation, OCBC, had to be ready to shed its cloak of colonial influence and dependency. In Chapter One we saw how Chinese banks in colonial Singapore adopted the practice of what Stanworth and Stanworth refer to as the 'short-termism' of British banks, by only providing short-term loans.[1] The Chinese banks essentially acted as money-lenders, loaning money to individuals and providing capital to sustain small businesses. Consequently, the lack of long-term financial support discouraged merchants from diversifying their economic interests, especially into manufacturing. Chinese capital remained structurally immobile and largely engaged in entrepot and compradore-type of activities. Tan Chin Tuan reckoned that, with the changing economic environment, the newly-formed OCBC had to venture into businesses beyond being 'simply money-lenders'.

Tan Chin Tuan saw how that the colonial economy of Singapore — before the war and even up to the 1950s — was basically controlled by a few big European (largely British) agency-houses and Chinese merchant compradores.[2] The British firms acted as 'safety nets' for British and European capital investments by virtue of their knowledge and experience in the region and by providing other essential services, such as banking, insurance and shipping. After the war, and once entrusted with the power to lead OCBC, Tan Chin Tuan 'adopted' their modus operandi of business creation. The outstanding feature of this strategy was the aquisition by Tan of the leading 'western-based' companies in the 1950s and their subsequent localisation into the OCBC network. He widened their horizons by transferring ownership and management to local hands.

While the impact of history is great, economic rationality also played a part in explaining the creation of an intermarket OCBC family. In his seminal work on a broad theory of the modern corporation, Oliver Williamson argued that '[t]he modern corporation is mainly to be understood as the product of a series of organisational innovations that have had the purpose and effect of economising on transaction costs'.[3] Hence, one main factor why firms integrate vertically is to reduce transaction costs. But what about a horizontal or intermarket type of economic organisation, such as the OCBC

Group, whose members have no necessary economic connection with each other? To the extent that they have business dealings with each other, the network as a whole could benefit from the transaction cost efficiencies. Group members know each other well and trust one another; to do business with a member of the group would not entail the same procedure and negotiation cost as buying from a company outside the group. The corporate business synergies — in terms of services, manpower, economies of scale and management — that could be produced within this inter-market network of companies are immeasurable. Companies within the Group could buy equipment from each other, borrow from the Bank, use its insurance services and its merchant banking advisers, and collaborate if necessary (the so-called 'synergy from size' argument) to negotiate with people outside the Group.

More significantly, however, is the role of OCBC at the centre of this network. As mentioned above, the Bank played an active role in the industrialisation of the young Republic. Hence, within this network, the bank could also provide access to capital at preferential interest rates to its 'family' members who wish to diversify their operations. Finally, the OCBC network is a larger, organisational personification of Tan Chin Tuan's philosophy of reciprocal moral obligation. He allocated much of his time and effort to developing a network of co-operative and reciprocal relationships among those people inside and outside the OCBC Group (see Figure 8.2).

As Chairman of several members in the 'family', Tan was able to gradually diffuse remaining traces of western colonial influences and stimulate an *esprit de corps* based on co-operation and mutual trust within the 'family' circle. The intensity of this feeling of togetherness as a 'family' permits the emergence of innovation in management and business practices and nurturing of a customer-focused culture.

Figure 8.2   The Chairman's Network

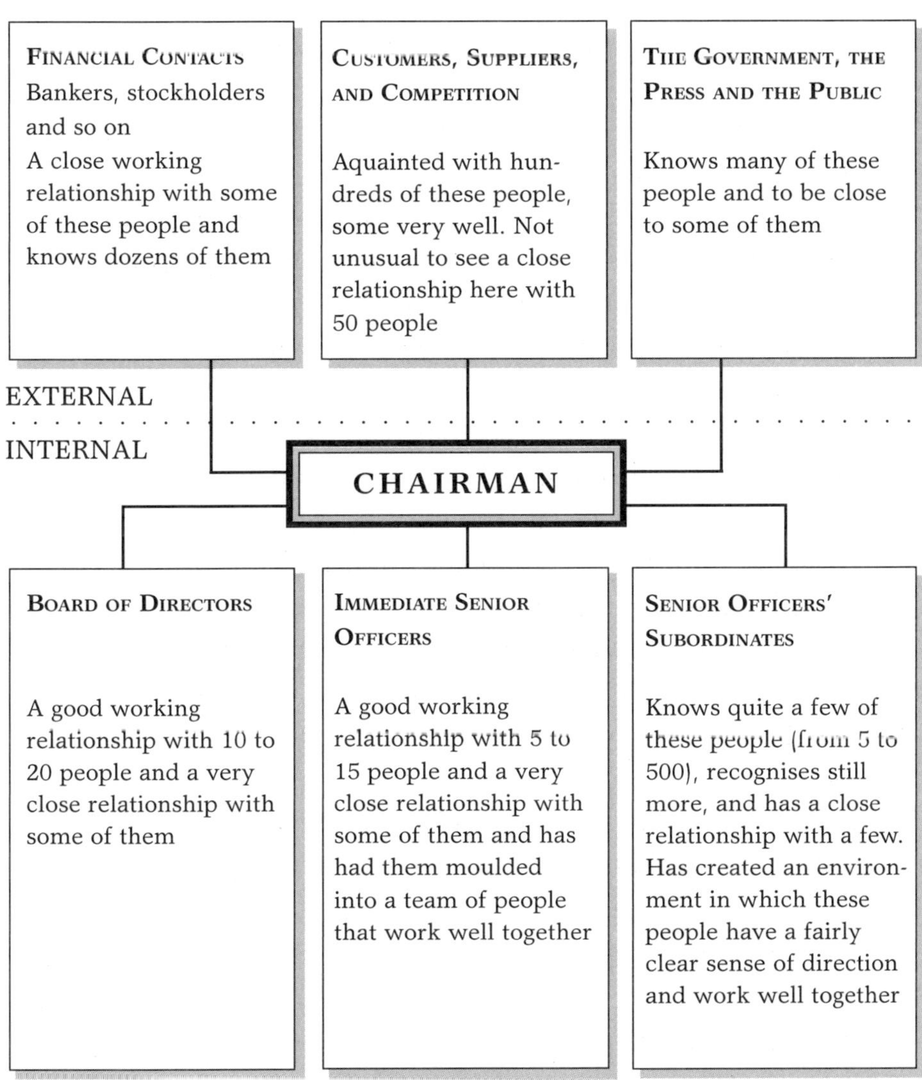

Source: Adapted from Kotter, 1999, Exhibit 7–3, p. 157

A Customer-Focused Culture through Technology and Training

Of the major local banks in Singapore, OCBC has the longest history. Before the War the Bank was a household institution for families and companies in colonial Singapore. Consequently, it has developed a strong customer service culture. Since the 1970s, however, other local banking corporations challenged her position as the premier bank in Singapore.

More significantly, from the late 1960s and into the 1970s, the world was experiencing a computer revolution. Business operations were profoundly altered by the capabilities of the computer. Corporations that responded positively and quickly to the utilisation of information and computer technology would stay ahead of their competitors. In the field of banking, information technology and computerisation became of considerable importance as the bank expanded the scale of its operations. Banks now recognised that in order to maintain a high degree of customer satisfaction they needed to computerise. The installation of computer systems meant that records of all customers of a bank's branches had to be kept in one central location, thereby eliminating the need for each branch to retain records of transactions on ledger cards. Gone were the days when it was necessary for a customer to go only to a particular branch to do transactions. 'On-line' and 'real-time' systems, whereby data processing is under the control of the central processor or 'nerve centre', enabled banks to maintain better management control and service to customers. With such a system, information on bank customers became accessible to any branch of the bank. As a result of these changes, inter-branch transactions are greatly facilitated. Continuing its tradition of serving its customers, OCBC, in the late 1960s, was already busily planning to introduce computerisation to synchronise vast range of services. Once again, initiative in this direction came from the Chairman himself.

The introduction of new technologies into the work place would often be met with resistance and scepticism from the employees. Research into the implementation of information technology in organisations, by scholars like Schien, has shown that chief executive officers are critical change agents or role models who have great power in getting the change process started.[4] They have the obligation to 'unfreeze' entrenched routines and work attitudes and to stimulate acceptance of the new technology. Contrary to popular reference to his conservatism in business strategy, Tan Chin Tuan was quick to move the Bank into the electronic age. He was not just obsessed with things financial, but was also fascinated with electronic gadgets (such as the camera) and inventions of all kinds. During his younger days, he used to experiment growing oil palm, decarbonised his own car and was himself one of the early proud owners of a radio in Singapore. Interestingly, one of his early mentors was also someone who held several invention patents — Tan Kah Kee. Hence, it was not surprising that OCBC should be at the forefront of adopting and adapting new but proven technologies.

On the deck of his sailing ship and looking at the horizon, the Chairman knew that he had to become a 'change agent' and initiate changes that would affect the attitudes and behaviour of his employees, from senior managers to the counter-staff. The motivation to change was obvious. His extensive contact with the external environment confirmed that the age of computerisation had arrived. As the Chairman and chief executive officer of OCBC, one of Tan Chin Tuan's most critical functions was to generate information or announce decisions having discomfiting effect, and subsequently initiating the change process. Previously-held operational routines and habits would no longer be effective in meeting the accelerated change in commerce and business due to progress in technological change. Only by computerising the Bank's services could it keep down the cost of handling the customers' business. In 1969 Dr. Tony Tan, a former university lecturer and Tan Chin Tuan's nephew, was asked by the banker to prepare a blueprint for the computerisation of OCBC. A plan was put into place, starting with the formation of Computer System Advisers (CSA). Specialists' Services Private Limited, a consultant company of OCBC, held 40% of the shares in the company.[5] CSA soon became a major systems company, actively involved in the introduction of computerised services both within the banking sector and in other areas throughout the region. It won several regional contracts, including a multi-million dollar deal from the Royal Hongkong Jockey Club.

The establishment of a modern, financially-oriented computer service facility in OCBC took place over three phases covering a three-year period. The first phase saw the provision of selected 'batch-processing' computer services since initial investment in equipment, personnel and facilities were kept to a minimum. During Phase Two, additional financial and commercial applications were gradually added to provide customers with basic industrial commercial computer services, for example, inventory control, production control, market forecasting, payroll, personnel records, movement control and general ledger. Finally, in Phase Three, with the purchase of additional equipment, full 'on-line' services were provided and this included low speed, medium speed, high speed and real-time teleprocessing. By the end of 1976, OCBC went fully 'on-line' and was one of the first local banks to offer advanced, modern, time-sharing, multi-programming service to its business community. This could not be said, however, of the general banking scene. On-line banking was not progressing in tandem with Singapore's growth as an international financial hub because the majority of the

70 banks (in 1976) with a total of 200 branches still took an apprehensive and cautious attitude towards information technology and computerisation.[6]

Rapid computerisation, however, could 'de-personalise' the banking business. Assuming people were comfortable with technological change, technology-based services and centralised processing centres help promote consumer banking and discourage customers from face-to-face encounters with banking staff. To continue making customers feel positive about the Bank, OCBC promoted a form of 'relationship banking', a customer-focused strategy which proved to be highly desirable in the service-oriented banking industry. Its excellent branch network and highly trained staff helped foster a more personalised service. Customer-focus meant serving clients, not controlling them. In line with this customer-focused culture, bank managers at all levels were trained to develop a more respectful, flexible, responsive and practical approach. Everyone walking into the bank was seen as a potential customer. However, to ensure some form of corporate control, senior managers and departmental heads were made accountable for their own behaviour and conduct. This approach ties in with Tan Chin Tuan's corporate philosophy of matching accountability with authority, holding decision-makers responsible for the quality of their decisions.

OCBC concentrated on developing its human resources, upgrading its staff on new banking procedures, and employing new technologies in its operations. Tan Chin Tuan took a personal interest in this area and initiated measures to prepare the staff for more sophisticated banking operations. In one annual statement, the Chairman wrote: 'Staff development is a prime objective [and] training courses are held regularly to up-grade the skills and knowledge of the staff at all levels.'[7] In the early 1960s, the Bank purchased a huge bungalow in Holland Park and used it as a staff residential training and recreation centre. Between July 1961 and March 1963, the Bank engaged W. Stanton, the retired principal of the Midland Bank Training School to train OCBC staff. Training courses for staff were not just 'knowledge-gaining' sessions. They were also geared towards developing corporate identity and a sense of camaraderie amongst staff. In January 1970, Tan Chin Tuan invited Lee Hah Ing, the retired principal of Anglo-Chinese School, to take care of all matters relating to staff training and development. When the OCBC Centre was ready for occupancy in 1976, staff training shifted to the huge complex. Training was provided for employees at all levels, from counter-staff to managers. Trainee bank officers, recruited mainly from the local universities, were expected to become professional bankers within three to four years. Promising staff members were sent on overseas attachment to some of the biggest banks in London and the United States. Monetary awards were also provided to encourage staff to acquire professional certificates and diplomas in banking. The Bank also created an Efficiency Council and courtesy campaigns or 'Good Customs Relations' campaigns were organised regularly.

To complement these activities, OCBC in 1975 produced a small 'customer service' caricature booklet (published in two languages: Malay and English) for all the staff. 'Through this light medium,' stated Lin Jo Yan, OCBC's General Manager, in the Introduction of the booklet, 'we will be able to laugh at our foibles and correct our errors as well as to pick up a few ideas to reinforce what we already know, so that we may provide more effective service to our customers.'[8] Interesting captions accompanied the drawings included: 'A friendly approach... makes all the difference to the mundane business of banking transactions'; and 'Be specially helpful to Mr Tan... and the Lims, Osmans, and Samys will flock to our bank. A satisfied customer is better advertisement than thousands of dollars spent on advertising campaigns.'[9] While the in-house, 'customer-first' handbook helped promote the name of the Bank, nothing could, however, match the gigantic 'billboard' that would rise from the site of the old OCBC building.

NOTES

1   John Stanworth and Celia Stanworth, *Work 2000: The Future for Industry, Employment and Society* (London: Paul Chapman, 1991).

2   G. C. Allen and A. Donnithorne, *Western Enterprise in Indonesia and Malaya: A Study in Economic Development* (London: Allen & Unwin, 1957).

3   Oliver Williamson, 'The Modern Corporation: Origins, Evolution, Attributes', *Journal of Economic Literature*, vol. 19 (1981): 1537–1568.

4   E. H. Schien, *Transforming Organisation* (Oxford: Oxford University Press, 1992).

5   Correspondence between Tony Tan and Tan Chin Tuan, *OCBC File*, 1 November 1972.

6   *The Straits Times*, 8 December 1976.

7   *OCBC Annual Report*, 1973, p. 8.

8   P. S. Png, *Kerja, Terhibur dan Sibur* [Laugh, Work and Grow] (Singapore: Pusat Latihan Kakitangan, OCBC, 1975).

9   Ibid., pp. 10 & 45.

CHAPTER 9

A Magnificient Obsession

The story of Tan Chin Tuan and the making of a powerful banking institution is incomplete if we make no reference to the OCBC Centre. This chapter documents the story of its construction and what it means to the man who described the building as his 'magnificent obsession'. The OCBC Centre became a symbol of Tan Chin Tuan's extraordinary vision in the re-defining of banking.

The Site

Befittingly, the OCBC Centre occupies an area known to be the 'birth spot' of modern Singapore: the place where Sir Stamford Raffles first embarked on the mouth of the Singapore River in late January 1819. It formed the south-west bank of the river and was given the name of 'Kampong Chuliah' under the Raffles Town Plan of 1822. The area had three major streets: Malacca Street, Market Street and Chulia Street (formerly Kling Street). Within this location, largely poor but what Raffles described as 'industrious' Chinese and Indian immigrants settled and provided the essential manual and commercial services which sustained the economic buoyancy of 19th century Singapore. Up till the 1860s, the span of offshore area between the Singapore and Rochore Rivers became the British port of call frequented by Chinese junks, Bugis prahus, British and American clippers, and mercantile ships of many nations. To facilitate this international arrival of ships, rows of godowns or warehouses belonging to British imperial merchants such as Edward Boustead and Alexander Guthrie and successful Chinese merchant-compradores such as Tan Kim Seng and Tan Kim Ching, lined the river bank known as Boat Quay.

Interestingly, Kampung Chuliah was also historically linked to the activities of Indian money-lenders, popularly known to non-Indian Singaporeans as *chettiars*. They often operated as one-man firms, occupying much of Market Street and Malacca Street. While the chettiars charged high interest rates, they performed an important economic role in providing essential start-up capital or expansion funds for small-time traders, including Chinese businessmen, who could not obtain any bank loans without security. By the turn of the century, the Chinese also ventured into banking in Singapore and Malaya. In that respect, Kampung Chuliah was the birth-place of the OCBC; and 60 years later, a giant monolith took centre stage on this very site. Since the 1930s, the head office of OCBC, the China Building, was located on 10 small shop- house lots. The building, designed by Major Keys (who also built the Fullerton Building) had become something of a national monument. It was promoted as a tourist attraction, and was featured on postcards and 20-cent stamps. In 1968, while Tan Chin Tuan was Chairman of the bank, the OCBC tendered for land adjacent to the China Building and amalgamated them into a single plot to develop the OCBC Centre.

On 15 November 1968, the Urban Renewal Department — formed in 1966 as part of the Housing and Development Board and then a separated Urban Redevelopment Authority in 1974 — released for sale, 14 sites within the financial and business district known as 'Golden Shoe'. The First Sale of Sites, which was held in June 1967, resulted in the outright sale of seven out of fourteen sites, attracting investments in land and building totalling $58 million. The First Sale demonstrated that, besides encouraging active private participation, Singapore's comprehensive Urban Renewal Programme could play an important economic role. This was done by providing opportunities for investment, employment, tourist promotion, increasing the Government's tax base, attracting foreign capital, earning foreign exchange, and activating the building industry.

Unlike the First Sale, which was mainly hotel-oriented, the Second Sale's focus was the development of good class office accommodation. Tenders were awarded based on a set of criteria, such as the level of capital investment involved, number of prospective jobs, revenue potential, architectural merits of the development proposal and premium offered. Incentives, such as a down payment of 20% on signing the Building Agreement, and the payment of the balance of 80% of the tendered land premium to be spread over ten years without interest, were offered by the government to stimulate sales. Fifty-seven tenders were received and all but two sites were successfully tendered for. All in all, the sale generated an estimated $233 million in investment and created more than 20,000 jobs. OCBC successfully tendered for a 44,600 square-foot site adjacent to China Building at $70 per square foot. The site had a 'guide value' of $50 per square foot. Initially, a local architect drew up the design for the proposed building but the design failed to excite the OCBC chairman. For Tan Chin Tuan, this building had to be very special, having the ability to capture the spirit and ideals epitomising the Bank. It had to be an eye-opener.

The Vision

It is difficult to miss the OCBC Centre. This monolith towers above the historical section of the Singapore River. Today, it is one of the major landmarks of Singapore's 'Golden Shoe', an area that has become a lasting symbol of the country's success in urban development. A symbol of corporate wealth and success, and de facto expression of urban diversity, the OCBC Centre quickly transformed Singapore's city skyline. Rising regally a staggering 198.12 metres from the ground, the OCBC Centre was in 1976 the tallest building in Asia outside of Japan. It occupied a total land area of 6,565.45 square metres and took, from the time sub-station works were started in September 1971, just five years to complete. The building cost was borne entirely by additional share-holder capital; not a single cent of customers' deposits was used. The fact that the building rose 52 storeys coincided with Tan Chin Tuan's 52 years of service to the Bank. On 1 October 1976 the $100 million, granite-clad OCBC Centre was officially opened and the OCBC and Singapore possessed the biggest banking hall in Southeast Asia, if not in the world.

The man responsible for the OCBC Centre was not trained as an architect, city planner or engineer. He was not even in the construction industry, nor in real estate development. The story of the OCBC Centre is really the story of a banker and his extraordinary vision. Tan Chin Tuan harboured a dream of building such a building for several decades. In his own words: 'I'd planned it 30 years ago. I was acquiring neigh-bouring buildings as and when I could. I always acquire buildings next to any of my branches.' It was, however, not merely a question of acquiring land and constructing the building. It took extraordinary courage on the part of Tan Chin Tuan to move away from the norm and venture into uncharted territory, especially in an area he had little training. Tan Chin Tuan pioneered a trend in Singapore to project a corporate image through spectacular architecture. As we have already seen, the OCBC chairman was always ready to do away with parochial and outdated ideas, images and processes. He was, on the other hand, always keen to explore new and exciting developments. Tan felt that the old headquarters premises had 'outlived' itself because, by the 1960s, OCBC was Singapore's leading local bank. He thought that the bank's reputation and its famous slogan 'Solid As A Rock' had to be reflected through the brick-and-mortar of the building.

What Tan Chin Tuan had in mind was something which went beyond the imagination of local architects, engineers and city planners at that time. He wanted a modern Singapore 'skyscraper'. Although skyscrapers have been a feature of American architecture since the 1930s (notable examples being the Chrysler and Empire State Buildings) the term was not one which was in common use in the Singapore of 1960s or even the 1970s. Etymologically, the word was meant to describe a building that was so tall as to literally 'scrape the sky.' Beyond its imposing height, a skyscraper had to be filled with space that could be used to commercial advantage. The structure had to be functional, productive and 'lucrative'. Above all, the banker wanted a superstructure that people would immediately identify as the OCBC.

During the formative years of this project, many of Tan Chin Tuan's close associates could not visualise what he had in mind. In any case, the mammoth project would require a huge financial outlay. The bank's corporate headquarters needed only a few floors; the rest was, in retrospect, one big speculative gamble that was probably not worth taking. But the chairman was not looking at the building's short-term impact. He thought a few steps ahead of many others in the directors' boardroom. The intangible benefits, in terms of publicity and corporate name recognition OCBC would receive for building Southeast Asia's tallest building far outweighed any possible loss the Bank might suffer from the venture. Tan Chin Tuan knew that all major newspapers and business journals in Singapore and the surrounding region would be there to cover the story of the OCBC Centre's official opening. The building would become a household name and even become essential sight-seeing for tourists. The monolith would also serve as a giant billboard, publicising the strength and efficiency of the Bank and its branches throughout Singapore. On this basis, OCBC's ability to finance and build the record-breaking building was a sound investment as a corporate undertaking. Tan Chin Tuan then began his search for the ultimate superstructure and the architect who could make his vision come through.

The architecture of the OCBC Centre is significant not only because it breaks new stylistic and technical grounds or that it was in the early 1970s, the largest urban renewal project ever undertaken. Tan Chin Tuan's vision gave Singapore planners and developers a new genre in office buildings or corporate headquarters construction. Besides exuding dignity, responsibility and affluence in the glossy finishes and luxurious interiors, the OCBC Centre symbolises an innovative, dynamic and progressive organisation. Besides the OCBC, the building houses hundreds of professional firms and this promotes an intra-networking of business contacts and opportunities. The eventual blueprint was a reflection of the combined geniuses of two of the most progressive minds of the time, one a banker and the other an architect.

The Blueprint

The renowned American-Chinese architect I. M. (Ieoh Ming) Pei was Tan Chin Tuan's choice to bring his vision to reality. Pei, one of the 20th century's most innovative and prolific architects, is noted for his ability to fuse a classical concern for elegance of form with a contemporary concern for functional efficiency. In America, he created the East Wing of the National Gallery of Art in Washington, DC, the John F. Kennedy Library in Boston, the National Atmospheric Research Centre in Boulder, Colorado, the Kirklin Clinic in Alabama, and many other buildings of major significance. Each of these buildings provided a memorable, abstract composition that, rather than literally representing the functions they housed, spoke instead of the qualities and aspirations of the institutions they embodied. They were buildings oriented towards human use, filled with light, organised around ample and clear gathering places, and yet larger than the mere conglomeration of their functions.

Not surprisingly, the services of a man of I. M. Pei's stature was not easy to secure. Indeed, when Tan Chin Tuan first approached Pei, the architect politely declined. But this made Tan even more persistent. In May 1969, on one of Pei's several visits to Singapore, Tan contacted him and asked him to convey his warmest regards to Pei's father, Pei Cho E, an old family friend. At the same time, he again expressed to Pei his desire to build a 'national monument'. The day after Pei left for Taiwan, Tan received a telegram from him confirming his acceptance of the commission; the design of the OCBC Centre was in good hands. The warm friendship between the two elderly gentlemen — Tan and Pei's father — and their families had triggered off the positive response. In early 1970, Pei presented one blueprint which was translated into reality six years later.

In retrospect, Singapore contributed much to the survival of the firm of I. M. Pei and Partners. In the 1970s the city-state was transforming itself into a business and financial hub. It was also during this period that I. M. Pei and Partners was in financial trouble.[1] Salaries of its 150 employees were frozen and debt mounted. The recession in the United States of the early 1970s forced a slowdown in the construction industry. Small architectural firms could survive the recession by taking up budget projects, but not I. M. Pei and Partners, which only handled large-scale prestigious projects. Pei was, however, a tough man and 'persevered in an Eastern way [and] adept at negotiating his way out of setbacks'.[2] Three major projects landed in his hands — OCBC Centre, the Raffles City complex, and an office building overlooking New York's South Street Seaport. A wealthy Singaporean shipping magnate awarded the last project to him.

Tan Chin Tuan's vision of the architectural features of the building was crystal clear. He wanted a structure that matched his famous dictum, 'Solid As A Rock'. The 'Rock' refers to the Rock of Gibraltar, which stands at the southern tip of the Iberian Peninsula and commands the western entrance to the Mediterranean Sea. In Greek mythology, the Rock of Gibraltar and ancient Abila (now Mount Acho) formed the two great Pillars of Hercules, the legendary hero noted for his strength and courage. At the same time, the building would also reflect the philosophy of OCBC — solid as a rock, conservative yet modern, dynamic and progressive in a calculated and stable manner, and efficient in service and prestigious in image.

The two great minds met on several occasions, reviewing many plans and models. Each time they met, Tan Chin Tuan was always enthusiastic about his vision of a powerful structure and often lifted his fisted arms bent at the elbows. The final blueprint was eventually agreed upon. The superstructure would be supported by a twin core structure — probably influenced by the lifted arms of the Chairman. Although nestled amongst rows of old shophouses and office buildings, the OCBC Centre was conceptualised not to reflect such 'antiquity'. In Pei's words: 'The OCBC Building has nothing to do with the shacks along Singapore River.'[3] It was a daring project which captured the imagination of hundreds of professionals, thousands of skilled and unskilled workers, and the population at large.

The Contractors

The OCBC Centre project was challenging but, at the same time, trying for many key people involved in it. Tan Chin Tuan's approach to its construction was straightforward — just as the best people were given the responsibilities to build up the assets and reputation of the Bank, the best people must also be recruited to erect its building. The OCBC Centre (Private) Limited, a wholly owned subsidiary responsible for the project, was formed and spearheaded by Goh Sin Tub. Tan handpicked the OCBC assistant general manager to head the Control Committee of architects and consultants. The search for the best brains in skyscraper construction began soon after. The strategy adopted was to integrate expertise from overseas and those within Singapore.

The OCBC needed a first-class builder, a general contractor who could successfully carry out the plans of the architects and structural engineers. The firm had to have a reputation for honesty and the ability to get the job done on schedule. However, at this time, skyscraper construction was still something new to Singapore. I. M. Pei advised Tan that the construction of 'highrise buildings require very special expertise; both on the part of the engineers as well as the contractors and labour. But you do learn quickly.

However, in order to learn quickly, you have to learn from others first, so you would not make the same mistakes.'⁴ It was decided that, instead of one, two main contractors would be engaged to handle the massive project.

In June 1973, Morrison-Knudsen International of USA and Low Keng Huat Construction Company of Singapore were invited to form a joint venture. The contract totalled US$22 million and was scheduled to be completed in 31 months. From its humble beginnings in 1912 in Boise, Idaho (in USA), Morrison-Knudsen became an internationally-reputed company with expertise in high-rise building knowledge and technology. They were also responsible for building such legacy projects as the Hoover Dam, the Vehicle Assembly Building at the Kennedy Space Centre and the Trans-Alaska pipeline. Construction of the Singapore project was under the overall direction of Harry Ackerman, their Far East vice-president, with Len Peterson as the project manager and R. D. Rowery as the business manager. The Singapore firm of Low Keng Huat was selected because of its experience in local labour and building conditions. Both contractors had excellent track records and for Low Keng Huat it was one project that would enhance its name in the local construction industry.

Right from the start, the contractors recognised that the construction of the 'highly sophisticated' OCBC Centre would present unusual problems.⁵ Architect Pei himself admitted that the OCBC Centre 'is a difficult building even for us in the United States'.⁶ The main contractors' modus operandi was essentially to decentralise work and provide a large measure of autonomy to the subcontractors. Unlike the centralised method which required the main contractors to engage a large staff of expediters to monitor the fabrication of materials and their timely delivery to the construction site, this strategy gave freedom and trust to the subcontractors and this motivated them to put their specialised knowledge and skill to work and to co-ordinate their effort with the overall operation. This also meant finding responsible subcontractors who would meet their part of the schedule and share the philosophy of working in a spirit of mutual co-operation. The main contractors, on their part, had to be totally familiar with the engineering problems presented at the site.[7] Ordinary building equipment would not do. More sophisticated machinery and equipment, such as tower cranes, had to be deployed. This meant learning on the job for many engineers, foremen and workers. They would take the drawing plans and specifications, and prepare an itemised list of materials, equipment, and supplies with subcontractors. Good record keeping, including costing of equipment, materials and labour, was very essential. They prepared detailed schedules for every stage of the construction process, estimated the labour required, and arranged to have materials fabricated and installed. Because the site was limited in terms of open space for storage, much of the material had to be prefabricated and installed or assembled at the building site.

Constructing Singapore's tallest building in the early 1970s also required the services of specialists. Goh Sin Tub and his committee scoured Singapore for qualified and reputable subcontractors and suppliers of materials. It is no exaggeration to say that the construction of the OCBC Centre had lined up the best of these local expertise into a 'Who's Who' list in the industry. All in, there were 35 specialists in construction and materials supply, each with his own task and schedule to accomplish.

The building presented problems to architects and engineers for which no precedents existed in Singapore. They had no bases upon which to find solutions. However, everyone in the project recognised that the accomplishment of the aspiration of having a hand in Southeast Asia's tallest building required friendly relations and open dialogue between parties at all levels. Goh Sin Tub and his Control Committee, consisting of 20 key architects, engineers, quantity surveyors, consultants and senior executives from the Bank ably marshalled the whole contingent of professional personnel. This 'backroom' team was instrumental in guiding the project to completion. More than 200 top-level meetings and sub-committee sessions were held to ensure that all problems were tackled quickly and efficiently. But it was not all work and seriousness. Sometimes a simple message teaser could ease the tension everyone in the Control Committee was experiencing. Goh related how worried he became when he received a note from Harry Ackerman, with the message '... there is a matter of some importance which we should discuss'. Frustrated, Goh reluctantly turned to the next page and broke out in a hearty laughter. Ackerman had enclosed a picture of the 'Leaning Tower of Pisa' with all its unusual specifications written and named it the 'OCBC Centre'. Goh Sin Tub commented on what made the core group tick:

> Along the way, we had our full share of disagreements and tensions, but we soon grew into a very closely-knit team ready to work hard and co-operate together, despite occasional sharp differences in opinion from time to time.... Before long we began to realise that this project was more than just another job. It absorbed our entire beings, body and soul. We often lost all sense of time as we discussed into the night and came back on site on Sundays and holidays to look into various things. [8]

The commitment displayed by Goh and his team was exemplary. Such intense desire to succeed and to rally the team towards a common goal was not extraordinary in the OCBC organisation. It was a common cultural norm nurtured amongst the managers, senior managers and directors who knew that the Bank would not be rated Singapore's premier financial institution and one of the world's top 500 banks if not for the resoluteness and passion shown by their long-serving Chairman, Tan Chin Tuan. He was the role model that everyone wanted to emulate.

Although Tan had, in the past, refurbished or developed old and new buildings on land acquired by the Bank, the OCBC Centre project presented him his greatest challenge. William Starrett, the contractor of the Empire State Building, once commented that the builder of a skyscraper could be compared to the general of an army.[9] He had to lead and in-spire his closest officers who would then transfer the same enthusiasm and pride to the thousands of soldiers under their control. This was exactly what the OCBC Chairman did. He personally spent three hours a week discussing the project with Goh Sin Tub, and other key architects and consultants who frequently flew into Singapore from all over the world — New York, Hong Kong, Sydney and Perth.

In the larger sense, the project was a great experience for local contractors, architects and sub-contractors — and for the Bank's real estate management arm. Prior to this, the Bank's expertise had been established in all kinds of projects including office buildings, shopping centres, residential and industrial sectors, warehousing, and hotel business. As project manager, Goh Sin Tub did well in co-ordinating the various teams and keeping to the construction schedule as well as, very importantly, contributing their expertise towards management of the project. Time was of great importance. A slight delay meant additional costs. Liquidated damages were high for the contractors. This had a bearing on the Bank as well: if the project was held up, it would be liable to pay penalties.

Building the the OCBC Centre

The project demanded a whole range of scientific testing in several key laboratories throughout the world. Soil foundation reviews were done in New York, computer runs on the structure in the United Kingdom, wind tunnel and wind deflection tests in Sydney, and granite hanging tests in Germany, Italy and London.[10] The grandiose project was delayed by about nine months for several reasons, such as shortage of building materials and labour (both skilled and unskilled), difficulties encountered in piling operations and other site works due to poor soil condition, bad weather and unfavourable market condition.

In many ways, the project became a pioneering example for the construction industry in Singapore. High-rise buildings, especially if it carries the name of the owner, have to justify the millions spent in creating a corporate architectural image. Leaving aside the technical details, there are several interesting features and 'firsts' which the construction of the OCBC Centre had produced:

- The OCBC Centre was erected by an innovative method that permitted construction to progress concurrently on three 14-storey increments, each supported by a pair of huge transfer girders spanning between two massive concrete service cores spaced 35 metres apart.[11] Each of the slip form-constructed cores was a semi-circular structure with an inside diameter of 20 metres. Besides supporting the transfer girders, the cores provided the space for lifts, toilets, air conditioning equipment, stairwells and storage.
- For the first time in local construction history, four passenger goods hoists called 'Super Scando' were deployed. These high speed and high capacity hoists could carry a maximum of two tons compared to the standard of one

ton and hydraulic drive with variable speed up to 315 feet per minute compared to the standard speed of 130 feet per minute.

- In many ways, the OCBC Centre is a piece of meticulously-sculptured granite rock. Granite was the best choice as the material itself was both hardy and lasting. Italy's Sardenia granite (thermal treated) and Italian glass mosaic were imported by Dobb & Company Limited who won the contract to carry out works on all exterior core walls, including the banking hall and plaza. Using steel anchors and Guthrie Mills' scaffolding, the mechanical installation of the materials was a first in the region.

- The building used Corbin locksets in conjunction with the 'under construction master-key system' security system. Sub-contractors and suppliers used the 'construction key' to open all doors. Then when the tenant or owner inserts his own key it reactivates the 'construction master key'. The owner of the building keeps the grand master key in case of emergency. The OCBC Centre is one of the first office buildings in Singapore to have this extra precaution as a security measure.

- The building contained Southeast Asia's largest banking hall, with a height of 12.2 m and a ground area of 1,300 sq. m. There is no fussy art display, no column and the hall is free from visual obstructions. The only things I. M. Pei permitted are the two logos of the Bank cast in aluminium with special buffing of the 'Chinese junk'. To further enhance the 'Solid As A Rock' image, mirror-like, polished, stainless steel panels manufactured by Tajima Metalwork (Singapore) Pte Ltd, specialists in highly polished stainless steel and jewellery, were used for the walls. The metal, instead of marble, is a new material used extensively in the United States and Japan.

The entrance to the banking hall is encased in glass. Although this glass façade is nothing but a separation of the outdoor environment from the controlled indoor environment, it has great aesthetic importance. It made the structure a volume rather than a mass.

- An antique-gold Tai Ping carpet, 4,000 sq. ft. in size, covered the polished, reddish brown granite floor of the banking hall. It was the largest, single-piece carpet ever laid in Singapore and was custom made by Singapore Carpet Manufacturers Pte Ltd.[11a] It was transported on a ten-wheel truck and took more than 30 workers to roll it into place.

- Otis Elevator Company was awarded what was then the largest lift contract in Singapore or for any single building in Southeast Asia — a total of 29 units including 26 passenger lifts, one goods lift and two dumbwaiters.

  Acoustics of the banking hall were handled by engineer Peter Knowland, designer of the famed Sydney Opera House's acoustics system. His task was made all the more challenging because he was specifically asked to 'ensure that the sound of a busy banking hall is maintained as OCBC feels that this would be in keeping with the traditional character of its working atmosphere'.[12] Combining the sounds made by customers, staff and machines with the unceasing sounds of traffic along Chulia Street which was allowed to filter into the hall would create 'a sense of the pulse of OCBC in operation'.

The **OCBC Centre** is also one of the few buildings in Singapore to have provisions for a helicopter landing pad in case of emergencies. The completed OCBC Centre has been described in many ways. *The Straits Times*, for example, gave this description:

It is simple — almost deceptively so. It is meant to impress, and it does, but not officiously. It has a rock-like strength that gives the impression of a powerful organisation, yet one not without vision. The straight lines are softened by rounded cylindrical edges and the monotony of height is broken by three tiers of windows that break out from the solid concrete form. Its purity of form was compared by one architect to the prestigious Cartier lighter — part of the accoutrement of the well-dressed, conservative and worldly-wise managers who work in the building.[13]

Another interesting description was given by an engineering journal, *Building Materials & Equipment*:

Thought of in terms of programme, OCBC Centre reflects the well calculated progression upwards... recalls the digital calculator, a mechanical style (a less than inspiring image, some say). Moreover, its sheer size makes it stand out like an adolescent bully on a kindergarten playground. But one thing is almost certain — observers have agreed that the 52-storey tower is a marvel of engineering.[14]

Whatever impression the building created on the thousands of passers-by every day, its construction produced a 'big push' to the Singapore economy, especially when the region and the world had to face up to the severe economic dislocations resulting from the oil crisis of 1973. The largest urban renewal project in the 1970s provided jobs to thousands of workers — from project managers, architects, engineers and contractors to steel-benders, concreters, carpenters, electricians, mechanics and finish-artisans — during the 30 months of its construction. At the peak of construction, about a thousand workers were employed at one time. Indeed, it could be said that the OCBC Centre project resulted in the awarding of more tenders to both local and foreign companies than any building projects during the period 1970 to 1976. However, many of the contractors lost money because of unexpected escalation of prices in materials due to the impact of the oil crisis in 1973.

The successful completion of the OCBC Centre produced a lasting legacy and boosted the knowledge, skills and confidence of local architects, civil engineers and contractors on the construction of high-rise superstructures. As the building was completed when Singapore was still climbing out of the recession, OCBC had some difficulty in filling the building with tenants. However, when fully occupied, the Centre housed about 5,000 workers from many organisations and, in the words of Goh Sin Tub, 'with such a big community, tenants can look forward to get in-house business through better chances of establishing rapport and being able to offer the convenience of in-house proximity.'[15] In addition to the external economies for firms, the mammoth collection of professionals within a single superstructure also led to a wider network of personal and inter-firm linkages and *guanxi* being cultivated within the 'client-oriented' financial and business stronghold in Singapore.

The Grand Opening

Tan Chin Tuan's 'magnificent obsession' — the OCBC Centre, then Singapore's tallest building — was officially opened on 1 October 1976. It was a day everyone in the Bank, especially its Chairman, had waited impatiently to arrive. More than 3,000 guests, headed by Lim Kim San (then-Minister for National Development) as Guest of Honour, were invited to share the glory of the occasion. The guests formed the entire business community leadership in Singapore. Included were also international financial executives and bankers who were on their way to attend the International Monetary Fund conference in Manila.

There was a carnival atmosphere, graced by swirling bagpipers, acrobats and prancing Chinese lions. The Bank had earlier sponsored an art competition with the theme 'Singapore Skyline 76', as part of the building's inauguration celebrations. More than 200 entries were received. As the guests streamed into the banking hall, walking on the red carpet which had been laid out, they were greeted by specially-trained reception guides in their smart blue uniforms. These young ladies were the front-line 'ambassadors' of the Bank, representing the fresh, efficient and professional image of OCBC. They represented the Bank's extensive training programme of grooming young staff members who were expected to attend to customers, from small account holders to heads of business organisations. At the opening of the OCBC Centre, their primary task was to offer visitors information on the Centre itself and to conduct a tour of the huge building, if necessary. Congratulatory messages poured in from 'friends of OCBC' during the time leading up to the opening ceremony. The Right Honourable Malcolm Mac-Donald compared the OCBC Centre to the Parthenon of Athens, one of the loveliest examples of ancient classical architecture. Although the Parthenon is a 'tiny pigmy beside this giant skyscraper in Singapore, the two buildings share a common distinction'.[16] Both marked the confidence of the city-state, the 'great abilities of its people, and the outstanding competence of its Government'. Dr Chang Kia Ngau, a banker, scholar and long-time friend of Tan Chin Tuan, highlighted the fact that the 'building cost of $100 million for the magnificent OCBC Centre is entirely derived from the additional capital of the shareholders without using even a cent from the customers' deposits [and this] clearly underline[s] the Bank's policy in pursuing a course of conservative safety for all its customers.'[17]

The final word of appreciation, of course, went to Tan Chin Tuan:

> My ambition has been to help build a strong and progressive financial institution worthy of the confidence of its constituents and capable of fully serving the big and small of these regions, and Mr I. M. Pei of New York has successfully translated into concrete reality our corporate aims and image of lasting strength, continuous growth and uprightness in his conceptual design of OCBC's Headquarters. It is up to the next generation in the Bank to make this the springboard for further growth and expansion, so that OCBC may become of even greater service to these regions.[18]

As in many of his other speeches, he acknowledged the contributions of people, including the founders and pioneers of OCBC. To mark the happy occasion, the Chairman announced the inauguration of the 'OCBC Centre Scholarships' to the University of Singapore, Nanyang University, University of Malaya, Universiti Kebangsaan Malaysia, Singapore Polytechnic and Ngee Ann Technical College. These scholarships were in addition to the 'OCBC Scholarships' donated by the Bank to four universities (University of Singapore, Nanyang University, University of Malaya, and Universiti Kebangsaan Malaysia) in 1973 to commemorate the 40th Anniversary of the Bank. These scholarships reflected Tan Chin Tuan's belief that institutions of higher learning are the primary source of knowledge and that the Bank has an important role to play in nurturing young citizens.

Au Revoir

In September 1983, Tan Sri Tan Chin Tuan retired as Chairman of OCBC. Word of the impending retirement of 'Mr OCBC' had circulated widely in the business and banking circles months before the official announcement. Speculation was rife as to who would be his worthy successor. A long and eventful chapter in the history of the Bank closed with his retirement, but his legacy continues. Entrusted with the survival of OCBC in his hands during the War, Tan managed to gain the confidence of the British administration to support OCBC when they returned to power in 1945. A strong obsession with the future of OCBC, a deep sense of moral responsibility towards the directors, shareholders and depositors, and faith in his fellow bank employees all helped Tan Chin Tuan to launch OCBC on a path of unprecedented post-war rapid growth.

Tan was a man of exceptional entrepreneurial talent and his early success in the banking business captured the admiration of the British rulers who invited him to sit in the Legislative Council. He used his increasing influence and power to consolidate OCBC. As Singapore moved into the turbulent 1950s, Tan Chin Tuan was constantly called to deal with labour problems. His abilities to resolve complex problems further strengthened his reputation, and hence, of OCBC. The banker embraced methods that enabled OCBC to expand beyond its financial businesses. Through the Bank, he acquired companies that were once the proud strongholds of the British and 'localised' them subsequently. This acquisition strategy strengthened the foundation of the OCBC Group or Family in the 1950s and 1960s. As the city-state of Singapore enjoyed its economic 'take-off' during the 1970s, OCBC grew in tandem and joined the rank of the top 500 banks in the world. The OCBC and its subsidiaries adopted prudent global and domestic expansionary strategies. Beyond being a clever entrepreneur and banker, Tan Chin Tuan lived his ideals and manifested his visions. In our final chapter we shall gain a deeper understanding of the ethical principles that drove Tan Chin Tuan and how these manifested in his management and leadership style.

NOTES

1 Michael T. Cannell, *I. M. Pei: Mandarin of Modernism* (New York: Carol Southern Books, 1995), p. 231.
2 Ibid., p. 232.
3 Interview, *Harvard Asia Pacific Review*, Summer 1998.
4 Interview, *Building Materials & Equipment*, September 1976.
5 *The EM-Kayan*, January 1975, p. 13.
6 Interview, *Building Materials & Equipment*, September 1976.
7 *Building Materials & Equipment*, November/December 1974.
8 *Building Materials & Equipment*, September 1976, p. 33.
9 John Tauranac, *The Empire State Building: The Making of A Landmark* (New York: Scribner, 1995), p. 180.
10 *Building Materials & Equipment*, September 1976, p. 33.
11 *The EM-Kayan*, April 1974, p. 10.
11a *The Straits Times*, 1 October 1976,
12 Quoted in *The Straits Times*, 1 October 1976.
13 *Straits Times Annual, 1989*, p. 29.
14 *Building Materials & Equipment*, September 1976, p. 31.
15 Ibid., p. 33.
16 Speech at the opening of the OCBC Centre, 1976 (Singapore: The Tan Foundation).
17 Ibid.
18 Ibid.

CHAPTER 10

ON ETHICAL PRINCIPLES AND MANAGEMENT LEADERSHIP

When a man of Tan Chin Tuan's stature retires after serving a gigantic corporation for more than half a century, an evaluation of his contributions is inevitable. The popular criticism levied against the Chairman by his rivals, critics and even some of his staff was that he was too conservative in his business strategies and dealings. This conservatism, they argue, resulted in OCBC losing its premier position among Singapore banks. But judging from the historical financial figures of OCBC and the OCBC Group, Tan Chin Tuan and his trusted generals created an economic empire they can be proud of. When he became joint managing director of OCBC in 1942, the Bank had shareholders' funds totalling $15.5 million. By the time he retired as chairman in 1983, OCBC's shareholders' funds totalled $1.2 billion. Fraser & Neave had only about $10.6 million in shareholders' funds when the banker took the reins in 1950. By the time he retired in 1983, the group's net worth had grown to $289.6 million. Great Eastern Life had total share-holders' funds of $16.9 million when Tan Chin Tuan became Chairman in 1969. The company's net asset base grew to $192.4 million when he retired in May 1992. Similarly, at the Straits Trading Company, shareholders' funds leap-frogged from $43.3 million in 1965 to $670.8 million in 1991 during the period of Tan Chin Tuan's chairmanship.[1] At the bottom-line, the banker and entrepreneur made a success of every company he led.

This book chronicles the rise and development of OCBC within the historical context of Singapore's modern history and the changing external environment. Specifically, it analysed the contributions of Tan Chin Tuan towards institutionalising OCBC. The banker is a man of patience, and he possesses a cool, thinking mind that allows him to handle complex situations and come out stronger than expected. It is therefore pertinent to end the book with a chapter that centres on legacies: What accounts for Tan Chin Tuan's transformation from apprentice to merchant banker, to business leader and to institution builder?

Philosophy of Life

What is Tan Chin Tuan's secret? It lies in a few popular slogans which inspired him throughout his corporate career: His philosophy of life was influenced by sayings such as 'Forbear, Forgive and Forget', 'Power tends to corrupt while absolute power corrupts absolutely', and 'Nothing but the best'. On the question of power, the banker argued that autocratic dictators in history like Adolf Hitler and Ferdinand Marcos were classic examples of individuals who wielded absolute power and yet plunged nations and peoples into chaos and suffering. As the all-powerful chairman, he had the final say in many matters but he says: 'I never tried to have full power but reminded myself that others must have something to say.' Nevertheless, he used his resources, formal authority and power to develop still more power. Unlike an unscrupulous dictator, he recognises that power comes with responsibility and certain moral obligations.

As a banker and chairman of OCBC, Tan Chin Tuan set himself a high standard in maintaining clearly-defined policies, moral leadership, sound management practices, nd regular reinforcement of ethical decision-making and behaviour so that top executives who have passed through the portals of the OCBC 'training school' could attempt to learn and emulate him. 'I try to give the best and then better than the best.' His desire for perfectionism pervades many aspects of life, including food. He would attempt to provide the best food for himself and his guests.

His advice to budding entrepreneurs and executives is also based on his personal perception of greed. A little success always leads to an obsession for bigger and quicker success. As he says:

> Greed is a prelude to downfall. Most people want to take [rewards]. To be successful, you should give before you take. I never asked what compensation I'd get. Started with a bank that was almost insolvent. It had almost nothing but once I got the bank on firm footing.... I took.[1a]

What he 'took' from OCBC was, according to Lee Seng Wee, 'far less than has been voted to him by the Board of Directors, and only a fraction of that paid to the chairmen of similar banks in Singapore [and] he has steadfastly refused to accept any retirement gratuity at all.'[2] For a man who worked all his life to institutionalise OCBC, Tan Chin Tuan's interest in the Bank is a mere 3% compared to the 30% stake held by the family of the late Lee Kong Chian.

There is no official figure on the personal wealth of Tan Chin Tuan but for those who have succeeded materially, he advises: 'Prosper but do not be arrogant', or 'Enjoy the fruits of hard work with humility'. He is proud of being told that he is considered scrupulous and, to him, he prefers 'having a good reputation to having all the wealth in the world'. His nephew, Dr. Tony Tan, says that '[Tan Chin Tuan] is completely honest — very unusual for Chinese business-man of the time.'[3]

Sharing Fortunes

The success of an entrepreneur is often measured by his or her contributions to society. Good corporate citizenship includes a commitment to uplifting the lives of the less fortunate by providing financial assistance to needy and deserving organisations. Tan Chin Tuan believes that one must always have a heart for ordinary people who are in need. As chairman of several companies within the OCBC Group, he strongly promoted the award of bursaries and scholarships to deserving children of employees. He also presented gifts and money to old folks during special occasions, such as Christmas. On one of his visits to a home for the elderly, he noticed that they had no exercise equip-ment. He bought the equipment, not only because of the importance of staying healthy but also because he believes that men of power and wealth often fail to understand what ordinary people, especially the elderly, go through in life.

At the corporate level, Tan Chin Tuan understood the need for corporate philanthropy because it is one major component of an enterprise's relationship to society at large. However, OCBC's first priority was to its shareholders, and as such, the Bank must consistently be profitable.[4] Tan stated, 'I got directors [of OCBC] to agree that we pass a rule that the bank must not give more than nominal amounts to charity because the money is shareholders' money. If we want to be generous, let's do it out of our own pockets.'[5]

The banker's personal efforts in helping local charitable organisations are, more often than not, not made public. Tony Tan commented that despite his heavy responsibilities, Tan Chin Tuan 'does a lot of good work, visits old folks home and helps those in need [and] yet [is] reserved and shuns publicity'.[6] A search in *The Straits Times* on reports relating to his contributions to social work during the 1970s draws a blank. Two foreign non-profit organisations also received his support. They were the Salk Institute and the Needham Library in Cambridge. The former is based in the United States and conducts biological and medical research. Tan Chin Tuan is the first Asian to join the prestigious International Council of the Salk Institute for Biological Studies. In June 1984, he gave US$100,000 to the Institute when a special research programme needed extra funding. The Needham Library is part of the Joseph Needham Research Institute which centres on the studies of the history and philosophy of Chinese culture and science. During one of his fund-raising trips in the Far East, its founder, the late Joseph Needham, was in Singapore and had the opportunity to meet up with Tan Chin Tuan. Needham had not been very successful in his bid to raise £350,000 to refurbish and expand the library in the Institute.

In 1984, Tan Chin Tuan donated £350,000 to the Needham Research Institute and the East Asian History of Science Library was named in his honour. He was not at the opening of the resource centre because he 'did not like travelling and did not want to publicise [him]self.'[7] The chairman of OCBC is himself a keen supporter of Chinese studies and culture. Indeed, it was said that Tan Chin Tuan derived much inspiration from the Tang poet, Li Bai, who said that men of power did not understand what ordinary people went through in life.[8] The act of giving is a key to lasting happiness.

Tan Chin Tuan's personal involvement in philanthropy exemplifies what many wealthy, self-made entrepreneurs throughout the world have been doing. The most notable example in Asia is Konosuke Matsushita who gave away US$291 million out of his own pocket and another US$99 million from corporate funds.[9] Such personal and corporate philanthropy instils pride in the employees who, in turn, show greater loyalty and attachment to the organisation.[10] According to Levy, '[i]n future, corporate philanthropists will be judged not only by the charitable performance of their business but also by how well employee contributions in time and treasure were encouraged and rewarded [and that] employees will take pride in knowing that the business that absorbs so much of their time and attention stands for something beyond the undiluted pursuit of self-interest.'[11]

More than anything else, Tan believes in a golden rule, which is, 'Do unto others what you want others to do unto you. Don't do to others what you don't want them doing to you'. This adage hails from the days of the Roman Empire when the Romans practised the principle of *do ut des* or 'to give and to receive' in their social relationships between patrons and clients. This basic rule ties in closely with the principle of reciprocal or mutual obligation. Harvard management professor, John Kotter points this out:

> One of the ways that successful managers generate
> power in their relationships with others is to create a
> sense of obligation in those others. When the manager
> is successful, the others feel that they should — rightly
> — allow the manager to influence them within certain
> limits. Successful managers often go out of their way

to do favours for people whom they expect will feel an
obligation to return those favours.[12]

The experienced banker and entrepreneur lived this principle to perfection especially in his handling of clients, business associates, dignitaries, employees and anyone whose path and his cross. Learning from his mentors during the early years of his banking career, Tan Chin Tuan understands the importance of upholding reciprocal obligation, not just in the world of banking but also in social relationships. Whenever a customer deposits money or borrows it, a relationship of reciprocal obligation is established between customer and bank. The customer expects the bank to safeguard the money invested and, in providing loans, the bank expects the customer to repay within a certain agreed period. Indeed, the concept of 'reciprocal obligation' lies at the heart of 'ethical' banking, and when a bank fails to abide by this concept it moves into the murky world of usury.

Applying this principle to other broader aspects of life, Tan Chin Tuan is able to create a wide network of friends and business contacts. He always strives to maintain the goodwill achieved. He has the ability to diffuse difficult and sensitive situations and, in the process, gained not only power but also long-term friendships. His view is this: 'If you can, make friends — if you cannot make friends, don't make enemies. I try not to make enemies and retain friends.' He recalled the days not long after the War had ended when, as the managing director of OCBC, he visited London and was only able to meet with the assistant manager of the international division of the Midland Bank. He did not fret or complain. Years later when he retired in 1983 he received good wishes from many heads of the largest banks in the world, including the chairman of the Midland Bank. Lasting friendships had been formed.

Finally, in life, one has to follow the 'Boy Scout Rule', which is to be prepared for any form of danger or unexpected news, for ups and downs, as in the business cycles of boom and recession. To illustrate his beliefs, Tan Chin Tuan relates an interesting real-life encounter:

> When I was Manager of the Properties Department, I often made visits to rubber estates in outlying corners of Malaya, and once encountered a tiger when I was only armed with an umbrella. In those days, I carried less meat than I do now, but to a hungry tiger I should still have looked pretty appetising. After eyeing me critically for some time, the tiger walked away, thinking, perhaps that a rock would be indigestible. Sad to say, such a hair-raising experience could evoke little response from me now!

The 'lunch-time' story was probably told many times in private but it was made known publicly in March 1975 during his speech to celebrate his 50 years of association with OCBC. While it drives home a subtle message, it also shows the humorous side of the banker who loves to include amusing anecdotes in his speeches. In his speech at the 50th Anniversary celebration of Tiger Beer, he concluded with the story of an American soldier who returned to camp in a drunken state and was ordered to report to his captain. 'There's no need for you to drink like this,' the officer lectured him. 'If you could stay sober, you might become a corporal, or even a sergeant.' 'Captain,' the soldier replied, 'the fact is that when I have a few drops of lager in me, I feel like a colonel!' There is also the story of a bank manager and his customer who was asking for a loan: 'If you can guess which of my eyes is false, I'll give you the loan,' said the manager. 'The left eye, Sir,' said the man, without any hesitation. 'You are absolutely right, but how on earth could you tell?' 'It looks far more sympathetic!' Stories and anecdotes (especially coming from the chairman himself) are not mere jokes to ease tension and work pressure. They serve as symbols or imageries underlining the strength and uniqueness of a progressive cor-poration. Using his own stories to motivate his colleagues, Tan Chin Tuan for more than half a century went through the vagaries of business cycles and each time his prepared-ness for the worst had led OCBC and its subsidiaries to greater heights.

Corporate Philosophy

Tan Chin Tuan did not operate a corporation for short-term gains. Throughout this book, we can see that his life-long ambition was to nurture a culture and management style that would ensure that OCBC remains a powerful banking and financial institution in the world, long after his retire-ment. Hence, his business model is based on a simple maxim, that for an enterprise to grow in size and stature, profit-maximisation should not be seen as the engine that drives the organisation. In neo-classical theory, the firm is usually an organisation that pursues short-run share-price maximi-sation for its principals: the stockholders. Tan Chin Tuan, on the other hand, was more concerned with a long-run market-share maximising strategy or growth. His innovative approach to sustainable growth led him to engage the Bank in cross-shareholding in non-banking enterprises. In this way, two objectives were achieved. First, the strategy ensured group solidarity, with the Bank at the centre of the stable of companies. Second, in the process, he (and, hence, OCBC) acquired more autonomy to act on behalf of the directors and employees of the newly-acquired enterprise by pursuing long-term growth.

Critics of Tan Chin Tuan's business policy sometimes question his conservatism. They argue that OCBC could fully maximise its potential, and hence its profits, if only the Chairman had been more aggressive in positioning the Bank in the financial retail market. The mid-1960s and 1970s were on the whole good years for the economies of Singapore and Malaysia. Banks were in a feverish mood to tap new opportunities and, by the end of the 1970s, OCBC was dislodged as the largest bank in both countries. During this period Tan Chin Tuan steered the OCBC Group almost single-handedly along what *Euromoney* magazine described as an

> ...unhurried pace that brooks no interference from out-side forces, ignores competitive pressures and does not seem aware of the chafing and frustration felt by ex-ecutives within the bank, who want to see the OCBC play a more active and aggressive part in the market.[13]

Some observers in the banking community accuse OCBC of having done next to nothing to help the growth of the Asian Dollar market, a symbol of national pride to many Singaporeans. Within the Bank itself, some disenchanted employees left for greener pastures. It did not matter to the experienced banker that OCBC was not in the pole position because, in his own words, 'like a sensible motorist, I prefer to drive at a speed which I consider the optimum. It is unwise to accelerate merely because of the fear of being overtaken.'[14]

While the Bank could gain short-run share-price maximi-sation for its stockholders through a less risk-averse lending policy, Tan Chin Tuan had a more lofty vision for the organi-sation. The Depression and the Pacific War had instilled in him a life-long principle. He saw himself as the guardian of the Bank's interests and those of its subsidiaries as well as the interests of the workers and shareholders. His view was shared by the rest of the directors. As the 'inner chamber' of the OCBC Group, the chairman and his fellow directors considered themselves as custodians, husbanding resources against any financial crisis. They regarded themselves as investors picking the winners in the long run. The 'Chairman's Statements' in the 1977 Annual Report clearly illustrates this corporate thinking:

> We have just emerged from another year of upheavals in exchange rates, sluggish economic growth, recurring threat of excessive inflation and stagnating world trade. In such circumstances, which have been described as 'chaotic', your Board has been more mindful than ever of the Bank's prime responsibility to depositors, and has accepted constraints on rapid business expansion to avoid exposure to abnormal risks. Your Board also believes in the long term policy of retaining the unwavering confidence of its customers and stockholders by striving for steady and continuous rather than spectacular and irregular rates of growth.[15]

The Bank was therefore committed to a policy of frugality, preservation of wealth and a reasonable return on capital — principles to which founder members of OCBC were themselves committed. The following anecdote made its round throughout the business circle regarding the Bank's idea of frugality:

> A charitable organisation mounted a donation drive. Major corporations and leading businessmen were approached for their generosity. Apparently, OCBC donated some trifling sum. When the acknowledgement to all donors was made, it was decided that as a matter of curiosity the organisers would go round the dinner

table to see how much each of the OCBC directors had given in his personal capacity. One gave $100,000 and another $1 million!

Hence, while thrift and prudence dictated the corporate philosophy, directors of OCBC knew very well their social responsibility to society.

Despite the economic downturn in the mid-1970s, the OCBC Group emerged stronger, with total shareholders' funds, assets and net profits attaining new heights in 1977. In retrospect, too, OCBC withstood well the slump that shook the Singapore economy in the mid-1980s, marked by the collapse of Chop Hoo Thye, a local abalone importer. The owners fled the country with unpaid loans of more than $100 million of loans from local and foreign banks. While local and foreign banks worried about bad loans, 'the beneficiary of this slackened period of growth may well be the Overseas Chinese Banking Corporation'.[16] This was due to the fact that the Bank had maintained the lowest loan-to-deposit ratio among the big four commercial banks and also frowned on providing unsecured loans. Instead of tightening its belt, OCBC, under its new chairman Yong Pung How, recruited 50 new bank officers and revised salaries when other banks were forced to cut cost. In 1982, Tan Chin Tuan reiterated that 'we have never forgotten that our custody of the deposits entrusted to us is sacred and consequently, while we always strive to employ our resources beneficially and profitably, we have often opted to forego more gain in exchange for reduced risks'.[17] Hence, the so-called conservative business approach was adopted with the shareholders in mind. Tan Chin Tuan instituted a system of rewards and benefits for employees — big bonuses for outstanding performance, quasi-permanent employment, seniority-based pay structure, and recreational benefits. As for the shareholders,

Tan Chin Tuan took upon himself to protect their interests and give them a sense of security for investing their savings in OCBC. At the end of the day, there were praises from the world's top bankers and business associates. For example, Walter Wriston, Chairman of Citicorp/Citibank, the world's second largest bank, wrote: 'I share your beliefs in the importance of strong capitalisation and prudent lending policies, and, above all, I admire your commitment to integrity and independent judgement, values which you have conferred upon OCBC.'[18] Harry Taylor, President, Manufacturers Hanover Corporation, added that 'over the past century, the bank's achievements, leadership and contribution to the banking community and Singapore as a whole have earned you (Tan Chin Tuan) deserved success and the highest respect of your many foreign banking friends.'[19] Indeed, the Singapore Government also emulated Tan Chin Tuan's prudent conservatism, which allowed the OCBC Group to ride comfortably against the waves of recession. The Monetary Authority of Singapore and the Government of Singapore Investment Corporation called for more selective diversification of their short and long-term portfolios, with an increasing emphasis on stable yields. The objective was to achieve more solid rather than spectacular growth.

The famous analogy associated with Tan Chin Tuan's corporate philosophy was that of the captain and his prized sailing ship. According to the banker, the captain sailing in the deep, blue sea 'must watch for the bad weather and the good'.[20] During the 1970s when the Singapore economy was generally buoyant and enjoying double-digit growth, the Chairman consistently avoided handing out money without good security, unlike many of his local rivals and much to the chagrin of his own officers. There was no urgent need to rush head-on into fine weather, hoping to gain distance quickly. Tan Chin Tuan's life experiences strengthened his senses and taught him to watch the elements with a critical eye. Looming on the horizon, the captain sensed the impending arrival of a powerful storm. To survive sailing in the wide ocean he trimmed his sails to match the weather. When the recession hit Singapore in the mid-1980s, OCBC's sailing ship inched slowly but surely towards its destination. Eventually, it touched shores safely, unscathed by the storm.

The analogy is apt not only because of the sailing ship logo of the bank. The Roman Empire was not built in a day. It was created because its generals consistently applied the Roman principle of *festina lente* — hasten slowly towards success. Similarly, for Tan Chin Tuan, 'the important thing is to reach one's destination safely', and OCBC's shareholders knew they had been spared the storm because measured by the market value of its shares, OCBC ranked 24th in the world in 1982.

Institutionalising OCBC

In Asian-Chinese societies, the basic level of economic organisation is the family-owned and family-managed private enterprise. These traditional Chinese firms tend to be rigidly hierarchical and resemble a military-type organisation in which the person at the top issues an order that is passed down the line until the person at the bottom does as he or she is told, without question or reason. According to Francis Fukuyama, the 'large, hierarchical, publicly owned, professionally managed corporation, which has been the dominant organisational form in Japan and the United States for many years, does not exist in culturally Chinese societies for all practical purposes'.[21] Studies have shown that the reason for the small scale of enterprises in Chinese societies, such as Singapore, Taiwan and Hong Kong, is that virtually all private-sector businesses are family-run.[22]

One striking feature of family businesses is the great difficulty they have in making the transition from family to professional management, a process that is essential for the enterprise to institutionalise itself and carry on beyond the lifetime of the founding family. An often-quoted case study is that of Wang Laboratories.[23] Founded by An Wang, the enterprise began as a small family business in Lowell, Massachusetts in 1951. By 1984, the computer equipment company had revenues of $2.28 billion and at one time employed 24,800 people. It was one of the great American high-tech entrepreneurial success stories. The highly autocratic An Wang adopted a typically Chinese, highly centralised hub-and-spoke management system, with all the organisation's various branches all reporting directly to the founding entrepreneur. Nevertheless, this management style did generate a successful corporate culture as long as he was at the helm. In the mid-1980s An Wang stepped down and passed the baton to his son Fred Wang who gained his position by leap-frogging over several more senior and experienced executives. This blatant nepotism destroyed the confidence and loyalty of these men and they left the company. In 1992 Wang Laboratories filed for bankruptcy.[23a]

The fact that large Chinese businesses are publicly listed do not make them any less family controlled. The founding families are usually reluctant to reduce their shares of their companies below 35% or 40%, which ensures them a major voice in the management.[24] Moreover, in most cases, many of the publicly listed shares are owned by a bank or financial company that is also controlled by the same family. This interlocking ownership often obscures the fact that a single family remains in control.

There are, however, exceptions to the rule. The World Wide Shipping Company of Hong Kong, owned by the late Sir Pao Yue-kong and the gigantic Li Ka-shing empire, also based in Hong Kong, are large corporations that were managed by professional managers. Nevertheless, they too remain family-managed. The Li Ka-shing empire was taken over by the elder Li's two Stanford-educated sons and the Pao empire was run largely by four sons-in-law.[25] The nature of Chinese familial loyalty dictates that only people within the family are to be trusted. Even if professional managers are recruited to run the affairs of the family business, their social and emotive affinity to the family-owners are often quite distant.[26]

In Singapore, OCBC and its stable of subsidiaries is one outstanding example of a successful corporation that is largely controlled by the Lee family. But there is one major difference. While the large businesses in Hong Kong and Taiwan remain family-managed, Tan Chin Tuan steered OCBC clear of family management and nepotism as early as the 1950s. In an interview with *Euromoney*, Tan explained:

> After the Japanese war, one of the first things I set out to do was to get and retain, as far as possible, the best people. This remains my policy. In any organisation people come first. Consequently, I set out to reduce nepotism. Previously, the bank readily offered employment to sons of directors and officers. When I was quite junior I was aware that some of the staff were dissatisfied because they feared that a director's son or a senior officer's son was likely to be treated preferentially. This was not the fault of the former management. It was simply the perpetuation of an old Chinese tradition. But this made the more promising bank officers feel that they might do better to seek other pastures. To set a good example, I therefore did not allow my son or my brother to join the bank. It was a painful decision.[27]

As in the case of Wang Laboratories mentioned above, misplaced trust or loyalty that overrides economic rationality often degenerates into nepotism, cronyism and generally bad business decision-making. Favouritism shown to an owner's children or a particular subordinate is certainly unhealthy for the organisation. Tan Chin Tuan set out to re-engineer the corporate structure and introduce professional management into the business system. He made a concerted move towards a modern management system with a formal division of labour, managerial hierarchy, and a decentralised, multidivisional form of organisation. This early innovative move allowed the corporation the time to institutionalise itself and carry on for generations to come.

In retrospect, Tan Chin Tuan short-circuited what business scholars describe as the distinctive three-stage evolutionary cycle for Chinese businesses.[28] In the first stage, the business is founded by an entrepreneur, usually an autocratic patriarch, who then places his immediate family members in key management positions. The second stage is the succession stage, during which the enterprise passes on to the founder's sons. Although they may inherit equal equity stakes, not all of them are equally competent or interested in running the family business. Unless one of the sons takes over the leadership of the company, authority becomes fragmented and this gives rise to disputes and, in some cases, eventual dissolution. The final stage arrives when the grandchildren of the founder assume control. Unlike the founding entrepreneur, they more readily take their prosperity for granted and are typically less motivated to sustain the business. More often than not, they pursue their own interests in other types of activities.

This gradual decline in entrepreneurial talent occurs not only in Chinese culture. Similar cycle affects many of the great American business families — the du Ponts, the

Rockfellers, and the Carnegies. This seemingly inevitable decline has been labelled the 'Buddenbrooks' phenomenon.[29] The big difference between Chinese and American (and Japanese) entrepreneurial families, however, is that the latter often succeeded in institutionalising themselves. This is precisely what Tan Chin Tuan tried to do during his long association with OCBC. At the helm of OCBC over a period of slightly over 50 years — including the last 17 years as its Chairman before retiring in 1983 — this *longue dures* gave him the opportunity to constantly review and innovate the OCBC's and its 'family of subsidiaries' expansion pathway. It is wrong, however, to say that the Chairman was not autocratic during his commanding years with the Bank. Indeed, as documented in the earlier chapters, history taught him that to get ahead of business competitors or to resolve difficult situations, one had to be resolute and decisive, to the point of being seen as autocratic by one's subordinates. During these decades, Tan Chin Tuan was able to refine his thinking on management issues and strategies that would contribute to the creation of an economic empire hinged on the nodal powerhouse, OCBC. More significantly, the long period ensured continuities — and changes, if necessary — of the successful corporate structure and culture that sustained the economic stronghold of the OCBC 'family'.

A Many Good Men

Writing in 1998, Harvard Professor Robert Reich, who was also an influential former US Secretary of Labour said, 'Ask leaders what their biggest challenge is, and you get the same answer: finding, attracting, and keeping talented people. Ask talented people what their biggest career challenge is, and you'll hear the same refrain: finding good people to work with — and to work.'[30] In the late 1960s and the 1970s, when the banking industry in Singapore was in a frenzy of expansion, Tan Chin Tuan decided to infuse OCBC with new ideas by recruiting men of exceptional talent and skills. He broke away from traditional sociability that required loyalty to be given to older, long-established social groups. Instead, he brought in the *novus homo* or 'new man' and entrusted these professional managers to lead OCBC into an era of prudent expansion — similar to those elite minority who did not belong to the inner circle of Roman nobility but were recruited to lead Rome to fame and glory.

Tan Chin Tuan had the extraordinary ability of picking the best brains for OCBC and its stable of subsidiaries. He head-hunted individuals who had a propensity to get 'involved in' and identify with groups which they join on a long-term basis. His objective was clear and straightforward; he wanted to institutionalise the Bank. In the eyes of talented and committed professionals, a powerful mission, according to Reich, is 'both a magnet and a motivator'.[31]

In the West, the 1970s was also a time when professional managers had gradually accumulated control of many large firms as public shareholding expanded and owners became too numerous and dispersed to retain effective control. Professional managers typically held little direct ownership stake in the firm. Yet many of them eventually wrested control of their companies on grounds that they would be more effective in serving ownership interests than the owners themselves. The enormous scale of operating new organisational forms in highly complex environments placed a premium on sophisticated leadership and training. The highly sought-after professional manager came to be viewed as someone with a university education and an excellent professional management track record. Tan Chin Tuan's decision to reorganise OCBC was in line with sweeping changes taking place in the West. This is not surprising because Tan always kept himself in touch with new developments through his reading and business discussions. In local circles, however, this move by the OCBC Group's patriarch to internally restructure the family business empire was seen by many observers as both timely and revolutionary.

Undoubtedly, 'OCBC Executives' were amongst the very best in the market. This was evidenced by the fact that the Singapore Government sought out a good number of its top senior officers for 'national service'. Some of the more high-profiled OCBC executives who went on to serve publicly with high distinction were Michael Wong Pakshong, Tony Tan Keng Yam and Yong Pung How.

Michael Wong Pakshong joined OCBC as assistant general manager in 1964, after spending four years in Price Water-house as a chartered accountant. Originally trained as an economist, Wong held an honours degree in economics from the University of Bristol. His 'national service' with the Singapore Government started in September 1970 when he left OCBC to become the managing director of the newly created Monetary Authority of Singapore.

Dr. Tony Tan, according to his uncle Tan Chin Tuan, 'came in on merit and gained promotion by merit entirely.'[32] An honours graduate in physics from the University of Singapore, and currently Singapore's Deputy Prime Minister and Defence Minister, Tan also holds an MSc in operations research from the Massachusetts Institute of Technology and a PhD in applied mathematics from the University of Adelaide. After a stint as a lecturer, he was recruited into OCBC in 1969. Tony Tan resigned from the Bank to enter politics on 11 February 1979.

Yong Pung How became one of OCBC's youngest directors in 1972. Educated at Victoria Institution, Kuala Lumpur, and then at Cambridge University where he obtained a law degree, he became chairman of Malayan Airways (MAL) (later to become the Malaysia-Singapore Airlines, or MSA) in 1964. From 1964 to 1969, he steered MSA through some of its most difficult years. He also became director in a number of other companies, like Guinness Malaysia, the Chemical Company of Malaysia, Harrisons and Crosfield (Malaysia), Malaysian Industrial Development Finance and the Southeast Asia Development Corporation. In 1970, he gave up legal practice and became, in 1971, chairman and managing director of OCBC's Singapore International Merchant Bankers Limited (SIMBL). Yong was seconded as Chief Executive to the Government of Singapore Investment Corporation Private Limited in March 1981. In August 1982 his concurrent appointment as Managing Director of the Monetary Authority of Singapore (MAS) made it necessary for Yong to resign as Director of OCBC. In 1989, after spending 18 years in the business sector, Yong was appointed Judge of the Supreme Court of Singapore, and in 1990, became independent Singapore's second Chief Justice, a post he continues to hold today.

Institutionalising a leadership-centred culture is the ultimate act of leadership and this was precisely what Tan Chin Tuan set out to do. Within five years, Yong sufficiently gained Tan's confidence for Tan to appoint him vice-chairman of OCBC. According to *Asian Finance*, the decision was an 'indication that Tan Sri Tan was preparing to relinquish personal supervision of OCBC operations, and had picked a man qualified to meet the challenge of modernisation'.[33]

The Chairman himself was glad that his men were special and gave his blessing readily, although by moving from the Bank to serve the government invariably increased his own load. He explained:

> Before making a senior appointment I usually obtained
> a verbal promise from the candidate that they will con-

tinue to serve the company loyally and not use the opportunity as a stepping stone to hop to another company. They readily promise because they appreciate that much time and effort has to be spent on grooming them. But I release them from such promises when they are required by the Government.[34]

Besides these 'new men', Tan Chin Tuan also depended on 'retirees' who joined the Bank through his personal invitation. Two of the more prominent ones were Charles Tresise and Lee Hah Ing. Upon his retirement as a senior partner of Cooper Brothers, Charles Tresise became Tan Chin Tuan's personal adviser. His wide-ranging experience in East Asia as a chartered accountant and businessman allowed him to serve as chairman and director of many companies within the OCBC Group. In the words of Tony Tan, the late Charles Tresise was 'always professional, dedicated and conscientious [and] he had in mind always the interest of the company, the shareholders and the employees'.[35] Retired Anglo-Chinese School (ACS) principal Lee Hah Ing was invited to join OCBC in January 1970 and stayed till August 1986, thus having the opportunity to serve under two chairmen. Like Charles Tresise, Lee's continued employment, as described by Yong Pung How, 'has provided strength and stability to our management structure during a period of transition towards a core of younger and less experienced officers'.[36] Lee was primarily responsible for the training and upgrading of staff and the Bank's Management Development Programme.

Recruiting people with leadership potential is only the first step. Equally important is managing their career paths. In 1978, a major internal restructuring of the top echelon of senior managers in OCBC occupied the business news in Singapore. The objective of the management restructuring was to delegate more responsibility to divisional heads.

Lin Jo Yan, retired as general manager in December 1977 and instead of finding a replacement, the Directors decided to abolish the single position of general manager and replace it with four general manager positions. The four new general managers were Choi Siew Hong (former adviser and principal executive for Malaysia) as general manager for the Malaysia division; Tony Tan Keng Yam as general manager for the investment division; Teo Cheng Guan (one of the longest-serving staff members) as general manager for the Singapore division; and Tjio Kay Loen as general manager for the international division. Except for Choi Siew Hong, the rest were formerly designated assistant general managers. The fourth assistant general manager, Goh Sin Tub, had earlier resigned from the OCBC Group.

A further reshuffle took place when Dr Tony Tan left to join the Singapore Government. A former Citibank vice-president, Wong Nang Jang, was made general manager of the international division of OCBC. Described by the Institutional Investor as a 'first class professional banker'[37], Wong's entry greatly strengthened the rank and file of professional managers in OCBC to meet the challenge of international competition and to ensure perpetual growth. The four general managers were ably supported by two deputy general managers who were promoted from their assistant general manager posts in 1981. They were Seah Buck Tiang and Ong Hock Chye. Both of them were in their thirties and considered the new breed of talent, although they were already veterans in terms of the number of years they served in the banking industry. Seah was with OCBC for 20 years and had undergone intensive overseas training in 1970 and 1979. Ong, like Wong Nang Jang, came from Citibank and represented the young breed of American-trained bankers who decided to join local banks during the late 1970s. He too had received overseas training in foreign exchange.

These highly-trained executives could well fit into what Robert Reich termed as 'symbolic analysts'. They are deft in 'problem-solving, problem-identifying, and strategic-brokering activities [and] their services can be traded worldwide'.[38] Symbolic analysts, such as investment bankers, financial consultants and organisation development specialists, usually 'spend long hours in meetings or on the telephone, and even longer hours in jet planes and hotels — advising, making presentations, giving briefings, doing deals... The bulk of the time and cost comes in conceptualising the problem, devising a solution, and planning its execution.'[39] One potential problem in hiring these professional managers and technocratic masters of problem solving is that their personal career considerations could intrude into their decision-making process, and this may not serve the interest of the directors and shareholders.

However, OCBC's senior executives have one common characteristic — loyalty and long-term commitment to their Chairman and the Bank. They developed a deep sense of pride, not just because they worked for a prestigious corporation, but also because of the opportunity of working with a legendary banker. Yong Pung How summarised the feeling well:

> [I]n the years to come, when the day's work is done, and there is time to be reminiscent with neighbours and friends, each of us will be able to look back with pride on our association with him [Tan Chin Tuan] and say 'I served with Tan Chin Tuan'.[40]

OCBC Executives thought of themselves as, and acted like, elders or 'guardians' to about 3,000 employees of the OCBC community and the shareholders at large. It was therefore not difficult for the Chairman to delegate much responsibility to his trusted officers. He said, 'I have been delegating as much as I can, otherwise I could not possibly cope with the multifarious responsibilities of the chairmanship of so many large companies.'[41] The top management concerns itself with the well-being of OCBC as an entity, a community of workers, with a future that may be more or less glorious, depending on their efforts. In management literature, this 'entity approach' has been considered instrumental in ensuring the survival and long-term prosperity of, not only Japanese enterprises, but American companies such as Johnson & Johnson and Hewlett Packard.[42]

Cultivating Trust, Honesty and Righteousness

It is no exaggeration to say that the hallmark of Tan Chin Tuan's success as a banker and entrepreneur is his ability in cultivating the 'human factor'. He recognised that the creation of modern business institutions and the adoption of innovative management practices were necessary, but insufficient conditions for the sustained development of an enterprise. Institutions need to be grounded in strong moral and ethical principles that allow individuals from different backgrounds to work at their best and operate as a team. Organisational culture and identity, however, are in themselves difficult to define. Generally, they refer to underlying shared values, beliefs, and principles that served as a foundation for an organisation's management system as well as the set of management practices and behaviour that both exemplify and reinforce those basic principles.[43] It is shaped not only by technologies and markets, but also by the cultural preferences of leaders and employees. As the economic world order becomes more 'borderless' and firms globalise their operations, 'future corporate leaders are likely to rely simultaneously on cultural symbols that support efficiency, entrepreneurship, and ethics to entice employees to remain within the extended family'.[44] Other studies have also revealed that relevant top management leadership behaviour include planning and communication about change, and strategic decision making that support innovation.[45] O'Reilly and Tushman, for example, recommended that managers exercise culture or social control to develop the norms that enhance innovation. This comprises two components — creativity (generation of a new idea) and implementation (actual introduction of the change) — and is done in a way that maximises the full potential of the employees and 'leaves them feeling motivated and engaged.'[46] The researchers stressed that innovative managers should provide support for risk-taking and change, tolerate mistakes, create effective group communication, and ensure speed of action.

Although the studies on management innovation mentioned above were done in recent years, Tan Chin Tuan had already put into practice the researchers' recommendations from the early days of OCBC. As OCBC's longest-serving Chairman, Tan Chin Tuan promoted a business culture with the following attributes:

(a) Develop and communicate a clear image of the Bank's reputation.

(b) Serve as a role model by sending consistent signals about the qualities of a leader and the importance of innovations in management.

(c) Build an executive team with technical, social and conceptual skills to accomplish diverse tasks and work actively towards envisioning a credible and exciting vision of the future.

(d) Hire senior staff on the basis of core competency rather than on relationships.

(e) Rewarding employees for loyalty and overall corporate
     performance.

Within the OCBC culture, decision-making is typically a
consensual, participative one. People are drawn into the shaping of important decisions, as evidenced by the numerous
correspondence and meetings between the Chairman and his
core group of senior officers. This participative process is one
of the mechanisms which provide for the broad dissemina-
tion of information and values within the organisation. It
must be noted that, although decision-making may be a collective process, ultimate responsibility for all decisions still
resided in Tan Chin Tuan as Chairman and Chief Executive
Officer. However, this overarching sense of individual responsibility also created tension within the rank-and-file of
OCBC's senior executives. This is because the consensual
process, as defined by Edgar Schein, is one in which members of the executive board may be asked to accept responsibility for a decision that they do not prefer, but that the
group, in an open and complete discussion, has settled
upon.[47] Tan Chin Tuan commented:

> The cornerstone of the OCBC's success lies in the unity
> and harmony prevailing among the Directors through
> all the years I have been privileged to sit on the Board.
> While matters brought up at our meetings are always
> freely and fully discussed, divergent views are invari-
> ably resolved without formal voting. It is this camara-
> derie and the urgings of my fellow directors that have
> made me stay so far beyond the retirement age.[48]

This combination of collective decision-making with individual responsibility and accountability demands an atmosphere of trust. The elements of trust, friendship and working

together are crucial to the way Tan Chin Tuan shaped OCBC's culture. Trust requires that organisations communicate with staff as people and not as mere cogs in a wheel. This is what researchers refer to as 'social capital',[49] or what Reich calls 'organisational glue'.[50] Hence, the 'more glue there is in a group, the better that group will function [and] the more willing people will be to share ideas.'[51] Fukuyama maintains that an enterprise with a strong heritage of social capital based on a common set of ethical norms, 'will be better able to innovate organisationally, since the high degree of trust will permit a wide variety of social relationships to emerge.'[52] Indeed, trust has an economic function. It serves to increase economic efficiency by reducing what economists term transaction costs which are incurred as a result of activities such as the search for creditworthy sellers and buyers and negotiate contracts. If trust exists between business partners then there would be less worry about unexpected contingencies and fewer disputes.

The upholding of the virtues of trust, honesty and mutual moral obligation was precisely how Tan Chin Tuan managed to sustain long business friendships and connections. Personal trust between a close network of friends was extended to a wider form of universalistic or business trust between associates. In practically all his public speeches and annual Chairman's statements, Tan never fails to mention his deep appreciation for his loyal and trusted friends and employees: 'OCBC has achieved its present exalted position through the united efforts of its dedicated and devoted Directors and employees, past and present.'[53] These included Lee Kong Chian, Tan Kah Kee, Chee Swee Cheng, Tan Cheng Lock, Lim Boon Keng, Lee Choon Guan, Tan Ean Kiam, Lee Choon Seng, Lim Peng Siang, Aw Boon Haw, See Boon Ih, Wee Theam Seng, Chew Hock Leong, Tan Lark Sye, Yeap Chor Ee, Yap Twee, Yeo Tiam Siew, Low Liang Quee, Chee Kah Hor and Khor Teow Koon. These individuals made a voluntary contract to uphold the strength and reputation of OCBC, based on shared ethical values and mutual trust.

As evidence of his ability to harvest friendships, Tan Chin Tuan received 42 congratulatory messages from leaders in the business and financial world to honour his 50 years of contribution to OCBC in 1982 — including a few from those who were not invited to the celebration or whom the Chairman did not know personally. In such high-trust relationships, parties do not even have to worry about maximising profits in the short run, because they know too well that, in the long run, they would stand to benefit. Rather than relying exclusively upon hierarchy and monitoring to direct behaviour, OCBC's senior officials were given sufficient autonomy to develop an attitude of egalitarianism and mutual trust in accomplishing their work targets. As such, there is an implicit assumption in the hearts and minds of OCBC's senior executives that they all hold basically compatible goals. No one engages in self-serving behaviour; each one accepts personal responsibility for group decisions and makes enthusiastic attempts to consolidate the position of OCBC as one of Singapore's and the region's top banking institutions.

Although observers commented on his authoritarianism, Tan Chin Tuan consistently strove to develop a sense of shared membership in the corporation. As already mentioned, he recognised the negative impact of absolute power. This collective sense of congeniality helped soften the adversarial nature of hierarchical relations so prevalent in family-based organisations. Such congeniality also gave more importance to managerial competence when authority is allocated. Hierarchy and the concentration of decision-making power in the hands of those who are most skilled and gifted in a large organisation like OCBC is unavoidable and indeed natural. But what Tan consistently demonstrated to his key people was the need to maintain a healthy balance between hierarchy and equality and, more significantly, to have a refined moral sense. Responsible officials and managers should not abuse their power. The story is told of how he prosecuted his own nephew who misappropriated some money when he was promoted to an assistant manager of a branch during the war: 'Small mistakes I tend to overlook but if it is corrupt or criminal, there is no sparing.'[54] One example of the Chairman's insistence on the need to be honest was his decision to close down the Indonesian branches of the Bank because he 'would rather forego any activity which is not strictly legal or ethical'. He added: 'There was a period when profits could not be repatriated, except illegally. After much deliberation, I recommended, and the Board agreed, to close down three of our branches in Surabaya, Palembang and Jambi.'[55]

Another anecdote highlights Tan Chin Tuan's personal conviction about justice and righteousness. He came across a newspaper article that reported on how a young vegetable seller, Wong Lai Fatt, killed a man who had forced his wife into vice and was subsequently sentenced to four years in prison.[56] In his letter to R. C. Hoffman of Allen & Gledhill, the well-known law firm, Tan Chin Tuan stated that the defendant 'was apparently trying to defend his wife from being raped by a scoundrel [and that] the apparent injustice in this case has so troubled me that I feel I should try to help this poor man, although he is a complete stranger to me.'[57] The case was brought to the attention of the Chief Justice who, after much deliberation, quashed Wong's conviction and sentence.

Such anecdotes, found in the annals of OCBC's history help reinforce the importance of trust, honesty and righteousness. OCBC officers were trained to exercise benevolence, show consideration towards their less-gifted workers, and, in general, not to gain wealth through dishonest means and at the expense of society. It is no exaggeration to say that the emphasis on this morally restraining code of behaviour advocated by Tan Chin Tuan and the training received in OCBC has produced individuals who were destined to contribute richly to the growth and stability of Singapore in the late 1980s and beyond.

Conclusion

The rise and expansion of OCBC provides an interesting case-study of the Chinese firm, a business model which still dominates the majority of business enterprises in Singapore and Southeast Asia today. We have shown that the role of leadership is of paramount importance in transforming the traditional family firm into a modern institution so that it can optimise opportunities within each new environment. It is useful to conclude with some generalisations pertinent to indigenous firms operating in Singapore and Southeast Asia.

A family-owned and -controlled economic enterprise can institutionalise itself successfully if the founding family is willing to accept a paradigm shift towards accepting a modern corporate structure largely controlled by professional managers. Few small and medium-sized, locally-owned |enterprises in Singapore have institutionalised themselves. Research into this phenomenon is still scarce but one can surmise that one important cultural obstacle to such institutionalisation is having a family-management with very short-term vision. This book has shown that for OCBC to last for generations to come, Tan Chin Tuan re-invented and re-defined the banking institution by moving it beyond the family-centric business model into the modern corporate form of organisation, making use of hierarchical management structures and professional managers. In so doing, he also transformed the traditional network-organisation of family or personal ties with other local, small Chinese or non-Chinese firms into a *keiretsu*-type of inter-market network that includes subsidiaries and associates way beyond the shore of Singapore.

For Chinese business enterprises to remain large-scale, vigorous and profitable, they must show great flexibility and tenacity in view of the changing domestic and international environment. From the 1930s to the 1980s, OCBC adapted itself to the challenges of each new environment and to business cycles in general. Yet, in spite of its enormous organisational network and the complexity of operations, the Bank remains a family-owned and controlled enterprise which still clings tenaciously to its well-tested prudent conservatism.

Size (and reputation) matters in determining the ability of an enterprise to engage in economic power-play, especially in the international arena. In the industrialised West, Japan and even Korea, economic development was stimulated by the power of large-scale corporations. Entrepreneurs in Singapore and Southeast Asia aspire to become the next Matsushita or Hyundai. In reality, however, this is unlikely to happen because capitalistic development had taken root historically in the region in quite a different manner as compared to the West or Japan. In the case of Singapore, its industrial and commercial structure was, as late as the 1980s, characterised by the dominance of small-scale private enterprises. Besides the government-linked companies, the OCBC Group proved to be one of the few exceptions. Even though the OCBC Group cannot match the size of Japanese *keiretsu* conglomerates, it managed to achieve a size at which economies of scale permitted them to compete effectively.

The transformation of a firm, from family-owned to a large-scale enterprise, does not mean the diffusion and eventual disappearance of traditional or core cultural traits and values that first allowed the family to establish a viable business. The OCBC's transformation into a modern, multi-business banking group illustrates how personal relationships, networking, prudent conservatism, ownership and control which the Bank first started off in the early 1930s remain very much intact within the OCBC of the 1980s.

Finally, behind the success stories of great enterprises lie the stories of unique personalities. This chapter has examined the ideals and thinking of the man who, in the opinion of many observers, is credited with the making of modern OCBC. While it is difficult or perhaps even unwise to suggest an Asian management model based on Tan Chin Tuan and his *tao* (or way) of business creation and management, it is nevertheless appropriate to highlight some of its essential characteristics. The so-called TCT (Tan Chin Tuan) model of business management has two key features. First is a disciplined and non-flamboyant style of business conduct. This should not be construed as business conservatism. Second is innovation through the application of modern economic institutions and management practices. Both these traits rest on a bedrock of traditional social and cultural values, key elements being trust, honesty and righteousness. Over and above this model is the invisible guiding hand of Tan's own ambitions and beliefs. Tan Chin Tuan would not be the icon that he is were it not for two overriding factors that shaped his ambitions and beliefs. First, he observed that self-made entrepreneurs in pre-war Singapore exhibited great humility and philanthropic traits, and second, he was deeply moved by the trust and confidence shown in him by the founding members of OCBC when war came to Singapore. Thus, Tan's personal commitment has always been first and foremost to OCBC and its major stakeholders (customers, employees, shareholders) and to society at large.

The events that shaped Singapore, the region and the world from the 1930s to the 1980s are now locked in memories and history books. Recently Singapore's economy went through a debilitating recession that destroyed the general prosperity of Southeast Asia and much of Asia. Continuing globalisation of the world economy and rapid technological change in the new millennium will change the format of competition for entrepreneurs and would-be entrepreneurs. What then is the relevance of Tan Chin Tuan's experiences? The generalisations that can be derived from the TCT model are these:

(a) A company, whether small or big, is made up of people. Harnessing employees' support requires reciprocal obligation from management. The result will be greater productivity, as employees feel more motivated and com- mitted to corporate goals. Besides employees, management will also need to recognise that customers hold the magic wand. A customer-focused corporate culture must be nurtured.

(b) The successful executive must possess not only entrepreneurial talent but also leadership qualities that can help institutionalise the company. Whether operating in the banking, manufacturing or other sector, he will need to internalise optimistic and ethical standards, possess broad-based knowledge and skills to make crucial decisions, and communicate his vision of a successful corporation to the whole organisation.

(c) It is important for the leader and management of a company to have big idealistic goals or visions. Equally crucial, however, is the need for them to exercise patience and prudence in developing strategies that will foster the achievements of these visions.

As this book goes to press, the local banking scene is undergoing some revolutionary changes. The Singapore Government announced in May 1999 that it would remove controls on foreign capital which until now have helped protect local banks from outside competition. The major banks are to be re-organised into just two mammoth entities to put them in better stead against stiff foreign competition. One of the two entities is the DBS Bank which has absorbed POSB Bank while the remaining four local banks (OCBC, UOB, OUB and Keppel-Tatlee Bank) would be potential targets for the re-organisation. This unprecedented change is founded on the argument that Singapore banks will need to be bigger to compete in the increasingly competitive financial market against foreign players that are world leaders in terms of the latest expertise and technology. In June 2000, Deputy Prime Minister Lee Hsien Loong announced that the Monetary Authority of Singapore would issue a directive to all local banks to unwind their cross-shareholdings and divest themselves of their non-financial assets within three years. This separation was designed to 'limit the risk of contagion from the non-banking businesses to the bank.' At the end of the three years, banks will still be allowed to hold investment stakes in various companies provided they have no management control and their stakes in such companies do not exceed 10%.

The financial sector liberalisation would also be effective in encouraging the realignment of the local banking scene by putting pressure on the domestic banks to break away from their family-centric governance and structure. Although many have grown beyond being family banks, there are still significant family shareholdings. No one can predict what the future holds for OCBC. But whatever happens, the annals of OCBC will be filled with the stories of one man who spent half his life grooming and institutionalising a bank that was born out of the Depression of the 1930s.

In his last Chairman's statement in the Bank's 1982 Annual Report, Tan Sri Tan Chin Tuan reiterated his fundamental beliefs in people who had given him the trust and the opportunity to uphold the famous motto 'Solid As A Rock':

> ...I wish to place on record my heartfelt gratitude to my mentors of years past and my colleagues, past and present, who have helped to elevate the Bank to its present eminence and whose loyal support has lightened my load and made my responsibilities less onerous and more gratifying. I also want to thank all constituents and customers for their unfailing goodwill and staunch support. I wish the new leaders of OCBC fair weather and smooth sailing.[58]

Whatever happens to OCBC in the new millennium, one thing is most certain to last forever. Entering the large banking hall, a young Singaporean gets the feeling of strength and grandness. He knows the mammoth structure is steeped in history — a history that reflects, powerfully, the visions of one man. Through stormy and sunny days, the captain of the legendary Chinese junk had slowly but surely guided the ship to a home as solid as a rock; a home of integrity; of trust and confidence in the future.

NOTES

1   See Oversea Chinese Banking Corporation Limited, *Annual Report, 1983*, p. 16; Fraser and Neave Limited, *Annual Report, 1983*, p. 22; Great Eastern Life Assurance Company Limited, *Annual Report, 1991;* and Straits Trading Company Limited, Annual Reports 1965 & 1991.

1a Interview, Tan Chin Tuan (n.d.), on file with authors.

2   Speech at OCBC's Farewell Dinner in honour of Tan Sri Tan Chin Tuan, 30 September 1983 (Singapore: The Tan Foundation).

3   Interview, Tan Chin Tuan (n.d.), on file with the authors.

4   As Peter Drucker maintained, 'Economic Performance is the *first*

responsibility of a business. A business that does not show a profit at least equal to its cost of capital is socially irresponsible. It wastes society's resources.' Quoted in R. Levy, *Give and Take: A Candid Account of Corporate Philanthropy* (Boston, Mass: Harvard Business School Press, 1999), p. 10.

5 Interview, Tan Chin Tuan (n.d.), on file with the authors.

6 Ibid.

7 Ibid.

8 Ibid.

9 J. P. Kotter, *Matsushita Leadership: Lessons from the 20th Century's Most Remarkable Entrepreneur* (New York: The Free Press, 1997), p. 211.

10 Levy, *Give and Take*, p. 3.

11 Ibid., pp. 193–194.

12 J. P. Kotter, *What Leaders Really Do* (Boston: Harvard Business School Press, 1999), pp. 104–105.

13 *Euromoney*, October 1982.

14 Ibid.

15 *OCBC Annual Report 1977*, p. 8.

16 *Euromoney*, March 1985, p. 177.

17 Speech at OCBC's 50th Anniversary, 30 October 1982 (Singapore: The Tan Foundation).

18 Correspondence between Walter Wriston and Tan Chin Tuan, 27 October 1982 (Singapore: The Tan Foundation).

19 Correspondence between Harry Taylor and Tan Chin Tuan, 24 November 1982 (Singapore: The Tan Foundation).

20 As quoted in the *The Business Times*, 30 October 1982.

21 Francis Fukuyama, *Trust: The Social Virtues and the Creation of Prosperity* (London: Penguin Books, 1995), p. 74.

22 Wellington K. K. Chan , 'The Organisational Structure of the Traditional Business Firm and its Modern Reform', *Business Review*, vol. 56 (1982): 218–235; S. G. Redding, *The Spirit of Chinese Capitalism* (Berlin: Walter de Gruyter, 1990); Stewart R. Clegg and S. Gordon Redding, *Capitalism in Contrasting Cultures*, eds (Berlin: Walter de Gruyter, 1990); Wong Siu Lun, 'Business Networks, Cultural Values and the States in Hong Kong and Singapore', in *Chinese Business Enterprise in Asia*, R. A. Brown, ed. (London: Routledge, 1995), pp. 136–153.

23 D. Brown, 'Race for the Corporate Throne', *Management Review*, vol. 78 (1989); 26–27; D. Cohen, 'The Fall of the House of Wang', *Business Month*, vol. 135 (1990): 22–31; C. Kennedy, 'Fall of the House of Wang', *Computer World*, vol. 26 (1992): 67–69.

23a Francis Fukuyama, *Trust*, pp. 69–70.

24 *The Economist*, 18 July 1992.

25 Ibid.

26 Gary Hamilton and N. Woolsey Biggart, 'Market, Culture and Authority: A Comparative Analysis of Management and Organisa-tion in the Far East', *American Journal of Sociology*, vol. 94 (1988): S52–94.

27 Interview, *Euromoney*, October 1982, p. 144.

28 Fukuyama, *Trust*, p. 77–78.

29 Ibid., p. 78, pp 83-95.

30 R. Reich, "The Company of the Future", *Fast Company*, no. 19 (November/December 1998): 128.

31 Ibid., p. 132.

32 Interview, Tan Chin Tuan (n.d.), on file with the authors.

33 *Asian Finance*, 15 September 1982.

34 *Euromoney*, October 1982, p. 150.

35 Remarks to congregation at Mr Tresise's funeral (Singapore: The Tan Foundation).

36 Correspondence between Yong Pung How and Lee Hah Ing, 10 April 1986 (Singapore: The Tan Foundation).

37 Quoted in *The Business Times*, 25 December 1979.

38 R. B. Reich, *The Work of Nations: Preparing Ourselves for 21st Century Capitalism* (New York: Vintage Books, 1991), p. 177.

39 Ibid., p. 179.

40 Speech at the Retirement of Tan Sri Tan Chin Tuan, 30 September 1983 (Singapore: The Tan Foundation).

41 Interview, *Euromoney*, October 1982, p. 147.

42 R. Dore, 'The Asian Form of Capitalism', in *The Corporate Triangle: The Structure and Performance of Corporate Systems in a Global Economy*, P. H. Admiraal, ed (Malden, Mass: Blackwell, 1997).

43 D. R. Denison, *Corporate Culture and Organisational Effectiveness* (New York: J. Wiley, 1990).

44 Charles J. Fombrun, *Turning Points: Create Strategic Change in Corporations* (New York: McGraw-Hill, 1992), p. 186.

45 Richard L. Daft, *Organisational Theory and Design* (St Paul: West Pub. Co., 1986); Mariann Jelinek and Claudia Bird Schoonhoven, *The Innovation Marathon: Lessons from High Technology Firms* (Oxford, UK: Blackwell, 1990); Charles A. O'Reilly III and Michael L. Tushman, *Winning Through Innovation: A Practical Guide to Leading Organisational Change and Renewal* (Boston, Mass: Harvard Business School Press, 1997); David Nadler and Michael Tushman, 'Beyond the Charismatic Leader: Leadership

and Organisational Change', in *The Human Side of Managing Technological Innovation: A Collection of Readings*, Ralph Katz, ed (New York: Oxford University Press, 1997);   M. Dodgson, and Y. Kim, 'Learning to Innovate — Korean Style: The Case of Samsung', in *International Journal of Innovation Management*, vol.1 (1997): 53–71.

46   O'Reilly and Tushman, *Winning Through Innovation*, p. 205.

47   E. H. Schein, *Process Consultation* (Reading, Mass: Addison-Wesley, 1969).

48   Speech at OCBC's 50th Anniversary, 30 October 1982 (Singapore: The Tan Foundation).

49   R. Reich, 'The Company of the Future', *Fast Company*, no. 19 (November/December 1998): 138.

50   Ibid.

51   Ibid.

52   Fukuyama, *Trust*, p. 27.

53   Speech at the TCT-OCBC-50 Celebration, *OCBC File*, March 1975.

54   Interview, Tan Chin Tuan (n.d.), on file with the authors.

55   Interview, *Euromoney*, October 1982, p. 152.

56   *The Straits Times*, 27 September 1982.

57   Correspondence between Tan Chin Tuan and R. C. Hoffman, 11 October 1972 (Singapore: The Tan Foundation).

58   *OCBC Annual Report 1982*, p. 8.

Bibliography

Primary Documents

Annual Report of the Labour Department, 1951. Singapore: Government Printing Office, 1952.

Annual Report of the Labour Department, 1953. Singapore: Government Printing Office, 1954.

Annual Report of the Labour Department, 1954. Singapore: Government Printing Office, 1956.

Annual Report of the Labour Department, 1960. Singapore: Government Printing Office, 1961.

Archives & Oral History Department, *The Japanese Occupation: Singapore, 1942–1945.* Singapore: Singapore News and Publications Limited, 1985.

British Military Administration. Singapore Advisory Council. Minutes of meetings.

Colony of Singapore. Advisory Council. Public Sessions, various years.

Colony of Singapore. Proceedings of the Legislative Council, various years.

CSO 0023/49. Appendix A, "Attachment to Political Report by Secretary for Internal Affairs", December 1949. Singapore.

CO852. Eastern Department, Original Correspondence, 1927–1946.

Department of Statistics, Singapore. *Singapore National Accounts, 1960–1973,* 1975.

Ministry of Finance, Singapore. *State of Singapore Development Plan 1961–1964,* 1961. *Ministry of Labour Annual Report, 1966.* Singapore, 1967.

Petir. *25th Anniversary Issue.* Singapore: Central Executive Committee People's Action Party, 1979.

Singapore Chinese Chamber of Commerce. Minutes of meetings, various volumes.

Singapore International Merchant Bankers Limited (n.d). *Merchant Bankers in the New Asia. SIMBL.*

Singapore. "Report of the Ritson Commission on Allowances, 1953". Singapore: Government Printing Office, 1954.

Straits Settlements. "Report of the Commission appointed by his Excellency the Governor of the Straits Settlements to enquire into and report on the trade of the Colony, 1933–34". Singapore: Government Printing Office, 1934.

Straits Settlements. "Report of the Commissions appointed by His Excellency the Governor of the Straits Settlements and the High Commissioner of the Federated Malay States to enquire and report on (a) the present state of trade depression brought about in the main, by the continued depression in the rubber industry and (b) the extension of credit facilities. 1921". Singapore: Government Printing Office, 1921.

Newspapers

The Business Times, 25 December 1979; 29 November 1980; 30 October 1982.

Nanyang Siang Pau, 15 October 1958.

Singapore Standard, various years.

The Sunday Times, various years.

The Straits Times, various years.

Straits Times Annual, 1989.

The Star, 25 May 1978.

Private Archives of Tan Chin Tuan (The Tan Foundation, Singapore)

Asia Pacific Breweries Limited. *Annual Reports*, various years.

Board of Commissioners of Currency press statement, 5 December 1968.

Board of Commissioners of Currency, Kuala Lumpur. Minutes of meeting, 15 December 1965.

Choi, S. H. "Notes of meeting with Deputy Governor Bank Negara Malaysia", 24 August 1976.

Fraser and Neave Limited. *Annual Reports*, various years.

Fraser and Neave. *Fraser and Neave: 1883–1983: The Great Years*. Singapore: Ho Printing, 1983.

Great Eastern Life Company Limited. *Annual Reports*, various years.

Letter from Gimson F. to the Secretary of State for the Colonies dated 24 November 1951 (confidential telegram).

Letter from Governor J. Nicoll to J. J. Paskin (Colonial Office) dated 11 December 1953.

Letter from J. R. Jones (HSBC, Singapore) to S. A. Gray (HSBC's London Representative) dated 16 November 1948.

Letter from Lien Ying Chow dated 25 October 1945, BMA HQ S Div 382/45. Reference Number 45/108.

Oversea-Chinese Banking Corporation Limited. *Annual Report*, 1973, 1977, 1982, 1983, 1989.

Oversea-Chinese Banking Corporation Limited. "Report of Directors and Statement of Accounts", 31 December, 1953, 1957–1959, 1961–1967, 1997.

Oversea-Chinese Banking Corporation. *Twenty-One Years: Growth and Progress*. Singapore: OCBC, 1953.

Overseas Assurance Corporation Limited. *Annual Reports*, various years.

Overseas Assurance Corporation. *The 51st Year Souvenir: 51 Years of Progress: The Overseas Assurance Corporation Limited*. Singapore, 1971.

Raffles Investment Limited, *Annual Reports*, various years.

Robinson and Company Limited. *Annual Reports*, various years.

Robinson and Company Limited. *The Story of Robinson*. Singapore: S. N., 1958.

Sime Darby. *Sime Darby 75th Anniversary (1985)*. Kuala Lumpur: Sime Darby Communication Department, 1985.

Sime Darby Holding. *J. M. Sassoon and Company Private Limited*. Singapore, 1973.

Straits Trading Company Limited. *Annual Reports*, various years.

Tan Chin Tuan personal correspondences. Singapore: The Tan Foundation.

Straits Trading. *The Straits Trading Company Limited: 100 Years of Growth 1887–1987*. Straits Trading Singapore, 1987.

The Great Eastern Life Assurance Company Limited. *Annual Reports*, various years.

United Engineers Limited. *Annual Reports*, various years.

Wearne Brothers Limited. *Annual Report 1996*. Singapore: Wearne Brothers Corporation Limited, 1997.

Wearne Brothers Limited. *Annual Reports*, various years.

Oral Interviews

Tan, Ee Leong. 27 December 1979, January 1980, 28 May 1981. Oral History Department, National Archives, Singapore.

Yap, Ee Chian. 13 August 1980. Oral History Department, National Archives, Singapore.

Yap, Siong Eu. 16 June 1983, 27 June 1983, 23 July 1983. Oral History Department, National Archives, Singapore.

Tan, Chin Tuan. 8 March 1999, 18 March 1999. Singapore.

Books

Allen, G. C. and Audrey G. Donnithorne. *Western Enterprise in Indonesia and Malaya; A Study in Economic Development*. London, Allen & Unwin, 1957.

Banyai, Richard A. *Money and Banking in China and Southeast Asia during the Japanese Military Occupation, 1937–1945*. Taipei: Tai Wan Enterprise, 1995.

Brown, R. A. *Capital and Entrepreneurship in Southeast Asia*. London: St. Martin's Press, 1994.

———, ed. *Chinese Business Enterprise in Asia*. London: Routledge, 1995.

Cannell, Michael T. *I. M. Pei: Mandarin of Modernism*. New York: Carol Southern Books, 1995.

Cameron, Rondo E. *Banking in the Early Stages of Industrialization*. New York: Oxford University Press, 1967.

Chan, King Nui. *From Poor Migrant to Millionaire — Chan Wing, 1873–1947*. Kuala Lumpur: Malaysian Branch of the Royal Asiatic Society, 1997.

Cheng, Lim Keak. *Social Change and the Chinese in Singapore — A Socio-Economic Geography with Special Reference to Bäng Structure*. Singapore: Singapore University Press, 1985.

Chew, Hock Leong. *When Singapore was Syonan: Being a brief account of what transpired during the three and half years' Japanese Occupation of Singapore*. Singapore: G. H. Kiat, 1945.

Chew, Melanie. *Leaders of Singapore*. Singapore: Resource Press, 1996.

Cho, Yoon Je and Kim Joon-Kyung. *Credit Policies and the Industrialization of Korea*. Seoul: Korea Development Institute, 1997.

Chou, Cindy. *Beyond the Empires: Memories Retold*. Singapore: Oral History Centre, National Archives of Singapore, Singapore Heritage Board, 1995.

Clegg, Stewart R. and S. Gordon Redding, eds. *Capitalism in Contrasting Cultures*. Berlin: Walter de Gruyter, 1990.

Cloake, John. *Templer, Tiger of Malaya: The Life of Field Marshal Sir Gerald Templer*. London: Harrap, 1985.

Clutterbuck, Richard. *Riots and Revolution in Singapore and Malaya, 1945–63*. Singapore: Graham Brash, 1973.

Compton, Eric. N. *Inside Commercial Banking*, 2nd ed. New York: John Wiley and Sons, 1983.

Cottrell, P. L. *Industrial Finance 1830–1914: The Finance and Organisation of English Manufacturing Industry*. London: Methuen, 1980.

______ . *Industrial Finance 1830–1914: The Finance and Organisation of English Manufacturing Industry*. Aldershot, Hamphire: Ashgate,1993.

Daft, Richard L. *Organisational Theory and Design*. St Paul: West Pub. Co., 1986.

Davenport-Hines, R. P. T. and Geoffrey Jones, eds. *British Business in Asia since 1860*. Cambridge: Cambridge University Press, 1989.

Davis, Steven I. *Leadership in Financial Services: Lessons for the Future*. Basingstoke: Macmillan Press Limited, 1997.

Denison, D. R. *Corporate Culture and Organisational Effectiveness*. New York: J. Wiley, 1990.

Donnison, F. S. V. *British Military Administration in the Far East 1943–1946*. London: HMSO (History of the Second World War: United Kingdom Military Services), 1956.

Dore, Ronald. "The Asian Form of Capitalism", in *The Corporate Triangle: The Structure and Performance of Corporate Systems in a Global Economy*. Edited by P. H. Admiraal. Malden, Massachusetts: Blackwell, 1997.

Drabble, John H. *Malayan Rubber: The Interwar Years*. London: Macmillan Press, 1991.

Douw, Leo and Peter Post, eds. *South China: State, Culture and Social Change during the 20th Century*. Amsterdam: North-Holland, 1996.

Drysdale, J. G. S. *Singapore: Struggle for Success*. Singapore: Times Books International, 1984.

EMF Foundation. *The World Competitiveness Report 1995*. Geneva, Switzerland: The Foundation, 1995.

Flower, Raymond. *Year of the Tiger*. Singapore: Times Book International, 1985.

______ . *Meet you at Raffles*. Singapore: Times Book International, 1988.

Fombrun, Charles J. *Turning Points: Create Strategic Change in Corporations*. New York: McGraw-Hill, 1992.

______ . *Reputation: Realising Value from the Corporate Image*. Boston, Massachusetts: Harvard Business School Press, 1996.

Fukuyama, Francis. *Trust: The Social Virtues and the Creation of Prosperity.* London: Penguin Books, 1995.

Gardella, Robert, Jane K. Leonard and Andrea McElderry, eds. "Chinese Business History: Interpretative Trends and Priorities for the Future", in *Chinese Studies in History*. New York: M. E. Sharpe, 1998.

Green, Edwin and Sara Kinsey. *The Paradise Bank: The Mercantile Bank of India, 1983–1984*. Aldershot: Ashgate, 1999.

Growing with Singapore. Singapore: United Overseas Bank Group, 1985.

Harada, Tadao. *List of Lee Kong Chian documents, vol. I.* Singapore: Nanyang University, 1979.

Hayward, Steven F. *Churchill on Leadership*. Rocklin: Forum, 1997.

Huff, W. G. *The Economic Growth of Singapore: Trade and Development in the Twentieth Century*. Cambridge: Cambridge University Press, 1994.

Jamann, Wolfgang. *Chinese Traders in Singapore: Business Practices and Organisational Dynamics*. Bielefeld Studies on the Sociology of Development. Saarbrucken, Germany: Verl. für Entwicklungspolitik Breitenbach, 1994.

Jelinek, Mariann and Claudia Bird Schoonhoven. *The Innovation Marathon: Lessons from High Technology Firms*. Oxford, UK: Blackwell, 1990.

Johnson, Hazel J. *The Banking Keiretsu*. Cambridge: Probus Pub Co., 1993.

Jones, Geoffrey. *Banks as Multinationals*. London and New York: Routledge, 1990.

______ . *British Multinational Banking, 1930–1990*. Oxford: Clarendon Press, 1993.

King, F. H. H. *The Hongkong Bank in Late Imperial China, 1864–1902: On an Even Keel, vol. 1*. Cambridge & NY: Cambridge University Press, 1987.

______ . *The Hongkong Bank in Period of Imperialism and War, 1895–1918: Wayfoong, the Focus of Wealth, vol. 2*. Cambridge & NY & Cambridge University Press, 1988.

______ . *The Hongkong Bank between the Wars and the Bank Interned, 1919–1945: Return from Grandeur, vol. 3*. Cambridge & NY: Cambridge University Press, 1988.

______ . *The Hongkong Bank in Period of Development and Nationalism, 1914–1984: From Regional Bank to Multinational Group*. Cambridge & NY: Cambridge University Press, 1991.

King, Sam. *Tiger Balm King: The Life and Times of Aw Boon Haw*. Singapore: Times Books International, 1992.

Kochan, Thomas A. and Michael Useem, eds. *Transforming Organisation*. Oxford: Oxford University Press, 1992.

Kotter, John P. *What Leaders Really Do*. Boston: Harvard Business School Press, 1999.

______ . *Matsushita Leadership: Lessons from the 20th Century's Most Remarkable Entrepreneur*. New York: The Free Press, 1997.

Kratoska, Paul H. *The Japanese Occupation of Malaya: A Social and Economic History*. London: C. Hurst, 1998.

Kua, B. L. *Xinhua Lishi Renwu Liezuan* [Who's Who in the Chinese Community of Singapore]. Singapore: EPB Publishers, 1995.

Lau, Albert. *The Malayan Union Controversy, 1942–1948*. Singapore: Oxford University Press, 1995.

Lee, Edwin and Tan Tai Yong. *Beyond Degrees: The Making of the National University of Singapore*. Singapore: Singapore University Press, 1996.

Lee, Kam Hing and Chow Mun Seong. *Biographical Dictionary of the Chinese in Malaysia*. Petaling Jaya: Pelanduk Publications, 1997.

Lee, Kuan Yew. *The Singapore Story*. Singapore: Times Publication, 1998.

Lee, S. A. *Industrialization in Singapore*. Camberwell, Victoria: Longman Australia, 1973.

Lee, Sheng Yi. *The Monetary and Banking Development of Singapore and Malaysia*. Singapore: Singapore University Press, 1974.

________ . *The Monetary and Banking Development of Singapore and Malaysia*, 3rd ed. Singapore: Singapore University Press, 1990.

Levy, Reynold. *Give and Take: A Candid Account of Corporate Philanthropy*. Boston, Massachusetts: Harvard Business School Press, 1999.

Lien, Ying Chow with Louis Kraar. *From Chinese Villager to Singapore Tycoon: My Life Story*. Singapore & Kuala Lumpur: Times Books International, 1992.

Lim, Richard. *Banking On A Virtue: POSBank, 1972–1997 Celebrating 25 Years*. Singapore: POSBank, 1997.

________ . *Building A Singapore Bank: The OUB Story*. Singapore: Overseas Union Bank Ltd., 1998.

Liu, Gretchen. *Raffles Hotel*. Singapore: Landmark Books Private Limited, 1992.

Lim, Linda Y. C. & Peter L. A. Gosling, eds. *The Chinese in Southeast Asia, vol. I: Ethnicity and Economic Activity*. Singapore: Maruzen Asia, 1983.

Lohanda, Mona. *The Kapitan Cina of Batavia 1837–1942: A History of Chinese Establishment in Colonial Society*. Jakarta: Djambatan, 1996.

Low, Linda. *The Political Economy of a City-State: Government-made Singapore*. Singapore: Oxford University Press, 1998.

Makepeace, Walter, Gilbert E. Brooke and Roland St. J. Bradell, eds. *One Hundred Years of Singapore, vol. 2*. Singapore: Oxford University Press, 1991.

Morais, John Victor, ed. *Leaders of Malaya and Who's Who, 1959–1960*. Kuala Lumpur: The Khee Meng Press, 1960.

Muirhead, Stuart. *Crisis Banking in the East: The History of the Chartered Mercantile Bank of India, London and China, 1853–93*. Aldershot, Hants, England: Scolar Press, 1996.

Nash, Gary B., Charlotte Crabtree and Ross E. Dunn. *History on Trial*. New York: Alfred A. Knopf, 1997.

National Archives. *The Japanese Occupation: Singapore 1942–1945*. Singapore Archives and Oral History Department, 1985.

Neenan, David. *Added Value Banking: Recruiting and Retaining Customers, Maximising Sales*. Dublin, Ireland: Lafferty Publications Ltd, 1993.

O'Reilly III, Charles and Michael L. Tushman. *Winning Through Innovation: A Practical Guide to Leading Organisational Change and Renewal*. Boston, Massachusettes: Harvard Business School Press, 1997.

Owyang, Hsuan. *From Wall Street to Bukit Merah — Strategies of a Corporate Leader*. Singapore: Times Books International, 1998.

Png, P. S. *Kerja Terhibur dan Sibur* [Laugh, Work and Grow]. Singapore: Pusat Latihan Kakitangan, OCBC, 1975.

POSB. *The Post Office Savings Bank of Singapore — Your National Savings Bank, 100 Years*. Singapore: International Press Company, 1977.

Pressnell, L. S. *Country Banking in the Industrial Revolution*. Oxford: Oxford University Press, 1956.

Prumbulavi, Vilasani & Wong Heng, eds. *From Singapore to Syonan-to, 1941–1945. A Select Bibliography*. Singapore: Reference Service Division, National Library, 1992.

Puthucheary, James Joseph. *Ownership and Control in the Malayan Economy*. Singapore: Eastern Universities Press Ltd., 1960.

Redding, S. Gordon. *The Spirit of Chinese Capitalism*. Berlin: Walter De Gruyter, 1990.

Reich, Robert B. *The Work of Nations: Preparing Ourselves for 21st Century Capitalism*. New York: Vintage Books, 1991.

Roberts, Richard. *Schroders: Merchants and Bankers*. London: Macmillan Press, 1992.

Rodan, Gary. *The Political Economy of Singapore's Industrialization: National State and International Capital*. Basingtoke: Macmillan, 1989.

Rose, Mary B., ed. *Family Business*. Aldershot, Hants, England: E. Elgar, 1995.

Sanger, Clyde. *Malcolm MacDonald: Bringing an End to Empire*. Liverpool, England: Liverpool University Press, 1995.

Schein, Edgar. H. *Process Consultation*. Reading, Massachusetts: Addison-Wesley, 1969.

——— . *Transforming Organisation*. Oxford: Oxford University Press, 1992.

——— . *Strategic Pragmatism — The Culture of Singapore's Economic Development Board*. Singapore: Toppan Company, 1996.

Scott-Ross, Alice. *Tun Dato Sir Cheng Lock Tan: A Personal Profile by His Daughter*. Singapore: Kefford Press, 1990.

Sharp, Ilsa. *There is only one Raffles: The story of a Grand Hotel*. Singapore: Times Printers Sdn. Bhd, 1981.

Short, Anthony. *The Communist Insurrection in Malaya, 1948–1960*. London: Muller, 1975.

Sim, Victor, ed. *Biographies of Prominent Chinese in Singapore*. Singapore: Nan Kok Publication, 1950.

Stanworth, John and Celia Stanworth. *Work 2000: The Future for Industry, Employment and Society*. London: Paul Chapman, 1991.

Stockwell, Anthony John. *British Policy and Malay Politics during the Malayan Union Experiment, 1945–1948*. Singapore: Malaysian Branch of the Royal Asiatic Society, 1979.

Tamaki, Norio. *Japanese Banking: A History 1859–1959*. Cambridge: Cambridge University Press, 1995.

Tan Beng Luan, *A Battle to be Remembered: Oral History Extracts of War — Time Singapore*. Singapore: Oral History Department, 1998.

Tan Chwee Huat. *Financial Markets and Institutions in Singapore*, 9th ed. Singapore: Singapore University Press, 1997Sim, Victor, ed. *Biographies of Prominent Chinese in Singapore*. Singapore: Nan Kok Publication, 1950.

Tauranac, John. *The Empire State Building: The Making of A Landmark*. New York: Scribner, 1995.

Teichova, A., G. K. Van Hentenryk and D. Ziegler, eds. *Banking, Trade and Industry: Europe, America and Asia from the Thirteenth to the Twentieth Century*. Cambridge: Cambridge University Press, 1997.

Khoo Kay Kim. *The Pacific Bank Berhad: Seventy-Five Years of Service to the Community, 1919–1994*. Malaysia: The Pacific Bank, 1994.

Tregonning, K. G. P. *Straits Tin: A Brief Account of the First Seventy-Five years of the Straits Trading Company Limited, 1887–1992*. Singapore: Straits Times Press, 1962.

Turnbull, C. M. *A History of Singapore, 1819–1975*. Kuala Lumpur: Oxford University Press, 1979.

_____ . *A History of Singapore, 1819–1988*, 2nd ed. Singapore: Oxford University Press, 1989.

United Overseas Bank Group. *The Singapore Bank with a Global Perspective, the United Overseas Bank Group: A Brief Profile*. Singapore: United Overseas Bank, 1988.

van Dongen, Y. *Brierley: The Man Behind the Corporate Legend*. Auckland: Viking, 1990.

Vogel, Ezra Felvel. *The Four Little Dragons: The Spread of Industralisation in East Asia*. Cambridge, Massachusetts: Harvard University Press, 1991.

White, Nicholas J. *Business, Government and the End of Empire — Malaya, 1942–1957*. Kuala Lumpur: Oxford University Press, 1996.

Wilson, Dick. *Solid As A Rock*. Singapore: Oversea-Chinese Banking Corporation Limited, 1972.

Woronoff, Jon. *Asia's 'Miracle' Economies*, 2nd ed. Armonk, New York: M. E. Sharpe, 1992.

Yap, Pheng Geck. *Scholar, Banker, Gentleman Soldier — The Reminiscences of Dr Yap Pheng Geck*. Singapore: Times Books International, 1982.

Yeap, Joo Kim. *Far From Rangoon: Lee Chee Shan 1909–86*. Singapore: Lee Teng Lay, 1994.

Yen, Ching Hwang. *A Social History of the Chinese in Singapore and Malaya, 1800–1911*. Singapore: Oxford University Press, 1986.

Yeo, Kim Wah. *Political Development in Singapore, 1945–1955*. Singapore: Singapore University Press, 1973.

Yeo, Siew Siang. *Tan Cheng Lock: The Straits Legislator and Chinese Leader*. Malaysia: Pelanduk Publications (M) Sdn. Bhd., 1990.

Yeo, Tiam Siew. *Destined to Survive: The Story of My Life*. Singapore: Toppan Printing, 1993.

Yong, C. F. *Tan Kah Kee: The Making of an Overseas Chinese Legend*. Singapore: Oxford University Press, 1989.

Xu, Yunqiao, org. ed. *Xinma Huaren Kangri Shiliao (1937–1945)* [A History of the Anti-Japanese Movement by the Chinese in Malaya (1937–1945)] Edited by Cai Shijun. Singapore: Wenshi Publishing, 1984.

Zheng, Bingshan. *Li Guangqian Zhuan* [A Biography of Lee Kong Chian]. China: Zhongguo Huaqiao Chubanshe, 1997.

Zhou, Mei. *The Life of Family Planning Pioneer, Constance Goh: Point of Light*. Singapore: Graham Brash, 1996.

Journals and Articles

Asian Finance, 15 September 1982.

Brown, D. "Race for the Corporate Throne", *Management Review*, 78, 1989, 26–27.

Brown, R. A. "Chinese Business in an Institutional and Historical Perspective", in *Chinese Business Enterprise in Asia*. Edited by R. A. Brown. London: Routledge, 1995, 1–26.

———. "Uses and Abuses of Chinese Business History and Methodology", in *South China: State, Culture and Social Change during the 20th Century*. Edited by Leo Douw and Peter Post. Amsterdam: North-Holland, 1996.

Building Materials & Equipment. Singapore: Trend Pub., November/ December 1974; September 1976.

Chan, G. G. "The Kapitan Cina System in the Straits Settlements". (Unpublished article).

Chan, Wellington K. K. "The Organizational Structure of the Traditional Chinese Firm and its Modern Reform", *Business Review*, 56, 1982, 218–235.

———. "Tradition and Change in the Chinese Business Enterprise", in Chinese Business History: Interpretative Trends and Priorities for the Future. Edited by R. Gardella, Jane K. Leonard and A. McElderry, *Chinese Studies in History*, 31(3–4), 1998, 127–144.

———. "Origins and the early years of the Wing On Company Group in Australia, Fiji, Hong Kong and Shanghai: Organisation and Strategy of a New Enterprise", in *Chinese Business Enterprise in Asia*. Edited by R. A, Brown. London: Routledge, 1995, 80–95.

Cohen, D. "The Fall of the House of Wang", *Business Month*, 135, 1990, 22–31.

Coleman, J. S. "Social Capital in the Creation of Human Capital", *American Journal of Sociology*, 94, 1988, 95–120.

Dodgson, M. and Y. Kim. "Learning to Innovate — Korean Style: The Case Of Samsung", *International Journal of Innovation Management*, 1, 1997, 53–71.

Gill, R. "OCBC: On Course with Banking Baron TCT at the Helm", *Insight*, September 1982.

______ . "KTP: The All-Weather Banker Runs his Rivals to the Ground", *Insight*, May 1983.

______ . "Mystery Shrouds OCBC Succession Syndrome, But Why?" *Insight*, July 1983.

Goh, Keng Swee. "A Socialist Economy that Work", in *Socialism that Works...The Singapore Way*. Edited by C. V. Nair. Singapore: Federal Publication (S) Pte Ltd, 1976, 77–85.

Fallon, P. "The tide in the life of Tan Chin Tuan", *Euromoney*, October 1982, 140–152.

Hamilton, Gary, and N. Woolsey Biggart. "Market, Culture, and Authority: A Comparative Analysis of Management and Organisation in the Far East", *American Journal of Sociology*, 94, Supplement,1988, S52 - 94.

Institutional Investor, May 1982.

Harvard Asia Pacific Review, Summer 1998.

Ishii, K. "The Role of Banking in Japan, 1882–1973", in *Banking, Trade and Industry: Europe, America and Asia from the Thirteenth to the Twentieth Century*. Edited by A. Teichova, G. K. Van Hentenryk and D. Ziegler. New York: Cambridge University Press, 1997.

Kennedy, C. "Fall of the House of Wang", *Computerworld*, 26, 1992, 67–69.

Khoo, Kay Kim. "The Contributions of the Chettiars in Malaya", *The Sunday Star*, 26 January 1996.

Lee, S. Y. "The Development of Commercial Banking in Singapore and the States of Malaya", *The Malayan Economic Review*, xi(1), April 1966, 84–100.

Lim, Mah Hui. "The Ownership and Control of Large Corporations in Malaysia: The Role of Chinese Businessmen", in *The Chinese in Southeast Asia, vol. I: Ethnicity and Economic Activity*. Edited by Linda Y. C. Lim & Peter L. A. Gosling. Singapore: Maruzen Asia, 1983.

Makepeace, Walter. "The Machinery of Commerce", in *One Hundred Years of Singapore*. Edited by Walter Makepeace, Gilbert E. Brooke and Roland St. J. Braddell. Vol. 2 (Reprint). Singapore: Oxford University Press, 1991.

Nadler, David and Michael Tushman. "Beyond the Charismatic Leader: Leadership and Organisational Change", in *The Human Side of Managing Technological Innovation: A Collection of Readings*. Edited by Ralph Katz. New York: Oxford University Press, 1997.

OCBC Journal, 2, 1972, 28–29.

Reich, R. "The Company of the Future", *Fast Company*, 19, November/ December 1998, 128.

Rudner, M. "The Organization of the British Military Administration in Malaya, 1946–48", *Journal of Southeast Asian History*, ix(1), 1968, 95–106.

National Archives. "Syonan — Singapore under the Japanese: A Catalogue of Oral History Interviews". Singapore: Oral History Department, 1986.

Pang, Wing-Seng. "The 'Double-Seventh' Incident, 1937: Singapore Chinese Response to the Outbreak of the Sino-Japanese War", *Journal of Southeast Asian Studies*, 4(2),1973, 269–99.

Schein, Edgar H. "The Role of CEO in the Management of Change: The Case of Information Technology", in *Transforming Organisation*. Edited by Thomas Kochan and Michael Useem. Oxford: Oxford University Press, 1992.

"Singapore's Lenders Get Tough", *Euromoney*, March 1985.

"Tan Chin Tuan OCBC-50", *Berita OCBC*, 6(2A), March 1975.

Tan, Yeok Seng. "History of the Oversea Chinese Association and the extortion by Japanese Military Administration of $50,000,000 from the Chinese in Malaya", *Journal of South Seas Society*, 3(1), 1946, 1–2.

The EM-Kayan, April 1974.

The EM-Kayan, January 1975.

"The Overseas Chinese", *The Economist*, 18 July 1992, 21–24.

Thio, Eunice. "The Syonan Years", in *A History of Singapore*. Edited by Ernest Chew and Edwin Lee. Singapore: Oxford University Press, 1991.

Williamson, Oliver. "The Modern Corporation: Origins, Evolution, Attributes", *Journal of Economic Literature*, 19, 1981, 1537–68.

Wong, Siu Lun. "Business Networks, Cultural Values and the States in Hong Kong and Singapore", in *Chinese Business Enterprise in Asia*. Edited by R. A. Brown. London: Routledge, 1995, 136–153.

———— . "The Chinese Family Firm: A Model", in *Family Business*. Edited by Mary B. Rose. Aldershot, Hants, England: E. Elgar, 1995, 621–635.

Unpublished Theses

Chung, W. Y. The Role of Commercial Banks in the Economic Development of Singapore. Unpublished B. A. Thesis. Department of Economics. Singapore: University of Singapore, 1976.

Lee, Y. H. A History of the Straits Chinese British Association 1900–1959. Unpublished B. A. Academic Exercise. Department of History. Singapore: University of Malaya, 1960.

Lee, S. Y. British Chinese Policy in Singapore, 1930s to mid-1950s: With particular focus on the public service career of Tan Chin Tuan. Unpublished Master's Thesis. Department of History. Singapore: National University of Singapore, 1995.

Ong, A. Straits Chinese Politics 1890–1942. Unpublished Honours Thesis. Department of History. Singapore: National University Singapore, 1989/1990.

Ong, T. H. The Straits Trading Company 1887–1937. Unpublished B. A. Thesis. Department of History. Singapore : University of Malaya, 1958.

Yam, C. T. The Role of Locally-Incorporated Banks in the Economic Development of Singapore. Unpublished B. A. Thesis. Department of Economics. Singapore: University of Singapore, 1962.

Zarinah Abdullah. The British Military Administration in Singapore. Unpublished B. A. Academic Exercise. Department of History. Singapore: University of Singapore, 1973.

INDEX

A

Abu Bakar, Tunku *58*
Abdul Rahman, Ismail bin Dato, *57*
Abdul Rahman, Tunku, *104*
Abdul Razak, Tunku, *143*
Ackerman, Harry, *211, 213*
Acquisition strategy, *148, 222*
Aggregate assets, *120*
Ahearne, C. D., *61*
Allen & Gledhill, *253*
Amoy University, *25, 26*
Anchor Beer, *132*
Anti-colonial politics, *91*
Approval of loans, *72*
Archipelago Brewery Company, *128*
Asian Bond Market, *161*
Asian Currency Unit, *167*
Asian Dollar market, *160, 161, 233*
Asian tiger economies, *160*
Assoc. of Banks in Singapore, *158*
Assoc. of Southeast Asian Nations
   (ASEAN), *180*
Automobile industry, *140*
Aw Boon Haw, *104, 251*

B

Bagnall, Sir John, *38*
Ban Hin Lee Bank, *13, 50, 53, 54*
Banana money, *50, 67*
Bank loans, *74*
Bank Negara Malaysia, *115, 116, 171*
Bank of China, *17, 114, 115, 116*
Bank of East Asia, *174*
Bank of Japan, *157*
Bank of New South Wales, *41, 56, 121,*
   178, 179
Bank of Singapore, *177*
Bank of Taiwan, *49*
Bank of Tokyo, *169*
Bank Ordinance, *9*
Bank's documentary records, *41*
Bankers Trust Company, *178*
Banking Bill, *99, 101, 102*
Banking industry, *1*
Banking system, *6*
Banking-related businesses, *121*
Bartley, William, *38*
Beatrice Foods, *130*
Big Four, *177*

Bing Sing & Co, *23*
Blocked accounts, *52*
Blue-chip companies, *147*
Boustead and Guthries, *123*
Branches in Indonesia, *117*
Brewery operations, *184*
Brierley Investment Ltd. (BIL), *186*
British birthright, *62*
British Military Administration
   (BMA), *68, 73, 79*
British Military Administration
   Advisory Council, *79, 112*
British-controlled firms, *146*
Bryson, H. P., *82*
Buddenbrooks' phenomenon, *241*
Bumiputra, *171, 172*
Butterworth plant, *136*
Byrne, K. M., *99*
Bywater, J. E., *143*

C

Campbell, J. W., *35*
Capital-intensive industrialisation
   programme, *178*
Carnation International, *131*
Central Bank of Malaya, *108*
Chaebol, *190, 191*
Chan Chin Cheung, *143*
Chan S. K., *70*
Chan Sze Jin (S. J. Chan), *36*
Chang Kia Ngau, *220*
Chartered Bank, *2, 42, 49, 73, 112, 172*
Chase Manhattan Bank, *105, 110, 111*
Chee Kah Hor, *251*
Chee Seng Rubber Works, *5*
Chee Swee Cheng, *21, 22, 27, 251*
Chettiar moneylenders, *8, 203*
Chew Hock Leong, *16, 24, 27, 31, 43,*
   70, 251
Chiang Kai-shek, *174*
Chin Peng, *92*
China Building, *41, 69, 203, 204*
China Relief Fund Committee, *40*
China Relief Fund, *39*
Chinese banker, *33*
Chinese Bankers Trust *30*
Chinese banks, *6, 7, 13, 14, 24, 31, 54,*
   64, 192
Chinese British subjects, *61*

Chinese capital, *145*
Chinese Chamber of Commerce, *76, 82*
Chinese Commercial Bank (CCB), *10, 12, 15, 21, 22, 24, 76, 82, 192*
Chinese Communist party, *39*
Chinese community, *7, 31*
Chinese insurance companies, *11*
Chinese Middle Schools, *92*
Chinese Nationality Law, *60*
Chinese-educated businessmen, *76*
Choi Siew Hong, *172, 246*
Chop Hoo Thye, *235*
Chrysler, *206*
Chu, W. H., *70*
Chung Khiaw Bank, *104, 172*
Chungking, *43, 56, 62*
Civil Defence of Singapore, *64*
Civil government, *76, 79*
Civil war, *174*
Coca-Cola franchise, *129*
Coconuts, *50*
Colonial government, *33, 55, 72*
Colonial Legal Service, *80*
Colonial Singapore, *2, 45, 192*
Colony of Singapore Advisory Council, *80*
Colour bar, *36*
Commercial Bank of India, *2*
Commissioner-General for the United Kingdom in Southeast Asia, *85*
Compradores, *4, 5, 193*
Computer service facility, *198*
Computer System Advisers (CSA), *198*
Computerisation, *196, 199*
Corbin locksets, *216*
Corporate business synergies, *194*
Corporate networks, *105*
Corporate philanthropy, *227*
Cost of rice, *84*
Credit Guarantee Corp., *171*
Curran, John, *164*
Currency independence, *158*
Currency problem, *47*
Customer-Focused Culture, *196*

D
Darby, Henry, *141*
Dally, J. D., *35*
Day, E. V. G., Colonel *61, 66*
Debtor and Creditor Bill, *84*
Defence (Companies Temporary Transfer of Registered Office) Regulations, *42*
De-monetisation, *74*

Deng Xiaoping, *174*
Development Bank of Singapore (DBS), *177, 258*
Dialect affiliations, *13*
Dialect groups, *8*
Diasy milk, *131*
Directorate of Civil Affairs, *67*
Diversification, *122, 124, 132, 158, 162*
Dobb & Company Ltd., *216*
Domestic banking, *1*
Drink products, *131*
Dual nationality, *60*
Dutch East Indies, *28*

E
East Asian History of Science Library, *228*
Eastern Realty Company Ltd., *30*
Eastern United Assurance, *11*
Economic development of Malaysia, *171*
Economic development, *154*
Economic nationalism, *171*
Edington, W. G., *106–108*
Ee Hoe Hean Club, *34*
Electoral registration exercise, *83*
Elias, John Aaron, *58, 109*
Emergency Regulations, *93*
Empire State Buildings, *206*
Eng Aung Tong, *105*
English colonial elite, *76*
Entrepreneurial talent, *257*
Equity interests, *123*
Eu Yan Sang Holdings, *168*
Eurodollar market, *161*
Euromoney, *179*
European banks, *2, 4, 5, 6, 8, 14, 64, 66, 75*
Executive Council, *125*
Expansion programme, *177*
Expatriate businesses, *125*
Export promotion, *158*
Export-oriented industrialisation strategy, *176*

F
Fair, A. A., *138*
F&N, *129, 130, 132*
Fancott, H. E., *58*
Fanta, *131*
Federated and Unfederated Malay States, *67*
Fergusson, Ewen, Sir *136*
Fergusson, Nicholas E. H., *169*

Financial hub, *178*
Financial sector liberalisation, *258*
Fire of 1972, *135*
First Legislative Council, *84*
First Malaysian Plan, *171*
First National City Overseas Investment Corp., *165*
First Oversea Credit Ltd. (FOCL), *165*
First Sale of Sites, *204*
Foreign capital, *257*
Foreign nationals, *60*
Four Seas Communications Bank, *177*
Four Seas, *177*
Fraser & Neave, *124, 128, 224*
Fraudulent practices, *5*
Free-trade principle, *3*

G

Gambier, *9*
Gambling, *48*
General Reconstruction Committee, *78*
George Champion, *111*
Gleeson-White, Michael, *168*
Gimson, Franklin, Sir *76, 79*
Godsall, Brigadier, *77*
Global investment, *137*
Globalisation, *257*
Globalising, *105*
Goh Keng Swee, *101*
Goh Sin Tub, *210, 212, 213, 214, 219, 246*
Gold bullion market, *162*
Gold Exchange of Singapore, *164*
Gold standard, *15*
Gold trading business, *163*
Golden Shoe, *204, 205*
Goodwood Park Hotel, *95*
Goodwood Park, *96*
Graduated tax, *81*
Great Depression, *15, 27, 136, 192*
Great Eastern Life Assurance Company, *124, 132, 138, 193, 182, 225*
Guan xi (relationship), *34, 103, 104, 108, 112, 155, 175, 219*
Guarantor, *72*

H

Heineken NV, *128*
Heineken, *129*
Henderson, Lauvence, *35*
Hoffman, R. C., *253*
Ho Hong Bank, *11, 15, 21, 22, 23, 24, 192*
Hokkien banks, *10, 11, 35*
Hokkien community, *74*

Hone, Ralph, *69*
Hong Kong and London, *121*
Hongkong and Shanghai Bank (HKSB), *112, 121, 172*
Hongkong and Shanghai Banking Corp., *2, 3, 5, 24, 42, 49, 174*
Hongkong Bank and Chartered Bank, *7*
Hotel Phoenix, *182*
Housing and Development Board, *204*
Housing conditions, *91*

I

Income Tax Bill, *82*
Independent nation, *116*
Indian Bank, *50*
Indian money-lenders, *203*
Indian Overseas Bank, *50*
Indigenous Chinese banks, *6*
Indonesia, *118*
Industrial capitalism, *156*
Industrialisation process, *156, 158*
Inflation, *48, 53, 68, 127*
Information technology, *196, 197*
In-house provident fund, *98*
Institutionalise, *237, 254*
Interlocking directorships, *148*
Internal Security Council, *97*
International Bank of Singapore (IBS), *177*
International economy, *127*
International financing, *161*
International markets, *159*
Internees, *74*
Investment strategies, *121*
Ismail bin Mohamed Ali, Tun, *172*

J

Jakarta branch, *118*
Jakarta, *117*
Jambi, *117*
James Reid Scott, *144*
James Spicer, *134*
Japanese aggression, *45*
Japanese banks, *50*
Japanese currency, *70, 74*
Japanese Inspector of Banks, *51*
Japanese Malayan Dollar, *47, 52*
Japanese Occupation, *49, 53, 55, 63, 72, 74, 104, 136, 140*
Japanese State Bank's office, *51*
Japanese war effort, *47, 48*
Japanese-based investment, *176*
John Little and Company, Spicer & Robinson, *134–135*

John, St. Island, *94*
Joint Supply Board, *82*
Jones, Irvins, *60–61*
Jones, S. W., *63*
Joshua Brothers, *3*
Judge, Bruce, *186*

K

Kambau rubber estate, *30*
Kampong Chuliah, *202, 203*
Kapitan China system, *9*
Keiretsu conglomerates, *255*
Keiretsu, *190, 191, 192, 254*
Keppel-Tatlee Bank, *258*
Keys, Major, *203*
Khor Teow Koon, *251*
King Edward Vii Medical College, *14*
Knowland, Peter, *217*
Kuomintang, *39*
Kwa Siew Tee, *24, 27, 43*
Kwong Yik Bank, *9*

L

Laycock, John, *58*
Lee Boon Tin, *70*
Lee Chim Tuan, *141, 142*
Lee Choon Guan, *11, 12, 251*
Lee Choon Seng, *23, 50, 55, 70, 251*
Lee Hah Ing, *200, 245*
Lee Hau-Shik, Sir Henry, *108*
Lee Kong Chian, *11, 12, 13, 23, 28, 41, 44, 55, 70, 71, 72, 103, 104, 124, 136, 146, 150, 251*
Lee Kuan Yew, *93, 94, 100, 102*
Lee Rubber Company, *23*
Lee Seng Wee, *226*
Lee Wah Bank, *50*
Legislative Assembly, *100*
Legislative Council, *36, 76, 83, 108, 112, 125, 222*
Leopard Brewery, *132, 133, 186*
Li Ka-shing empire, *238*
Life insurance industry, *138*
Lim Bock Kee, *24, 43*
Lim Boon Keng, *47, 127, 251*
Lim Kim San, *219*
Lim Nee Soon, *11, 127*
Lim Peng Siang, *12, 251*
Lin Jo Yan, *200*
Lion Breweries Ltd., *186*
Liquidity demands, *8*
Loans, *52*
Local banking industry, *33*

Local banking, *257*
Local banks, *8, 50, 52, 178*
Local Chinese banks, *6, 8, 15*
Long-term finance, *2*
Long-term loans, *8*
Lottery, *48*
Low Keng Huat Construction Company, *211*
Low Keng Huat, *211*
Low Liang Quee, *251*

M

Malcolm MacDonald, *85, 220*
Malaya (Unallocated) Account, *81*
Malayan Airways (MAL), *243*
Malayan Banking Assoc., *52*
Malayan Breweries Ltd. (MBL), *124, 132, 128, 186*
Malayan Civil Service, *36*
Malayan Communist Party (MCP), *92*
Malayan Exchange Banks Assoc., *100*
Malayan Glass Factory Berhad, *130*
Malayan Planning Unit, *66*
Malaysia Smelting Corp. Berhad, *137*
Malaysia-Singapore Airlines, *244*
Mao Tse-tung, *174*
Market forces, *159*
Matsushita, Konosuke, *229*
Mckerron, Patrick, *64, 69*
Meadow Gold, *131*
Mercantile Bank, *2, 3*
Merger, *114, 177*
Merger-separation years, *162*
Meritocracy, *149*
Metal Box (Singapore), *130*
Metro, *168*
Midland Bank Training School, *200*
Midland Bank, *106, 108, 178*
Modern corporate multinational banking, *170*
Monetary Authority of Singapore (MAS), *160*
Moratorium Proclamation (Repeat) Ordinance, *85*
Morrison-Knudsen International, *211*
Mouhtbatten, Louis, Lord *68*
Municipal Commission, *38, 39, 41*

N

Nanyang University, *14*
National economy, 158, *162*
Nationalist Party of China, *39*
Needham, Joseph

Research Insitute, 228
Nepotism, *28, 238*
Networking, *103*
New Court Merchant Bankers Ltd.
   (NCMB), *163*
New Economic Policy (NEP), *171, 172*
New Malayan notes, *68*
New Malayan post-war currency, *73*
New Zealand Breweries, *186*
Newly-industrialising economies, *157*
Ng Sen Choy, *38*

O

OCBC Bullion Ltd., *164*
OCBC Centre Scholarships, *221*
OCBC Centre, *202, 205, 207, 210–217,
   219–220*
OCBC Group, *177, 178, 183, 186, 193*
OCBC shares, *70*
OCBC, *28, 31, 43, 50, 54, 62, 66, 72,
   98, 115, 167, 180, 196, 197, 203, 204,
   224, 254, 256, 258, 259*
OCBC's 50th Anniversary, *170*
OCBC's post-war development, *63*
Occupation, *64*
Oil Crisis of 1973, *155, 171*
Ong Boon Tat, *127*
Ong Eng Guan, Major, *114*
Ong Hock Chye, *246*
Ong Piah Teng, *24*
On-line banking, *178, 196, 198*
On-line, *178, 196, 198*
Operation Cold Store, *97*
Organisational culture and identity,
   248
Organisational glue, *251*
Otis Elevator Company, *217*
Oversea-Chinese Bank, *10, 11, 13, 21,
   22, 24, 34, 47, 192*
Oversea-Chinese Banking Corp. Ltd.
   (OCBC), *17, 21, 22, 86*
Overseas Assurance Corp. (OAC), *11,
   127*
Overseas banks, *105*
Overseas Chinese Assoc. (OCA), *47, 58*
Overseas Union Bank (OUB), *177, 258*
Owner-directors, *71*

P

Pacific Bank Berhad, *171, 172*
Palembang, *117*
Pao, C. J., Dr. *59*
Pao, Yue-kong, Sir, *238*

PAP government, *116*
Passive Defence Council, *40, 41, 43*
Peck Pia Jim, *69*
Pei Cho E, *208*
Pei, I. M., *183, 208, 209, 216, 221*
People's Action Party, *99, 124, 154*
Personalism, *13*
Peterson, Len, *211*
Philanthropy, *229*
Phoenix and Framroz, *129*
Pinder, D. W., *142*
Po Chiak Keng Tan Clan Assoc., *40*
Political independence, *158*
Population increase, *91*
POSB Bank, *258*
Post-war baby boom, *91*
Post-war Singapore, *65*
Poverty, *92*
Professionalism, *149*
Prudent conservatism, *236*
Public life, *76*
Public service, *75*
Pulau Brani smelter, *136*
Purcell, Victor, Lieutenant-Colonel *66*
Puthucheary, *95, 96*

Q

Quality of rice in Singapore, *84*

R

Raffles City, *182, 183*
Raffles College, *14, 37*
Raffles Holdings, *182*
Raffles Hotel, *94, 95, 109, 110, 124*
Rayman, Lazaru's, *38*
Real-time, *196*
Recession, *127, 237*
Recruitment policies, *71*
Registration of Foreigners Act of 1939,
   60
Reid, J. S. W., *61*
Relationship banking, *199*
Remittance business, *31*
Rendel Commission, *112*
Restructuring, *178*
Richard O. Winstedt, *37*
Robert Kuok, *130*
Robinson & Company Ltd., *96, 124,
   134*
Robinsons, Philip, *134*
Rockefeller, David, *111*
Rowery, R. D., *211*
Rubber estate, *10, 34*

Rubber industry, *16, 22, 24, 125*
Rubber prices, *11, 27*
Rubber, *2, 23, 27, 46*

S

Sago factories, *2*
Salaries Commission Report, *80*
Salk Institute for Biological Studies, *228*
Sampson, A. J., *140*
SBEU, *100*
SCBA, *37*
Schroders, J. Henry, *168*
Scott, A. W., *142*
Seah Buck Tiang, *246*
Second Legislative Council, *85*
Securities Industry Council, *160*
See Boo Ih, *16, 35, 251*
Self-government, *78*
Seow Eu Jin, *56*
Seow Poh Leng, *10*
Separation from Malaysia, *154, 158*
Servicemen, *74*
Shared membership, *252*
Shareholders' funds, *128, 224, 225*
Short-term borrowing, *81*
Short-term credit, *2, 4*
Short-term loans, *192*
Sime Darby, *40, 141, 142, 143, 144*
Sime, William Middleton, *141*
Singapore Advisory Council, *76*
Singapore Bank Employees Union
    (SBEU), *99*
Singapore Carpet Manufacturers Pte
    Ltd, *217*
Singapore Chinese Chamber of
    Commerce, *82*
Singapore City Council bond issue, *112*
Singapore economy, *167*
Singapore Gold Clearing House Pte.
    Ltd., *164*
Singapore International Merchant
    Bankers Ltd. (SIMBL), *164, 167, 168,
    244*
Singapore Legislative Council Elections
    Bill, *82*
Singapore MasterCard International
    Incorporated, *180*
Singapore Post and Telegraph and
    Uniformed Staff Union, *93*
Singapore Ratepayers' Assoc., *82*
Singapore Skyline *76, 220*
Singmas Ltd., *164*
Smelting, *136, 137*
Smith, J. D. M., *81*
Social capital, *251*

Solid As A Rock, *206, 209, 258*
Sook Ching, *46*
South Pacific Brewery, *132, 133*
Southern Regions Development Bank
    (SRDB), *50*
Specialists' Centre, *182*
Staff welfare package, *98, 99*
Standard Chartered Bank, *174*
Starrett, William, *214*
State of Emergency, *92*
Stanton, W., *200*
Sterling exchange standard, *3, 4*
Stock exchange, *122*
Straits Chinese British Assoc. (SCBA),
    36
Straits dollar, *15, 47*
Straits Settlement Legal Service, *80*
Straits Settlements, *38, 67*
Straits Trading Company (STC), *124,
    135, 137, 225*
Straits-born Chinese, *36, 83*
Strike, *93–95*
Sunkist, *131*
Super Scando, *215*
Surabaya, *117*
Symbolic analysts, *247*
Syonan Chinese Banks Joint Board of
    Control, *52*
Syonan-to, *46*
Sze Hai Tong Bank, *28, 50, 177*

T

Taib bin Haji Andak, Tan Sri, *143*
Tajima Metalwork (Singapore) Pte
    Ltd, *216*
Tan Cheng Lock, *12, 29, 36, 58, 59, 70,
    104, 141, 142*
Tan Cheng Siong, *34*
Tan Chin Tuan, *16, 24, 25, 30, 33, 34,
    37, 42, 44, 55, 57, 63, 64, 69, 71,
    74–76, 79, 81, 84, 86, 93, 97, 98,
    101, 102, 108, 109, 116, 137, 149,
    183, 184, 186, 192–194, 197, 202,
    205, 207, 209, 214, 220, 221, 223,
    224, 227, 256*
Tan Ean Kiam, *12, 21, 13, 17, 127, 251*
Tan Kah Kee & Co., *24–26*
Tan Kah Kee, *12, 13, 16, 25, 26, 34, 39,
    42, 103, 150, 197, 251*
Tan Lark Sye, *103, 251*
Tan Siew Sin, *59, 143*
Tan Tock Seng, *9*
Tao (or way), *256*
Tapioca, *23*
Technological change, *257*

Technology-based services, *199*
Teo Cheng Guan, *158, 246*
The Chartered Bank, *3*
The OCBC Echo, *29*
The Singapore and Straits Aerated
    Water Company, *128*
Three-stage evolutionary cycle, *240*
Tiger Balm Factory, *105*
Tiger Balm King, *104*
Tiger Beer, *128, 132, 231*
'Tiger' economies, *156*
Tin, *2, 27, 46, 135, 136*
Tjio Kay Loen, *162, 169, 176, 246*
Tan, Keng Yam Tony Dr., *198, 227, 243*
Total equity interest, *122*
Trade unions, 92
Travellers cheques, 180
Treasury, *73*
Tresise, Charles, *169, 245*

U

Union Bank of Calcutta, *2*
Union militancy, *92*
United Chinese Bank, *50*
United Overseas Bank (UOB), *177,
    258*
University of Malaya, *14*
Urban Redevelopment Authority, *204*
US dollar crisis, *163*
US-based capital, *176*

V

Varied investment portfolio, *121*

W

Wall Street Crash, *15*
Wang, An, *238*
Wang Laboratories, *238, 240*
War effort, *50*
War Office, *66*
Wartime currency, *67*
Wartime financial transactions, *84*

War-time internees, *74*
Wartime Japanese notes, *70, 73*
Wearne Brothers, *124, 139, 141*
Wearne, C. F. F., *139*
Wearne, T. J. B., *139*
Wearne, W. J., *140*
Wee Swee Teow, *36*
Wee Theam Seng, *251*
Weisberg, H., *42*
Westpac Banking Corp., *121*
White superiority, *49*
Widespread unemployment, *91*
Wing Loong, *38*
Wong Ah Fook, *9*
Wong Lai Fatt, *253*
Wong Nang Jang, *246*
Woodhull, Sandrasegaram, *96*
Wong, Pakshong Michael, *243*
Wong, S. Q., Dato *47, 138*
World War Two, *39, 56, 86, 136, 157*

X

Xin yong (trustworthiness), *34*

Y

Yamaichi Securities Company Ltd.,
    169
Yap Chor Ee, *13, 53*
Yap Pheng Geck, *12, 15, 16, 27*
Yap Siong Eu, *13, 53*
Yap Twee, *17, 23, 28, 251*
Yeap Chor Ee, *251*
Yeo Tiam Siew, *175, 251*
Yokohama Specie Bank, *49, 52, 157*
Yong Pung How, *124, 143, 167, 235,
    243, 245, 247*

Z

Zappel, *131*